BULLETINS

To The Alex Brown.

from "The Other Alex"

3 June 1998

BULLETINS

A.L. Brown

Published in 1989 by
Dr A.L. Brown
29 Geraldine Road,
Malvern, Worcs WR14 3NT.
in association with
The Self Publishing Association Ltd
Lloyds Bank Chambers,
Upton-upon-Severn, Worcs.

British Library Cataloguing in Publication Data

Brown, A.L.
Bulletins.
1. World war – Biographies – collections
I. Title
940.54'8

ISBN 1–85421–053–X

Designed and produced by The Self Publishing Association Ltd.
Printed and bound in Great Britain by Billing & Sons Ltd, Worcester.

INTRODUCTION

The letters contained in this book were written whilst I was a Regimental Medical Officer attached to the 51st Medium Regiment, R.A. (T.A.). After the war they were packed away in a box, and I did not read them again for nearly forty years, by which time I had retired from general practice. I tried them out on my daughter and grandsons, who seemed to find them interesting, and this gave me the idea of publishing them. I have reproduced them completely unaltered except for the insertion of certain place names and other facts which had to be omitted from the originals for reasons of security. I have resisted the temptation to alter opinions which I had held at the time, some of which have been altered by post war events.

For security reasons, and in order to pacify the censors, the letters were written about three months after the actual events had taken place. They were, however, based on notes I took every day.

Readers may be interested to know that the bonds of comradeship forged during my time with the 51st Medium Regiment are as strong as ever in 1989. Reunions of the two batteries are held every year, and a Regimental Reunion every three years. At the last Regimental Reunion over seventy officers and men attended, a testimony to the high regard we have for each other. I was indeed fortunate to share the comradeship of such a fine body of men, hence my dedication of this book to them.

I am most grateful to Mrs. Mary Thomas, whose expert typing from my original letters has enabled me to publish them.

Malvern - June 1989

BULLETIN ONE

"All at Sea" — August to October 1942

Well here it is folks, the only family newspaper with no policy, no price and no morals. All shall be told (censor permitting) in plain English though not, I fear, in plain handwriting.

We embarked as planned with no hitches. The ship, the *Sibajak*, is modern, fairly fast and very comfortable. I have a cabin on the boat deck shared with the Padre and another Officer of the Regiment. The only snag is the shortage of fresh water which is only turned on for a total of 5 hours a day and mostly at times when one is eating or sleeping. One of my first visits on my tour of exploration was to the ship's shop. Here there are stocked most of the things which make life bearable on board ship in the tropics - talcum, lavendar water, soap etc, plus many things now unobtainable at home, such as sweets galore (unrationed) and a certain amount of cigarettes. The latter were South African and rejoiced in the name of "C to C" meaning Cape to Cairo. They sold very well for the first few days but after a short interval we renamed them "Camels" (C to C = Camel to Consumer) and they were no more seen (or smelt). Actually, there turned out to be plenty of English cigarettes of good brands on board and as the ration is 50 per day nobody is really short.

Soon after embarkation grim reality raised its head with the issue of the usual Board of Trade life jacket, guaranteed to break the neck of the wearer if he jumps into the water from any great height - unless he braces it very carefully with his arms. I soon exchanged mine for an inflatable rubber one guaranteed to keep the wearer upright in water indefinitely (as if that mattered!). It is much smaller than the Board of Trade one which is the point, as one has to carry it everywhere with one (yes, Everywhere!) when the ship is at sea. The Board of Trade variety forms a useful cushion for impromptu deck sitting or rail leaning.

This is not a British ship so, of course, it is spotlessly clean and the food and service are wonderful. It is amazing to sit down to fish and meat at the same meal and to be able to peel an orange once again. We get fresh fruit at least once a day. Drinks, of course, are fantastically cheap. Whisky is 6d per glass (cheaper than beer) and other drinks are proportionately as cheap. So a round which would cost about ten bob in the Old Country works out at about 2/6d. Cigarettes are 1/8d for 50!

As she was on a tropical route in peacetime, the ship is fitted with electric fans in the cabins and public rooms. We need them as all windows have to be closed at blackout. The fug has to be experienced to be believed. What it will be like when it gets really hot I shudder to think. There is quite a good library on board but deck space for the officers is somewhat restricted, so games are difficult. I am doing PT each morning when I feel like it but we shall all be rather flabby by the time we reach the other end - wherever that may be.

Well, as you will have guessed by now, we set sail. The convoy numbers between 1 and 100 ships and is escorted between 1 and 50 vessels of HM Navy and is proceeding at a speed somewhere between 1 and 40 knots. The first few days were awful. This ship rolls and pitches more than any other I have sailed in. Add to this the fact that we have had to sleep in our clothes and you can imagine how I felt. My well known tendency for sea sickness soon made itself evident and I spent three days flat on my back living on barley sugar. It was so rough that even the O/C Troops, a hardened sailor, "felt the motion of the ship" as he so daintily phrased it, while the attendance at meals fell off markedly as did quite a lot of the crockery. The C/O received a plate full of hot soup full in the lap - very sticky and very wetting. However, after a time, things became very much better and the sun appeared, although the sea was still fairly rough. Everybody staggered on deck looking pale and wan; some had lost false teeth (either overboard or down the lavatories) and there was no prospect of them getting any replacements until we reached the end of our journey so I feared that there would be a fair amount of indigestion to deal with. We soon recovered and ate very heartily for the next couple of days. One thing about sea sickness, it gives you a terrific appetite!

The improvement in the weather and in the morale of the ship generally produced a sort of prep school atmosphere in which it became fashionable to feign ignorance of nautical terms. People talked about leaning on the palings at the blunt end and references were made to the flag pole and the chimney. But worse than these were the ship's wiseacres. They could tell you the date of sailing, the destination, etc, and knew the names of every ship in the convoy in spite of the fact that they were all painted the same uniform grey and had all names obliterated. Being an old hand, I knew what the opinions of these false prophets were worth but many lambs were led to the slaughter. I found that I was developing a "when I was in the old Memnon" complex and had to curb my tongue a bit - a super human task as all you who know me will realise.

After we had been going a few days more we changed into Tropical Kit or K.D. (khaki drill) as they call it in the Forces. Everybody spent a great deal of the day putting in buttons, badges, etc and the scene in the smoke room that evening looked like a Hollywood set. However, this did not last long as the stuff soon gets creased and untidy; it makes everybody look very different and many a handsome officer lost his film star glamour when shorts revealed his spindly calves or knock knees.

The next day we put into Gibraltar. There was no shore leave for us so I could not send a cable. We sailed the next evening under a nearly full moon. The place as we left was a glorious sight and, as we turned away, a great four engined plane zoomed overhead just above mast height. We could see the blue flames from the exhaust quite clearly.

Now we are really in the tropics. A day or two ago we passed Madeira. It is very hot, especially at night, and I have taken to sleeping on deck on my li-lo. It is very comfortable and very restful to gaze up at the funnel outlined against the milky way, as it was last night. One's thoughts are freer than they ever can be on land and one gets quite a different outlook on things. The old shipboard feeling of "never do today what you can put off till tomorrow" has returned, so I hope you will appreciate the effort required to write this as I can appreciate the effort required to read it.

There is a sweep on the day's run at noon each day. I won a fifth share in it of 21/6d and, even after the customary round of drinks, I still have ten bob left much to my relief. Last time I won a sweep (on the Derby in the mess at home) the drinks cost me five bob more than my winnings, which was a bad thing!

Laundry looms large on the horizon at the moment. I did my own last week in cold water with Persil. It comes out very well and none of the woollens have shrunk, much to my surprise and pleasure. The ship does a certain amount of laundry but their charges are exhorbitant.

I will now describe some of the more colourful personalities on the ship, so laying myself open to several actions for libel and finally setting the seal on the success of this periodical!

Well, to start with, they sent us five Padres. FIVE! In addition to our own Arthur Gee (of whom more anon) there are four others. There is "Noddy" in the RAF. He came out of a monastery to join up and can't let you or himself forget it for more than five minutes. Then there is "Ginger" - RAF again. He was a wholesale draper before entering the church and has rather a draperish outlook on things; he announces his hymns as if they were a special bargain in ladies underwear at 3/11 three! The other two both belong to the Army and are a direct contrast to each other. "Gorgeous George" is a very handsome RC Padre, lately an art student (mostly nudes, I should think). 6 ft tall, a champion boxer and sunburnt so much that we were all afraid he would be offended by the colour bar in South Africa; hail-fellow-well-met with everybody. "Smudge" C of E is small, wizened, 5 ft 4 ins tall and weight 7 stones. He eats more per meal than any other man I have ever seen; where it all goes to nobody knows; he must have hollow legs!

In addition to the Church, there are one or two other notables. "Twitchy" is in the RAF; so called because his moustache worries him and he is always pulling faces. Drunk every night, he is very noisy and generally trying to find out in a raucous falsetto voice "who killed Cock Robin?". We told him very firmly the other night but he still persists. "George" is a very witty RAF officer of exalted rank who makes up good rhymes in the Billy Bennett manner. "The Eastern Brothers" are a pair of Army officers who make up excellent verse of topical subjects in the style of the Western Brothers and have a fund of risqué but drawing-room stories (sent in plain envelope on request, price 6d per story, let us put you on our mailing list). Finally, there are Dave, Steve and Joe - three special pals of mine in the RAF. We play draughts together each evening and discuss everything from socks to Spitfires. There are some other people too numerous and uninteresting to mention.

Our next port of call was Freetown where we were stuck in the river for ten days. Life was dull to say the least though we were allowed on the sports deck and got in some good deck tennis. As I suspected, we are all getting terribly flabby. There was a great scare about mosquitoes and all sorts of contrary orders were issued about sleeping with windows shut etc. But after I pointed out that the local variety bit by day as well as by night things were relaxed somewhat.

Just about this time I began to reflect on whether I hadn't brought rather too much kit with me. I seem to have rather a lot and, of course, you do stand to lose it under active service conditions; on the other hand, I might have a chance of some golf or some tennis and these things seem to disappear mysteriously anyway if left at home!

The concert party urge is rampant at the moment. I enjoy a good show but it loses a lot of its novelty when you have heard the bits being rehearsed for the past week ad nauseam. However, I suppose that is inevitable on a ship. There is generally a (very) male voice choir booming away somewhere in the distance. (It's "Hearts of Oak" at the moment). While closer at hand the favourite crooner is extolling the merits of a certain type of orange. ("Tangerine" I think, but this orange seems to have lips and eyes).

Disaster overtook us the other day when that seemingly bottomless cornucopia, the ship's shop, suddenly ran out of sweets; I had laid in a small reserve fortunately, but others less wise had been caught bending and are having to make do with the sticky goo purveyed by the men's canteen. Owing to the delay at the last port, food is also getting a bit short and we are having to put up with only four courses at dinner instead of the usual five or six! The heat is awful and we shall be glad to get out to sea again.

Soon after sailing we crossed the equator and, life being what it is, crossed it with due ceremony. I was duly ducked - my crime being that I had caused excessive wear and tear to the ship's draughts board! I have a very interesting and decorative certificate with a snapshot of the ship on it. Soon after crossing the line, the weather rapidly changed for the worse and it became so cold that we had to change back into our serge clothing again. Everybody was sniffing and coughing and we all felt quite miserable. However, life had its compensations. We had quite interesting lectures by individual officers, including a very popular one on "wines and spirits". We have a General Knowledge Bee once a week and are going to start a debating society. Incidentally, I saw my first albatross today - a lovely bird like a large gull but with an enormous wingspan, it flies almost touching the water. A beautiful sight.

One day stark melodrama raised its head; we had a case of acute appendicitis and had to operate. A young New Zealand surgeon did the job and I gave the anaesthetic. The patient did very well. I heard later that a similar case occurred on another ship and they buried the patient at sea, so I think we have some cause for self-congratulation!

Every now and then the officers get together with the sergeants and have a party. We had one such a little time ago at which one fellow (more than somewhat under the influence) made a meal of a couple of electric light bulbs and some razor blades. I can positively state that there was no deception - he really swallowed everything. (Yes, I was sober at the time!) The cream of the show, however, was the horror struck expression on the face of the Javanese wine steward while the trick was being performed.

You will all no doubt be suitably amused to hear that I am now singing in the Regimental Choir and I must say that I enjoy it very much, purely from the musical angle. I generally sing soprano but do tenor and bass as well as a sideline on an "as required" basis.

In due course we reached Durban and left our ship. We were all bustled away to a tented camp somewhere outside the town and in this operation an awful mess-up was made of the baggage. I had only two articles of baggage but when I at last located them they were over a mile apart at different ends of the camp! Some people spent nearly a day locating all their property.

I forgot to mention that, as our ship entered port, we had a singing welcome from a lady with the figure (but not the voice) of a prima donna. She started with "Land of Hope and Glory" and this was followed by (yes - you've guessed it) "There'll Always Be an England" - both bellowed fortissimo through a megaphone. However, it was nice to be welcomed by someone and it went down well with the troops.

The first day was far too wet to wander round the shops. We all went into town and were reduced to that last resort of all people with nothing to do on a wet afternoon - the pictures. "Mrs Miniver" was on and, as I had already seen it, I went and saw some awful American "musical". The shops shut at four so there wasn't much to do and we all returned quite early and very sober. The next day I window shopped in the afternoon but didn't buy much as we knew there was plenty of time (or so we thought).

However, the next day we were hoofed off again and are now on another ship, the *Ekma,* much smaller than the last, and nearing the end of our 11,000 mile journey. We had a singing farewell ("We'll Meet Again" - heaven forbid! - and "There'll Always Be an England" again) from the same buxom lady who had welcomed us.

This ship has only just room on it for the Regiment but we are all fairly comfortable. It is a small ship of the B and I Line used for carrying passengers up the coast from South Africa to Egypt and Mozambique. It rolls frightfully and the sea is pretty rough at present. I noticed that, unlike other ships in the convoy, we did not seem to be zigging and zagging in the usual manner. Inspection of the steering gear in the stern revealed that this was so decrepit that it had to be lashed and was only used when entering or leaving port and on gross changes of course. As you can imagine, this increased my confidence no end! This was further increased when I was consulted in my professional capacity by the Captain who turned out to be completely blind in one eye and suffering from advanced cirrhosis of the liver! There was also the episode of the breakaway barrage balloon. Each vessel in the convoy carried its own barrage balloon and, one fine morning with a blue sky and sunshine above, ours started to misbehave itself, yawing from side to side and showing every sign of coming down in the sea. It was winched in hastily but at about 100 ft from the deck one of the fins came off the back end. It was therefore decided (in my view very sensibly) to shoot the thing down and the Lewis gunner (our sole defensive gentleman on the ship) brandished his gun which, of course, jammed after about five rounds as they always do. Efforts were then made to sink the thing with rifle fire but in the end we had to cut it loose and it drifted away southwards.

The final straw came when our Commanding Officer, who was also O/C Troops, was dissatisfied with the general hygiene of the ship and relieved the ship's medical officer of his duty and appointed me in his place. This was doubly embarrassing as I was sharing a cabin with the said medical officer!

Apart from the foregoing, there wasn't much to do except to sleep and eat and read good books but some of us were putting in some heavy work with the medicine ball to try and get really fit. We are all looking forward to reaching our destination and getting down to work again. It will be four months since I did a really full day's work.

BULLETIN TWO

October to November 1942

Once more your editor and only contributor greets you. Any falling off in the quality or quantity of this number, in comparison with the last one, can be ascribed to the cares of fatherhood - newly thrust on the editorial shoulders. I need hardly say how proud I am of both mother and child and I am sure the latter will nobly uphold the traditions of the Brown family, whatever they may be.

Well, to resume this saga at the place where I left off, we soon disembarked at Suez which had grown enormously since I was there the day war broke out in 1939. We got off pretty quickly and were hoofed into a train Egyptian style where we waited, grilling steadily in the sun, for three hours. The carriages (German) were primitive to say the least and after so long at sea the flies were an absolute pest. After an interminable wait we at last got moving, at first in fits and starts punctuated by long waits during which hawkers offered us out-of-date magazines and papers at exorbitant prices. Later we really got cracking and were soon burning up the sands of the desert at a great pace. As it grew dark the choir got together with a few old good ones and the time passed quite pleasantly. During this journey I learned one tip about opening tins of bully beef in hot weather; when one end is opened it is NOT necessary to invert the can and tap it to loosen the contents. I lost a whole tin of bully beef in a squidgy mess on the carriage floor by this means.

We arrived at our destination, Cairo, in the bright moonlight (fortunately for us) and were faced with a three-mile route march to the camp. I found this really very enjoyable; the Padre and I brought up the rear of the column singing "Ilkley Moor B'aht'at" at the tops of our voices just to let Egypt know we were there. We finally "kipped down" at about 2 am. It was perishingly cold and we were quite glad to get up again at 6 am. We were in a large camp at Almaza of which we occupied a small part miles away from any exit, amenity or convenience. The first day was pretty chaotic whilst all our equipment and stores were being sorted out and checked. I had my first sight of the Regiment's guns, very inspiring. Everybody was very helpful and full of hints and tips about life in the desert. I am afraid many of the tales were a good deal exaggerated.

I have a brand new Ford three-ton truck to carry my equipment, myself and three men. This is twice the usual size of truck a medical officer gets and is very palatial, but very bumpy on the roads here which are universally vile after three years of war traffic.

I managed to get into Cairo a couple of times to do some shopping. Things are very plentiful but very expensive. One of my first purchases was a "flea bag" to keep me warm when the sands of the desert grow cold. I also got a small grip to contain odds and ends as I shall have to leave my tin trunk behind when we move on. Everybody here is very confident about the present push which had started two days before our arrival. (This was the Battle of Alamein). I only hope their confidence is justified.

The Egyptians are a curious people, very degenerate I should say. The men are very effeminate and the women beautiful at fourteen but look like English women of forty by the time they are twenty - only not so good looking. (A quick recovery from a bad faux pas that!)

Apropos of nothing at all, that reminds me of the best funny story heard since landing here. It concerns a pushing young commando officer who went out into the desert disguised as an Arab with only a camel and a wireless set for company. His idea was to capture Rommel single-handed and bring him back alive, so to speak. After three weeks a code message was received, and after the cipher people had decoded it, it was sent to the brassiest of brass hats. His astonished eyes read "Rommel captured; send truck at once". The brass hat was as bucked as a bronco and the truck was just ready to leave when another man came hurrying over from the cipher department. Quoth he, "Sorry sir, there is an amendment to that message; for "Rommel captured" read "camel ruptured"!

To resume; after a few days we moved on again to another place, a bit more desert-like this time and I had my first experience (in the Army) of sleeping in a bivouac. This is a little tent 6 feet by 4 feet by 2 feet high, made in two identical halves. Each man carried one half and two men sleep in each bivouac. Officers get one each;

my little low camp bed just fits in nicely and I am very comfortable.

Whilst we were in this area, we learned to drive vehicles in the sand and to dig them out when they got stuck and the gunners also learned to fire the guns over open sight at targets less than 500 yards away! We hope we will never be placed in this situation because it isn't a usual one for our type of gun.

The day's routine goes roughly as follows: 05.45 hours - roused by batman. 0600 hours - roused by batman, get up, shave (thank goodness for the old electric razor worked off a couple of wireless batteries), wash and dress. 0630 hours - sick parade. 0700 hours - breakfast. 07.15 - kill flies. 0800-1200 hours - work of various sorts. 1200-1230 hours - light lunch. 1300-1800 hours - more work. 1800-1830 hours - dinner. 1900 hours - kip down; maybe read in bed for a bit. It is dark at 6.30 pm so bed is the only place to go and very welcome it is too.

During one of our journeys we passed the pyramids. Ruined (like most other ancient monuments) by advertisements for whisky, beer and other less romantic commodities in close proximity; I found them very disappointing. A much more thrilling sight is the enormous number of aircraft and other items or war material which we see from time to time. It makes you feel good to see it all and to know that this is just the beginning. The organisation is good too.

Flora are conspicuous by their absence but there are some interesting fauna about. There is a grasshopper affair about 4 inches long; it jumps a yard and can also fly. There is also a bird with a call exactly like a police whistle; the first few times I heard it, I thought it was some sort of air raid alarm! Then there are one or two odd lizard-like animals, our friend the mosquito (but no malaria) and, of course, the flies. I now know where they go from England in the winter time; they are all out here!

I have been doing a sick parade for some negroes from the Seychelles; they haven't much English and it has given me a chance to give my once excellent French a badly needed airing; I get on quite well. During this time I had a trip to Alexandria but didn't see much of it as I was too busy. It struck me as a much nicer town than Cairo. The sea is very refreshing after the desert dust. During this time I tried to see Tom Smith, my cousin; his unit was quite close to us but he had been moved to another one miles away a fortnight before. His nickname, not unnaturally, is "Lofty"; as he is so tall. Perhaps I shall run across him again later.

A few days after this we moved out even further away from civilisation to Alam Shaltut, and settled down to some real desert training. We are now living in our trucks and each truck does its own cooking. The food is top-hole and I like the life very much. I am lucky in having a pretty good lorry crew, there are five including myself. I will try to give you a thumbnail sketch of them all. Blythe, the driver, is a dour near-Welshman from Frodsham in Cheshire. He does things when asked politely but doesn't like obeying orders. Scruffy and untidy, I have to chase him constantly to make him keep himself and the truck clean and in good order but I think he will turn up trumps if we ever get in a tight corner, which seems unlikely as things are at present.

Lance Bombadier Harold Jones is my medical orderly. Aged 36 he was a male nurse at Bicton Mental Hospital near Shrewsbury and knows his job inside out. He is large and phlegmatic, makes tea as I like it and also cooks well. A pearl without price, nothing shakes him and he really runs the whole show like a good butler. I am sure of him in any crisis. Bill Brain, my batman, is a native of Stone, Staffs, and is universally known on the lorry as "Prim" because his second name happens to be Primrose. He has tried to live it down but hasn't managed it so far! He is aged 36 and has done every job under the sun; he was working for Joules Brewery as a drayman when war was started and knows my cousins, who live at Stone, very well. He is another slow and steady fellow, a deep thinker and loves an argument, so he is an excellent companion. He is also a very good batman and looks after me like a mother - only better. HE doesn't put things away where I can't find them! Johnny Ellard is Dan-Dan the sanitary man. He was a glazed-tile maker and comes from Longton. He is a good worker and takes pride in doing really well any job he is given. His chief defect is that he has little or no roof to his mouth, a distinct handicap in an argument! So you see I am very well off in my immediate companions and I am getting on well with the Regiment as a whole.

One of our chief tasks in the past few days has been to learn desert navigation. There are absolutely no landmarks in the desert and one has to find the way by compass, both by day and night. By day we are all well spread out and the navigator is out in front; I occupied this privileged position the other day and did pretty well. But the real fun happens at night when it is as good as a Marx Brothers film. The vehicles form up in a square with 15 yards only between them, and the navigator is about 20 yards in front of the square. Bear in mind that it is pitch dark, the navigator has to steer dead straight come what may (more or less) on a compass bearing and after three years of war the place is strewn with slit trenches, rubbish dumps, barbed wire, old iron and what-have-you, and you will see the possibilities.

We set off in formation with a grinding of gears and were soon spanking along at 12 to 15 miles an hour. I stand with my feet on the passenger seat and my head through a hole in the roof of the cab; my back and sides are protected from bruising by stretcher pillows tied round my waist (trust me to attend to this little item of personal comfort!). All I can see is the back of the truck in front of me and the truck 15 feet away on each side; there are no lights, of course. At first all goes well and the sand beneath is hard and smooth; suddenly everybody in front slows down and there is the crash of hastily changed gears. All this means that there is soft stuff in front and the wise man slows down a bit and leaves himself space for a good run at it. The truck in front moves slower and slower and finally gets stuck; if you aren't awake and moving fast enough to get round, you get stuck too. I am not moving fast enough. There is a quarter of an hour's hard digging and the air becomes hot with the flow of language. Fortunately, it's quite cold in the desert at night so we don't get too hot digging, just uncomfortably warm. At last we get going again after a few false starts and the trucks reform. We go tonking along over some more good ground. Suddenly there is a yell from up in front, or maybe nearer, accompanied by a dull thud (if the fool has run into a slit trench) or the rending sound of tortured metal (if he has hit a stanchion or rubbish dump). Everybody who is alert swerves to left or right;

to stop is fatal as one is almost inevitably rammed by the following vehicle which can't stop in time. So this nightmare yet side-splitting journey continues; some of those fallen by the wayside are picked up by the breakdown gang who follow at the rear. Others less fortunate are condemned to a night out of camp; this hasn't happened to me yet but I never go out now without my bed on board, just in case, and some tinned food as well.

As I write this, news of the Allied landings in North Africa is coming through. It certainly looks as though we have really started at last. Perhaps the regiment will return across Europe instead of by sea; I certainly hope so. If I have to be away from home, I want to move about and see as much as I can; you can see from all the above that life isn't half bad and very safe. I don't think we shall be needed here now.

Up to now, this personal history of the war to end all personal histories of the war has dealt with the novelties of desert life and training. I am now going to deal with the incredible boredom and sapping of initiative which occurs after the novelty has worn off and in the absence of fighting; some of the methods of relieving the boredom will be described. A recent order permits the recounting of personal experiences so I will just emphasise, for the benefit of the censor and some others, that these are my own personal experiences and do not necessarily refer to those of any other officers in the unit in which I serve.

Well, to be brief, I have done sweet F.A. to speed the progress of our glorious army; in fact my life out here has been an exact repetition of the last two years without any of its compensations. In other words, I have sat upon that portion of my anatomy designed for the purpose and contemplated nature in the raw, or rather the sand. There is no doubt about it, the desert gets you after a bit, especially if you have little to do. Meals and the arrival of the post become the major events in a day which is spent killing time and flies in that order of importance. This is even more so in my case as my day's work, apart from the odd casualty (from football), is over within an hour or so of sunrise. One result of this "desert brain" is that everything becomes too much fag to be worthwhile. Even the offer of some leave produces only a lukewarm response; fixing up trains and hotel reservations seem herculean tasks; the noise and crowds of a busy town have little attractions after the quiet of the sands. Don't forget that all this is my own feeling; had I been fighting I daresay things would have been different; I can only describe things as they affect me in my own situation. Of course, this feeling only comes over one gradually and is relieved from time to time by various incidents, some of which I will now attempt to describe.

One of the first things that happened was the elaboration of my sleeping accommodation. You may or may not remember that I started with the idea of living hard, sleeping in a 6 foot bivouac at night and eating in the truck with the men. That was soon changed. My bivouac soon acquired 2 foot walls of canvas made from odd bits found in the desert, while many of the others started using full sized tents. I held out against this for a long time but finally gave way and now share a tent with the Padre. There is, needless to say, a pukkah Officers Mess and we eat off china. In addition to all this, I got back the de luxe part of my kit which had been left in my tin trunk in a safe place; I thus had my camera available again in addition to various sports clothes and other creature comforts.

While this mushroom growth was proceeding in the camp area, training was not neglected. We were all out once or twice a week learning to find our way about the desert and how to get free when bogged down. Training culminated in a week during which the unit carried out the various tasks it would be called upon to do in battle; brass hats and instructors were two a penny, and though my professional services were never actually needed it was a near thing once or twice and I shall have a tale or two to tell when I get home.

While all this was taking place, the Battle of Alamein had been fought and won and Rommel's rout from Egypt was taking place. We heard the artillery barrage on the night of October 23rd; it was like continuous thunder throughout the night and gave rise to much speculation. We knew we had the stuff but not one of us in the unit imagined that Jerry would be chased so far or so fast. When the news of the landings at North Africa arrived we realised something big was in the air, the end of which we had yet to see. Everybody imagined we should be in it soon ourselves but the weeks have gone by and we have done nothing. Futility has once again raised her foul head and there are parades and spit and polish. However, all this will go again when we get a real job to do.

During trips in the desert one finds dumps of the most amazing salvage, whole tents, ammunition boxes (these make ideal containers for rations and belongings) belts of live cartridges, crashed aircraft, water tins and even an ordinary domestic bath of all things, in addition to the inevitable "non returnable" petrol tin which is actually very valuable salvage. We collect as much of this as we can and make dumps in the camp area for collection by the salvage people later. We haven't seen anybody yet, in spite of the blitz on salvage which is going on out here at present. During a stroll the other night I even found a perfectly good football; it was in perfect condition and only needed blowing up in order to be ready for the game. Why it hadn't been found before and why it was left there in the first place one can only guess. Some luckless unit probably had to move off suddenly at night and left it. The propensity of the English for kicking a ball about is amazing; whether the temperature is 98° or 0° in the shade they still play football. Frank Ommaney, in his book *South Latitude*, tells of the crew of the *Discovery II* who played football on the pack ice of the Antarctic whilst waiting to see whether the ship would be wrecked by the pressure of the ice surrounding her!

Once the novelty has worn off, there is little to break the monotony. We have an occasional sing-song in the truck when my mouth-organ comes into its own and is much in demand. About once a week we manage to get into Alexandria where we can get a game of tennis, a bath and a decent meal. Thank goodness it is still possible to eat fried chicken, peach melba and sticky cakes with real cream in them without feeling an absolute criminal - though it costs, if anything, more than in the black market at home. The unit of currency out here is the piastre. A newspaper costs a piastre and everything else is pro rata so most things cost about two-and-a-half times what they did in England in peacetime and a decent dinner costs at least ten shillings. So living out here isn't quite as cheap as you might think, especially when there is plenty of spare time to kill.

Returning from the town after dark presents some problems (or used to until the camp blackout was relaxed a bit). After one very late night we got hopelessly lost (I was driving and NOT navigating) when somebody in camp accidentally showed a light. So anxious was I to reach him that I failed to keep a sufficiently sharp look out dead ahead and committed the classical blunder of driving into a slit-trench at about 25 miles an hour. When the noisy recriminations of those in the back died down, and we had dug them out from the pile of greatcoats, rifles, kit and parcels under which they were buried, we had to leave the truck to be dug out in the morning and walked the last mile on foot. I learned my lesson, and never get out of third gear now unless I am very sure of my route. It is amazingly easy to lose one's way at night, and even in the camp area I have spent ten minutes trying to find a truck or tent less than half a mile away. A compass is the only answer.

Another (and very unwelcome) relief from monotony is the periodical sand, or more accurately dust, storm; we have another and much less polite name for it. It is impossible in mere words to do justice to this most unpleasant of all desert phenomena. The one we had the day after I got back from leave surpassed all previous ones in violence and unpleasantness. It started in the night with a bitterly cold wind which gradually grew stronger until it was blowing half a gale. With it came more and more dust. It was impossible to see one end of a tent from the other and the dust formed great drifts at every crevice. To venture outside was not only silly but apt to be extremely hazardous. The wind became so strong that 44 gallon petrol drums were being blown about the camp like balloons; every few minutes the rumble of one could be heard approaching the tent, and it was a tense few moments until the noise began to recede in the distance. Many bivouacs were torn to shreds and several tents came down. One party whose bivouac got blown away became hopelessly lost while making their way to a truck which they KNEW was not more than 10 yards from them, and when things died down they were half a mile away.

The Padre and I were lucky, though we spent a restless night; the ridge pole of our tent parted early in the proceedings, and though everything else held we spent an anxious time watching the bellying canvas and wondering how long it would be before an extra strong gust lifted the whole issue or brought it down on our heads. The storm continued most of the next day; it was impossible to venture outside except upon the most urgent pretext; no cooking could be done, and we had to live on chocolate, which was all we had in the tent, washed down with neat lime juice as we had no water. Try it some time; I had heartburn for days after! When we did finally emerge the scene of desolation which met our eyes almost beggared description. Torn and bulging canvas flapped drearily in what breeze was still remaining; everything in the open was covered with drifts of sand as with snow at home; every lorry and truck had about six inches of sand on the floor, and the stuff had penetrated everywhere, even between the pages of note books and this writing pad. It was a couple of days before things were anything like straight again and the officers mess has only just started to function properly again today, six days later. One of the trucks was out late that evening and got caught; the driver and his mate got out to see where they were and when they tried to mount again each received a series of violent electric shocks. The damp sand had short circuited the ignition system, and all the metal parts of the truck were alive. So you can see on all counts a sandstorm is an experience to be dreaded.

On this dreary note I will end this bulletin and in the next one I hope to deal with Christmas and New Year celebrations and further desert doings.

BULLETIN THREE

December 1942 to February 1943 (approximately)

It was Christmas Day in the desert; it was all very dull and pathetic really. It was a dull grey day and the sun only shone for about an hour in the middle of the day. There was a football match in the morning; we were afraid nobody would be able to stand up later in the day. We had a good dinner of pork and plum pudding but it was really very dull with an awful air of false gaiety; everybody's thoughts were obviously elsewhere. Everybody tried to drown their sorrows in strong drink, with various degrees of success. I retired early after a very dull party which the officers gave to the sergeants in the evening. Boxing Day was much better however. Four of us went into Alexandria and had an excellent game of tennis and a blow-out afterwards.

After the mild flutter at Christmas life settled down to its dull routine again; I didn't even see the New Year in. After a bit, everybody begins to get on each other's nerves; every statement provokes wordy and acrimonious argument and one is apt to retire to one's tent and brood in dudgeon.

The next relief to the trivial round came in the shape of an opportunity to visit the El Alamein battleground and positions further forward. This was a most interesting experience; I cannot say much because of the security question but I think I can safely say a few things. One thing that immediately struck me was the difference between the markings on British and German graves. The Germans usually use a big ornate Maltese cross with a big black border and large lettered inscription "Died for the Fatherland and Freedom". The Allied graves bear a simple white wooden cross with just the soldier's name, rank, number and unit and sometimes his steel helmet. I thought the contrast summed up rather well the difference between the Allied and Axis idealogies.

Some of the war equipment we saw was very interesting; the new Sherman tank is a wonderful job. I saw several which had had chunks knocked out of the armour without the shells penetrating. We did not see much enemy stuff as most of it had been taken back for examination; what there was looked pretty good especially the

German motor transport. I had a ride in a Volkswagen (the people's car); it is a pressed steel job with a four cylinder engine, air cooled, at the rear and torsion bar suspension instead of springs. It rides marvellously over rough country and did about 60 on the road. It was funny to see the names of well-known English and American firms on the equipment - Solex carburettors, Dunlop tyres and Ford trucks were all much in evidence, all made in plants in Germany and occupied countries, which just shows how international this war is. I had a field day among the abandoned aircraft on the landing grounds. There were dozens of fighters all practically intact, several bombers and one Gotha troop-carrying glider which interested me very much. The landing grounds were pitted with bomb craters made by our bombs.

I saw many other things, pleasant and unpleasant, but the whole impression left on me was one of horror at so much wastage and destruction both of material and lives. It made "homo" seem very far from "sapiens" if you take my meaning. However, it left no doubt in my mind that the Germans were decisively beaten by better soldiers and better generals, not only by superior war material. The Alamein victory must have cost him a lot of equipment and aircraft which he could ill afford. By the way, I was surprised to find so little sign of human habitation at the famous El Alamein. All it is is a small railway station (it would have been called a halt at home) and a few tents. It is the same at El Daba and the other places.

Soon after the foregoing I had three days leave in Cairo and that was quite enough! I went down by road with the survey officer who was going on a course, thus saving me from a heavy bill for the train fare; the privilege was dearly bought however. We were in an open truck and it was perishing cold; we stopped at a NAAFI half way and thawed out with coffee; by the time we reached the pyramids at Mena it was 12.30 so we adjourned to the Mena House Hotel for a good lunch. This hotel is definitely one of THE spots; I should like to stay there for a bit one day but we had already booked at Shepheard's, so resisting without difficulty the importunities of the dragomans (plural of dragoman - I have always thought it was dragomen, didn't you?) to visit the pyramids on a camel, we hoofed off into Cairo and took over our rooms at Shepheard's. This is an enormous mausoleum of a place and was earmarked by Rommel as his headquarters. We had a very nice room on the fourth floor at 6/6d a day and feed yourself. It was really astounding to wash in a hand basin with taps, brush your hair in front of a full size mirror and sleep again in a bed with sheets, after so long in a tent.

After a good wash and brush up we met a former officer from the Regiment and had dinner (turkey!). Later on we went to an extremely good concert of classical music, the debut of the newly-formed Cairo Symphony Orchestra. They were an amazing mixture of members of all the forces and civilians, and we thought we had bought a pup, but they were really good. And so to bed.

The next morning was devoted to "a look round"; after a visit to Barclay's bank to draw heavily on our accounts we went shopping. I bought several copies of Punch and Flight and a couple of books; my companion fell for a pipe. Cairo was very crowded and we soon got fed up with the pestering attentions of hawkers, dragomans, etc, so took a tram out to Mena and had lunch at the hotel again. After lunch we "did" the pyramids in the usual way; I found them very disappointing, and was much more interested in the tombs which a party from Harvard University are still excavating. Most of the contents had been removed, but the wall carvings and paintings were perfectly preserved, embarrassingly so in a few cases. The engineering feat carried out in the building of these tombs would be amazing today; how the ancient Egyptians managed them is miraculous. For instance, many of the ceilings were made of blocks of granite 20 feet by 10 feet and 4 feet thick, which must have been brought hundreds of miles and then raised on pillars. The Sphinx too was quite impressive.

After bathing in ancient history, we returned to modern convenience in the shape of tea in the lounge at Shepheard's, the waiter being summoned with a couple of hand claps. I am going to do this in Barrows or some other café when I get home just to see what happens! In the evening we went to an Egyptian cabaret, just so we could say that we'd been to one. It was really quite good and there was one marvellous dancer there who did things with her hips which I would have thought anatomically impossible. The Egyptian music is very noisy and squeaky with a tendency to wobble from note to note like Chinese and Japanese tunes. We left at 11.30 and fell into bed very tired after a hot and dusty day.

Next morning we had a look around a couple of museums including one which contained a panorama of the Suez canal; looking into a sort of illuminated box, one was made to feel like a passenger on a ship traversing the canal. The illusion was most lifelike, and the whole thing was very well done.

In the afternoon we set off to visit some of the mosques in the city but got fed up with waiting for trams, and went to the pictures instead! We saw "This Above All" and thought it awful tripe. In the evening we went to an excellent gramophone recital of classical music.

And that's all. I saw a friend for an hour and had lunch with him at the hospital next morning and left for the desert the same afternoon; I had had quite enough of the flesh pots and was quite looking forward to the desert again. I arrived back just in time to get involved in the dust storm which I have already described. When that died down, I soon settled once more into the eat, sleep and moan routine of the day.

Soon after this, began the period of alarms and excursions which always precedes any eventful happenings. We are going to so-and-so and so-and-so. We were being broken up (true, to some extent, as the transport was suffering from a lot of desert driving by amateurs!). We were going to do this, that and the other. Even (from the wishful thinkers) we were going home! After a period of this coupled with an outbreak of mild jaundice in the Regiment, solid proof that we really were going to do something came in the shape of some new trucks to replace old ones and an order to be ready for anything by a certain date.

Then the flap started! We had been in one spot for so long that nearly everyone had begun to think that we would never move. Enormous quantities of extra kit - tables, chairs, etc - had made their appearance and nearly everybody had too much of nearly everything. Fortunately we had remained fairly mobile-minded on the MO's truck and weren't caught napping when the move finally came; we spent what days remained in getting things really ship-shape. We put in a couple of good big shelves and a 16-gallon water tank which was to stand us in good stead later on, as you shall hear. I also found time to visit some ancient Roman ruins, some distance from the camp. Only the foundations remain but they are excellently preserved, especially those of the main church. There are the ruins of a whole city called Abu Mina, with some really gigantic wells, one of which we reckoned was nearly 200 feet deep, by dropping a stone down it and timing how long it took to fall, and heated Roman baths. The whole place was quite unspoilt; I don't suppose many of the thousands of travellers who come to Egypt each year have ever heard of the place, let alone visited it. So I came back with a feeling of conscious superiority! Soldiers from the last war and this had scribbled their names on the walls. I did NOT add mine!

I think this is a good point at which to end this edition of the family bulletin and I will detail the saga of our voyage to war in the next one. For now - farewell.

BULLETIN FOUR

Into Battle

When I left you at the end of Bulletin number three you will remember that we were about to leave camp and move forward at last - we hoped into the battle area. My birthday occurred three days before we were due to break camp, and it was accompanied by certain disquieting symptoms which made me pretty sure that I was about to develop jaundice. This placed me in a quandary. I knew the sensible thing to do was to report sick and go back to hospital in Cairo. I was reluctant to do this, as I knew it would mean losing the Regiment to which I had become very attached. Besides, I might get posted to an infantry or tank regiment which would be much more dangerous! So I decided to keep quiet and hope for the best.

We were due to leave at about 6.45 am on February 1st and I was wakened by Brain at 5 with the news that Blythe, my driver, was taking somebody else's places and he (Brain) was to drive instead. As Brain hasn't touched a truck for two years (apart from driving mine on one or two occasions) I foresaw an anxious and irritating journey. However, I could do nothing but look pleasant - difficult at 5 am on a cold dark morning, when I was already beginning to feel a bit groggy.

I travelled in the rear of the regimental transport column so that everybody would know where I was if I was needed. This was an advantage in one way, as it meant that I started nearly an hour later in the morning, and stopped at NAAFIs and other beauty spots en route without being found out, but it meant getting into camp correspondingly late which was a snag - especially as I had to hold my sick parade in the evening.

A more or less typical day on the road runs as follows, with minor variations according to the mileage to be covered, the number of NAAFIs en route, etc. We are woken at 5 and breakfast is 5.15 ready to move off at 6. Once on the road there are no planned stops until 10.30 when we have a 20 minute break. At 1.30 we have an hour's break for lunch, shave and wash and brush-up, after which we go on till reaching our camping area for the night, usually at about 5 pm; it is dark by 6 so we don't get much time to pitch tents, etc. Forseeing this, we had scrounged half a tent, which we fixed to one side of the lorry. It forms a good waterproof lean-to, and can be let down or rolled up in five minutes after a little practice. I had my own little bivvy, which only takes a few minutes to erect, so we were well away. We generally turned in at about 7.30 pm as there was little else to do.

There are, of course, many stops in the day additional to those above, due to traffic hold-ups, obstructions, etc, and if we got fed up with a specially dull or bad piece of road I just stopped and we had a brew of tea; nobody was any the wiser as I was last vehicle, and I could always plead a petrol stoppage if anybody inquired. I am afraid my truck had a very bad reputation for petrol trouble by the end of the trip, though actually we had an almost trouble free run!

As I had anticipated, Brain proved to be a most irritating driver, though quite safe. The coast road, on which we travelled, was pretty worn after all the army traffic, and an additional hazard was provided by the many craters which the Germans had blown in it. These had been filled in roughly by the Royal Engineers, but had sunk, so traversing one at any speed was disastrous. I soon discovered that Brain was short-sighted and applied the brakes far too late, accompanied by the sound of breaking glass and many expletives from the unfortunate passengers in the back. All this meant that I had to keep a sharp look out and couldn't relax, so in the end it was less of a strain to drive the truck myself.

We followed the coast and had the sea on our right hand most of the time. We spent the first night at Fuka, beyond Alamein and near the aerodrome where a large number of German fighters lay abandoned, practically undamaged. As we pitched camp I began to feel horribly sick and had a high temperature and severe abdominal pain. Finally I was sick and felt a lot better. I felt better the next morning and by living on a fat-free diet consisting of biscuits, Palestinian chocolate and milkless tea, I managed to carry on, though the shaking we got in the truck didn't improve matters. My eyes went yellow a couple of days later, but that was all.

On the second day we pushed on past Mersa Matruh on a still

good road; apart from a few burnt out tanks and lorries here and there the country we saw bore little sign of the battle which had been fought so recently; it was clear that little attempt had been made, at any rate on the coast, to fight more than a rearguard action. Most of the abandoned tanks were Italian, whilst a good many of the burnt out trucks were British ones which had been captured either in France or in the previous June advance to El Alamein. We spent the second night between Matruh and Sidi Barrani, in what were for us idyllic surroundings. There was actually grass about and a few flowers as well! Some stalwarts walked a couple of miles to the sea for an evening swim, but I (as you have no doubt guessed) was not one of them!

The next day was very wearing. The road was still good when we started and remained so until we had passed Sidi Barrani - nothing but a small group of buildings, none with a roof and most of them with a wall or two down as well. It was an awful scene of desolation in the early morning sun. Then the road became terrible, or so we thought at the time; later we realised it must be classed as comparatively good; I have seen NO road so bad in England; there was a large pothole every two or three yards. After a few miles of this going I was scared stiff that some of my medical stuff would get broken, so we stopped for a brew of tea whilst we repacked it. We repacked it to such good effect that we came all the rest of the way at the cost of only one small bottle broken - a good record, as anyone who has travelled the same road will agree.

By the time we had done this, the convoy had got well ahead, so we went in our own time, and stopped at the NAAFI at BuqBuq for a good lunch. Most of these places, like Buq-Buq, Gazzala, etc, are just names on the map, sometimes with a building or two, most often with nothing to mark their position except a sign. After a good lunch of pork chops (I had to stick to biscuits and chocolate!) we were fortunate to get hold of a dozen tins of various assorted fruits which we put away in the locker and decided that we would only use them if things got really bad.

After this we bumped and rattled our way along the coast to Sollum and up the famous Halfaya Pass; this is steeper than anything in England and the guns took hours to get up, so we waited at the bottom and lay on the beach for an hour's well-earned rest. It was 3.30 pm by the time we reached the top and the view back over Sollum bay was glorious, though too hazy for a photograph. On our way up the Pass we saw the caves in which the Germans lived during the siege of 1941, when they were surrounded and held out for so long. To our relief, Graziani's road started at the top of the pass and we had a smooth run for the rest of the day on tarmac, though it was a bit narrow. We left Bardia, a nice looking little spot with a lighthouse, on our right and leaguered for the night on what we later found out was a minefield! However, nobody got hurt and there were no explosions, so the mines must have been either very old or non-existent.

Next day we pushed on through very uninteresting country past Gazzala (one building only!) and on towards Tobruk. However, Fate decreed that we were not to visit this famous shrine of so many memories. During the siege of Tobruk the enemy built a road round the perimeters to bypass the town and called it the Axis Road. We called it many other things! It really was dreadful; I didn't think any vehicle could stand up to such a surface. We just bounced along from ridge to ridge at 10 miles an hour. The seat of my truck was far too springy, and every jerk of the road springs meant three or four bounces; I finished the day with a raw place on my back where the centre button of my greatcoat had pressed into the skin. We bumped and bashed our way along, gradually getting further and further behind the main body of the convoy. Trucks were passing us at 15 and 20 miles an hour making an awful row, but in sheer desperation I at last tried it myself and found that the truck rode much better at a higher speed. The afternoon we passed the roofless buildings of El Adem aerodrome, and the smoking wreck of a Hudson aircraft which had crashed early the same day. We were very tired when we reached camp that night.

The next day we left the Axis Road and rejoined the main coast road for which relief we gave much thanks. At the point where the bypass joins the main road the I-ties had erected a pillar of what looks like brown mud, with a bas relief showing the building of the road, and ornate yellow letters which spell out "Strada del Asse" to the horrified observers of this hideous edifice; I was reminded of the decorations in the old Empire Theatre in Hurst Street, Birmingham.

Once on the good road again, we made excellent time to Tmimi, were we pulled in to what turned out to be a fairly long stay in a very delightful spot. There were lots of bright little flowers and birds and butterflies galore; the only blight in the picture was our old enemy the mosquito who was a bit of a nuisance at night. When I walked into the officer's mess on the first night, the CO (whom I hadn't seen for six days) took one look at my yellow eyes and blew his top! He resented the fact that I had sent five of his officers to hospital when they got jaundice but had not gone myself! After I explained that I realised my own case was very, very mild and that I was not infectious he calmed down a bit; but he was a bit grumpy for the next few days.

We had a grand time here during our stay, and were well looked after in the matter of canteen supplies, comforts and welfare; we had a good wireless set and plenty of cigarettes, chocolate, tinned fruits, etc. During our stay here the last signs of my jaundice gradually disappeared; I tried to wangle a transfer to a Field Ambulance and the famous 'combined shoot' of the three non-artillery officers took place. The Field Ambulance transfer didn't come off so I am going straight on to a description of the shoot. The Regiment had a couple of days practice shooting and, there being a few spare rounds left at the end of the first day, the CO allowed the Padre, the Signals Officer and myself to have a go. We had all been paying careful attention all day, and had a pretty good idea how things were done; we worked everything out to such good effect that our first round was dead right for line and one thousand yards too far; the third around landed plumb on the target - one of the best shoots of the day! The Divisional Commander of the Royal Artillery (who was watching) was tickled pink, and the CO stood us a bottle of whisky that night in the mess on the strength of it.

Well, in due course the time came for us to pack up and move on; we had enjoyed our stay, but were glad to be on the move again. In an attempt to improve the riding on rough roads, we had packed the driving seat of the truck with waste paper and rags until it was board hard; the improvement in riding comfort was immense. Our journey now took us through the Jebel, the most wooded and lovely part of Cyrenaica. For the first day or two the road had an excellent surface, and passed through wooded scenery which gladdened our desert-weary eyes. On either side plantations of trees and wooded slopes were to be seen, and the road wound up hill and down dale. Every mile or so we saw a little white villa, one of the houses erected by Ente Colonizzazione Libia, an Italian organisation formed to exploit the land. The immigrant from Italy got the house and an area of land already ploughed, and paid part of his profits back to the organisation as the purchase price. They have certainly cultivated the land well; the scheme was a Government racket and really it took thirty years before the immigrant actually owned the property.

After this we got diverted round Derna on to more awful roads, where most of the officers mess crockery, renewed at Tmimi, was broken. We spent one night in a setting strongly reminiscent of Welsh Wales; it was very high up, there was a heavy dew, and great difficulty was experienced in starting the vehicles next morning owing to dew on the plugs. Towards evening of the same day, we descended Barce (pronounced Bar-chay) Pass, a magnificent road cut in the escarpment above the town. The Germans had done some excellent bridge demolitions here, which we had just as cleverly circumnavigated. The view over the plain below was magnificent, but was marred by the Ente farmsteads previously mentioned, which were symmetrically placed and looked like a small white army drawn up for review. That night was spent on an Ente farm, the officers mess being the principal room. It was a peculiar sensation to walk on a stone floor again, eat in a room with a door which shut, and hear voices echoing, things we had quite forgotten after so much tent life.

The next day, as I had a couple of patients to take to hospital, we set off for Benghazi just in front of the main convoy, travelling independently - a great relief. We had a good road with no traffic to speak of, and bowled along at a steady 40 miles an hour. We were soon at the top of the Tocra Pass above the town of the same name. Similar to Barce Pass in geography, the view from it was much finer; no Ente buildings marred the view over a magnificent plain to the sea. The road at the bottom was lined with trees, and dead straight for a couple of miles. On the way down we saw an old overturned British tank on whose flat bottom the I-ties had painted "British Built, American equipped and Italian mined". The I-ties plastered their language everywhere; nearly every Ente building had daubed on it "Duce Duce Vinceremo" or some other slogan.

Before it received such a bashing from both armies, Benghazi must have been a very fine town, though rather smelly, as it is built on a causeway and has a lake in the centre. The airfield was one of the largest and finest I have seen outside England. I went to the officers shop in the town and was able to buy a few necessities, and one luxury - a pair of brown knee-length boots which will be grand if we meet any mud; they were so good and so cheap (£2) that I just couldn't resist them. We stayed a couple of days on the Tripoli side of Benghazi in a field of sweet-smelling flowers, while we got everything tuned up for the next lap of our journey, which was to be somewhat faster.

When we started out again, the road once more ran across the desert; it had a METALLED SURFACE, but this was in poor repair in many parts. For a day or two the journey was quite uneventful, not to say monotonous; in due course we passed Marble Arch, or to give it its high-sounding Latin title, Arae Philandrum, on the borders of Tripolitania and Cyrenaica. The Arch is a white stuccoed-looking affair which straddles the road; I was irresistibly reminded of Shelley's poem "Ozymandias". We passed all the famous places on the coast road, like Agedabia, Nofilia and El Agheila - the latter still enveloped in wire and minefields. The minefields were so dense that we had to camp right on the edge of the track, which meant that we got covered in dust from passing vehicles.

The next day I had my first taste of shellfire - from our own shells! You will remember that I travelled near the back of our convoy; in front of me on this occasion was an ammunition truck, which stopped very suddenly one evening about 4 pm. I was quite close to it before I had managed to pull up; everybody was getting out in a great hurry, but it wasn't until I saw a great flame lick up the side of the canvas cover that I realised the truck was on fire. I couldn't pass, as I was afraid my own truck's cover would catch fire because the road was very narrow, and I couldn't reverse far as there were a lot of vehicles piled up behind me. I knew there were forty rounds of ammunition on the truck, and believe me I spent a nasty ten minutes waiting while everybody behind reversed; finally I managed to put about 100 yards between my truck and the burning one before the stuff started exploding. We all dived for cover under trucks; we daren't go off the road, as there was considerable danger of mines, so we had to wait two hours while the truck burned itself out. Every few minutes there was a colossal bang and large bits of metal buzzed through the air in every direction; I was scared stiff on my own account, and also afraid my truck would be hit by a hot fragment and set on fire; however, nothing happened. The Regiment was not popular, because the explosions cut off all the communications between the Eighth Army and base in Cairo because of damage to the telephone lines which ran alongside the road. They seemed disposed to make a joke of the matter when I got into camp (very late); I am afraid I failed to see any cause for laughter!

At Buerat, another small placed covered with minefields, we left the main road and took to the desert again. The track was very narrow and ran a lot of the way through minefields. We thought all this was rather a scare until a truck coming the opposite way pulled out to pass one of ours and had its rear wheel blown off! After that, we kept scrupulously to the track, which later degenerated into a dust track. The wind was blowing dead astern so that we got all the dust from the column in front, we all finished up looking like chocolate coloured coons. We had two days of this and on the second night we had actually to pitch our tents on the track, owing to the danger of mines.

I must finish this now. It is really far too long anyway. The next edition will follow as soon as may be and I hope will tell of our last lap up to the front, and as much as I can tell of what took place there. Cheerio for now.

BULLETIN FIVE

March/April 1943

This is your editor Alex writing to you in English, though you may not be able to read it. Censorship having been relaxed somewhat, I am now allowed to talk a bit about events which have happened some time ago, so on with the saga.

As we closed edition four I was left on the side of the road wondering when somebody was going to tread on a mine. We were to have stayed one night only in this God-forsaken spot, but plans miscarried and we were faced with another day there. Convoy after convoy passed us, covering us with dust until we looked like a gigantic nigger minstrel show off on a tour. We expected to stay another night but got a sudden order to move in an hour. Thus began the terrible two night journeys which were to end our advance of the forward areas. We were all prepared on our truck, and had tested all the lights that morning to make sure they were OK. Our annoyance can be imagined when, on turning them on for a last minute check-up, the whole lot fused except for the side lights! As we were in convoy, the absence of a rear light was distinctly awkward; the Padre, who was to follow us, took a very dim view of the matter (naturally enough!).

We set off at last light in the usual cloud of dust and as it got darker it became clear to me that we were in for a sticky time. The dust was so bad that it was impossible to see the truck ahead until we were right on top of it, and when HIS rear light went out (as it very soon did) we were really in the soup. Brain's eyesight (nothing to write home about in daylight) was much worse at night, and he was literally driving with my eyes, which meant that I never got any rest even when I wasn't actually at the wheel. For the first three hours the route lay along an indefinite sandy track. Fortunately, we moved only in fits and starts, as otherwise somebody would certainly have been hurt; we did exactly 18 miles in three and a half hours! After we regained the main road things got better in a way. There was a fairly full moon, and we tanked along at 20 miles an hour, which seemed like 40 with no lights. My eyes felt as though they were on foot-long stalks with peering through the windscreen at the truck in front. The trouble was that a good bit of the road was tree lined on each side, and you couldn't see a thing because of the shadows. The Germans had carried out pretty good demolitions, and the diversions were sometimes perilous in the dark; several people went off the road and there was no rest for me; every two minutes Brain would want to know "how much room is there on your side, sir?". However, we finally made it, and went into a camp about 11.30 am just east of Tripoli. By the time we had cleaned up, had breakfast/lunch and got sick parade over, it was 2.30 pm; there were still the lights to be fixed. This took an hour and just as we were finishing off reading our mail (the first letter for seven days) the order came through to move off in three hours! Sleep was out of the question owing to the heat and the flies, so we just relaxed and had a jolly good grouse!

We were at the back of the column as usual, so it was nearly dark when we got moving; I tried to sleep in the back of the truck, but the road was too rough. As we left Tripoli the nightly air raid was in progress and the tracer bullets from the ack-ack made a lovely pattern in the sky. It was practically the first sign of enemy activity since leaving home, and everyone was a bit windy though interested! After dark the road improved a bit, and we went along at a good pace. It wasn't long before the lights let us down again and we only had side lights. Our chief trouble again was with the diversions round enemy demolitions; Brain nearly put us in the ditch, and I had to take over. The road soon became worse again. There were no kerbs or verges, and the road was narrow. One of our guns and its tractor went off the road and down a 20 foot drainage ditch, falling on its side. They sent an SOS back for me, but only the driver was hurt; he had a cut forehead which I had to stitch up to stop it bleeding, but nothing worse. Lucky 51st Medium Regiment again! Soon after this incident, we had another petrol stoppage - genuine this time, and our first for a long while. It took us a long time to clear it and while we were doing the job the side lights went out! This was really TOO much, and I felt like bursting into tears. After many harsh words we decided to carry on; by this time what was left of the convoy was well ahead; trucks were falling out right and left with odd troubles and several went off the side of the road, which was raised on a sort of causeway most of the time. None of them were damaged and they all came in next day, which was a very good show. We bumped and banged on our way and dawn found us on the Tripolitania/Tunisia border, a few customs houses and some barbed wire. We were far too tired to experience even the mildest thrill, and once over the border the road got much worse; pothole after pothole, some of them 4 feet in diameter and a foot deep. The shaking up produced two more petrol stoppages, the last within sight of the spot where everybody else was having breakfast. However, we eventually reached Ben Gardane, first outpost of the Mareth line, and paused to repair the ravages of the journey. Here we learned that Rommel had made a desperate sally from the hills on to the plain of Medinine, and had been repulsed with very heavy losses. Later we were to learn that he had lost 4,000 troops, murdered by our artillery and machine gun fire. It was an enouraging moment for us, on the eve of our baptism of fire. While we were at Ben Gardane, I was able to inspect an example of one of the Mareth strongpoints. It was well built of concrete and was a self-contained post, all sanded-up, a relic of the "Maginot Mind". While here we also had what we hoped would be our last sandstorm.

We were soon on our way forward again on atrocious roads with many diversions; soon the Mareth Hills appeared in front of us. It seemed strange after so long to be seeing enemy held territory for the first time; I think all of us paused mentally to look back and to speculate on the future; a turning point had been reached in the career of most of us. That night we were within sight and sound of German artillery for the first time; it was a nasty feeling but we were soon to get used to it! We weren't shelled, but it was amusing to hear the news bulletins from home - "patrol activity on the Mareth Line". The next day we moved into a battle position and soon our guns were firing on the enemy for the first time; I fired one round, just to show willing! We had nothing back, and it was really very peaceful, just a few dog fights and our bombers going over to make life interesting. However, something was in the wind we knew, and after a few days the plans came through. We moved into a new position in a nice deep wadi (a dried up river bed) and waited for zero hour. I had my R.A.P. (Regimental Aid Post) well dug in in a little grove of palms, nice and handy to the guns.

As zero hour approached the silence seemed to become deeper; a German bomber droned away over towards Mareth and the frogs croaked in the stream in front of our position. It was a brilliant moonlight night, and it was difficult to associate war with the peaceful beauty of the scene. At zero hour, the medium guns opened up; I already knew their friendly "woof" and it didn't scare me. Soon after, the twenty-five pounder field guns joined in. It was the first time I had heard them, and I was scared stiff; they make a terrific crack and the shells go whistling overhead so that I thought at first it was Jerry replying. After a bit I got used to the noise, and was able to look round again. As far as one could see the sky was lit with the flash of the guns, the deep red of the twenty-five pounders and the bigger yellow flash of the medium; even the moonlight was dull by comparison The field artillery were firing terrific salvos, sounding more like machine guns than twenty-five pounders. The noise was hideous, like some giant boiler maker's shop in the infernal regions.

During this barrage the Regiment sustained its first fatal casualty. One of the guns had a "premature"; this happens when a shell explodes before it has left the barrel of the gun. There is a lot of metal flying about and unfortunately one of the gunners was hit in the side of the head and killed instantly.

The barrage ceased as suddenly as it had begun, to be succeeded in contrast by a deathly stillness, broken only by the ringing in my ears. Soon the enemy began to send a few rounds back at us - so few and so inaccurate that it was obvious our guns had done their work. During the barrage an endless stream of vehicles of all descriptions passed along the track near my Regimental Aid Post, sharply silhouetted against the bright sand. So ended the Regiment's first barrage, and we learned from the news next day "the Eighth Army had been successful in straightening their line!". The big show was yet to come. Plans came through soon; we were to move to a new position at night, so I went up by day to have a look-see and took a digging party with me. The place was as bare as your hand and right under Jerry's eyes, as usual, so we needed little encouragement to dig deep; it was risky to move about after mid-day when the light was in the enemy's favour; he sent us on our way with a couple of rounds as we left, but they both fell short.

We moved in that night; a thin drizzle helped to reduce visibility a bit which was a comfort, though it made the hole we had dug very damp. We got there with no hitch, and spent some time admiring the beautiful effects of Jerry's tracer and searchlights; our aircraft were giving his front line stinko, the weather cleared up and we could see them quite clearly hovering around. We put the tent up over our hole. and tried to get some sleep, but it was very damp and cold, and I slept in the cab of the truck.

After a while I got fed up and went to my bivouac for a spot of sleep. I got to sleep all right only to receive the most horrid awakening that I hope I shall ever experience. Jerry was sending them back. Wheeeee-crump! Wheeeee-crump! they seemed to be landing just on the other side of the bank beside which I was dug in. I cowered beneath the clothes wondering how soon it would stop. After about twelve rounds had landed the shelling stopped, and I scuttled across to join the others in the R.A.P. Curious how the herd instinct operates on these occasions! We all waited with bated breath for the casualties to arrive but none appeared, and we found next morning that nobody had been hurt and none of the stuff had come within a hundred yards of the R.A.P. I felt a trifle sheepish when I thought of my terror of the night before, and after this I was never quite so scared again. I had learned the rookie's first great lesson; the bark is worse than the bite.

We stayed in this position for a couple more days after which, so far as the Regiment was concerned, the war became one of movement, and as far as I and my minions were concerned, one of excavation. In other words - we dug. How we dug! We never seemed to have completed one R.A.P. and got comfortably settled before we were up and off. We dug in sand, clay, rock, soil and gravel, and in a mixture of all five which is worst of all. In five days we broke one pickhead and two shafts; I don't think I shall ever get blisters again from holding a golf club! We were getting a bit depressed about the war, which didn't seem to be going too well, but we little knew that Monty's "left hook" was on its way, planned from the beginning, as he told us later. All WE knew was that one morning we woke up and Gerry was gone. So ended our part in the battle of the Mareth Line. The Regiment had done well, and had already learned a lot which was to be useful later. I personally had got used to the idea of being shelled and knew more or less how I stood with regard to my R.A.P. staff. I had also proved the wisdom of taking a look-see at positions myself, and of digging-in no matter how safe the place looked. My training at home was beginning to bear fruit.

During the battle the Regimental officers had been too busy to run the men's canteen and I took it over, though I didn't like the idea much. As soon as we finished fighting, a spate of buying commenced and I was kept very busy. I got in an awful mess with the accounts, and when I handed the canteen account over again after three weeks, it was thirty bob short, which, of course, I had to pay!

We pulled out for a rest in delightful surroundings, an olive grove in the foothills of Mareth. It was pleasant to sleep above ground again, and not to have to dig holes or worry about enemy action. The area was very green and fertile and we climbed one of the hills for a look round. The view at the top put into my head two good opening lines for a small piece of verse. I struggled hard with it for two days, but couldn't do much with it. The weather was now getting too hot for comfort, and we were all glad when the order came to change into khaki drill. The men's shirts have been redesigned this year and are made of thinner material. They are in the form of a safari jacket, to be worn outside the shorts. They are very cool and comfortable, but rather shapeless, so most of the men wear them tucked in inside the trousers, thus defeating the object for which they were designed!

During this time Rommel's forces had been going back steadily towards the Gabes Gap where they were expected to make a stand on the Wadi Akarit. In a few days we moved up again towards the front line, taking a cross country route away from the coast road, which was already crowded with northbound traffic. The next day we reached our new position, astride the coast road just outside a little village called El Melah a few miles south of Wadi Akarit. It was very hot, but as the road was an obvious target for bombers we needed little encouragement to dig really deep. At this position our defences against enemy action reached a new stage of elaboration. In addition to the R.A.P. and my bivouac, which were both well below ground level, I also dug a really deep and narrow slit trench with a top cover of sandbags as a protection against machine gunning and splinters from our own ack-ack barrage, which was pretty dense at times. We were expecting a noisy time and we got one. Sure enough, enemy bombers were over at dusk and they came singly all through the night, dropping flares and bombs of various types, but they did singularly little damage and we all felt very safe in our funk holes. One of our trucks had a narrow escape. It was always parked in one position, but at the time in question it had been moved, which was lucky, for a bomb landed right between the wheel marks of its former position. One night the bombers hit an ammunition truck or dump away to the south of us, and we had a firework display for a couple of hours. By day we had a grand view of our own fighter and bomber boys going over, with an occasional enemy fighter patrol. On one day we had quite a busy time; enemy fighters were active and they ran for their own lines right across our position, so I was able to check up on my aircraft recognition; I had a really close view of an FW190 for the first time. The climax came one evening when a formation of fighter bombers flew into the most intense light ack-ack barrage I have ever seen; they were all shot down in the space of a couple of minutes, and from then till the end of the North African campaign we hardly saw another German machine in the air. There were plenty of mosquitoes about at night but, fortunately, not malaria carrying so we weren't worried about their bites.

During this stage of the battle we had under our control a captured German big gun, variously known as "Adolf","Hermann" or (inevitably) "Big Bertha". We kept firing away industriously with it every night at colossal range, just to let the Germans in the back row of the stalls know we were there.

Things built up in the usual way and one morning the barrage started at 4.30 am. It went on for over three hours, and when it ceased the RAF took over with a record number of fighter bomber sorties. It was a glorious sight to see our chaps go over right "on the deck" and return unmolested time after time. The medium bombers joined in later, with wave after wave of eighteen plane raids, and very rarely was a plane missing when they returned. It was all over in a matter of hours; the Germans had expected us to wait for the moon before we attacked; our tanks went through a prepared gap and outflanked the enemy, who had to run for it, and was soon past Mahares on his way to Sousse. We, as usual, didn't follow very closely in pursuit, but stayed where we were for a few days. I took the opportunity of going up to the recently evacuated enemy front line trench and positions. Wadi Akarit itself was a truly formidable natural obstacle, and every yard had been sown with mines and barbed wire. In addition, our own front line was overlooked by the usual ridge of hills, and a hefty anti-tank ditch had been dug at the only weak spot. Yet we breached the line by direct frontal attack in 24 hours - a wonderful show.

The part of the line I explored had been held by Italian troops; they had obviously left in a hurry, for in one place we found an anti-tank gun with a round up the spout already to be fired. Shell holes every few yards bore testimony to the nerve-racking qualities of the British barrage. It must have been a noisy time. The amount of equipment lying around was incredible, most of it brand new. There were enough new shirts and underwear to fit out a battalion, and the gas masks were still in their original packing and hadn't been opened since they were made; the troops in this sector could only have been in the country a few days. Amongst other interesting material I came across "Mein Kampf" and "The Destiny of the Axis", both in Italian. The I-tie is a great bloke for getting really "dug-in"; the trench systems were very elaborate and the dugouts large. Both were filthy and littered with little red devils - hand grenades which also act as booby-traps for the unwary. They make a helluva bang but don't do much damage unless you get one under your foot.

All this time trucks had been passing our R.A.P. on the main road, full to the brim with prisoners; we all thought Jerry had been caught napping, and this was borne out by what we saw later on, on our way up towards Sousse. It was twenty miles before we came to the first demolished bridge, although there had been several obvious places before that where the road could have been blown up had the enemy had time to do so.

It was at this time that I renewed my acquaintance with men of the Luftwaffe, of whom I saw quite a lot during the Battle of Britain. The individual concerned was shot out of the sky by a couple of patrolling Spitfires; caught napping nicely, in fact. He landed by parachute near one of our batteries, and was brought to me because he had been wounded. He was most fortunate to be alive; the bullet had entered low down below the angle of his jaw and had come out through his open mouth, chipping one of his teeth in the process! An inch higher at the outset and it would have pierced his brain. He was the vainest human being I have ever come across - myself not excepted! All the way down in the truck (and on several occasions while I was attending to him) he kept pulling out a small pocket mirror and looking to see the extent of his wound; one look I could have understood, but he kept on at it. After I had dressed his jaw I noticed he had a cut on his scalp, probably where the cockpit hood had caught him as he baled out. In order to get a clear view of the wound, I told my orderly to cut away the hair (very long and auburn) round it. At the first snip, our prisoner leapt into the air, yelled "Nein, nein, nein" at the top of his voice and made for the door. I thereupon washed my hands of the matter and they took him down to a field ambulance where I learned later they shaved the whole area completely!

This was the last item of interest at the Akarit position. I forgot to mention that it was here that Regimental Headquarters were shelled for the first time; no injuries, but they made a few holes in the mess tent and smashed a cup or two, which rather annoyed us.

In due time the call came for us to move forward, and we got on the move one bleak morning at 6.30. We crossed the Wadi Akarit by a long diversion round the blown up viaduct. It was only a few days since the battle, but already the place had been cleared up; minefields were all wired off and marked and the wonderful South African engineers were already at work making a good surface to the diversion. There was little sign of the war, except for an occasional truck abandoned or burnt out, the odd crashed aeroplane, and German and Italian signs at the side of the road. It was twenty miles before we came to the first crater, and there were no signs of any attempt to organise defence works. We had surprised the enemy without a doubt. The road up was pleasant, and the country gradually became less pastoral and more orchard-like; the road was bordered in many places by banks reinforced by giant cactus plants - soon to become a familiar sight, and an even more familiar sensation when we fell over them in the dark! Mahares, the first place of any size we passed through, was a little fishing town, a picture in the bright morning sunshine, with a blue sea on our right, and a water-logged JU52 seaplane (the first I had ever seen) on the foreshore. After a luncheon stop to pick up some guns from another regiment, on we went. We had a royal welcome as we drove through Sfax that afternoon, and we all enjoyed the sight of a few pretty faces (and figures) after so long away from the sight of a white woman.

Our bomber boys had left the part of the town we passed through absolutely untouched. Indeed the only signs that war had been that way were the telegraph poles. Every third one had been torn off with military precision at exactly the same height - about three feet from the ground. I heard later that the docks had been pretty well bashed about by our airmen, who were feted in the town because of their good aim.

Our way now lay through miles of groves of olive trees, planted in long straight rows. Most of them looked very old and unproductive to me. That night we camped in one of the groves. I treated the local big-wig, who had a bad case of the itch, and we dined off some excellent eggs and goats milk (boiled of course) as a result. The local populace were glad to see us, but weren't above making a good thing out of us if they could. We got tired of turning away offers of eggs in exchange for tea or sugar or V cigarettes (a vile issue cigarette, which the men only smoked when they could get no other, and which they were forbidden to swap for food). From this point on, I was frequently asked to treat members of the local populace, and have a photograph of some of my young patients. A large percentage of the Tunisians live near the starvation level and go about in rags. The main roads are good, but villages are old and in poor repair for the most part, even allowing for the ravages of war.

We got off to an early start the next day, but were held up soon afterwards by a really good Jerry demolition; single-line traffic only was possible, and there was a jam both ways for about five miles - eloquent testimony to our command of the air. Near the demolition we passed General Montgomery's own personal Grant tank with "Monty" written on the side of the turret. We had fallen behind the main body a bit, but after the demolition the traffic thinned out and we cracked along at a nice steady 40 miles per hour to El Djem, where we stopped to look at the Roman amphitheatre. This was in a fair state of preservation but was ruined from the aesthetic point of view by all the native dwellings clustered around it. There was also a squadron of Tomahawks on the flat ground all around. This was the largest and finest amphitheatre in North Africa, and rivalled that of Carthage in capacity. After El Djem, we had an uneventful trip on to the little village of Bourdjine where we stopped for the night.

That's all this time, folks. Next issue tells all about the last battle and after.

BULLETIN SIX

Ever Onwards — April 1943

I last said, in Number Five, that we were at the little village of Bourdjine, and just catching our breath before the last run up to the fighting line again. George Blythe (our driver) had now returned to the truck; going over it he found we had a broken front spring, and the fitters worked all night to get the truck roadworthy again. We got off the same morning. As we neared the main road we passed a graveyard; it was Saturday, and the widows from the village were sitting beside the graves of their menfolk. Every Saturday these women come to the graveside and sit in silent communion with their loved ones, sometimes staying all day.

I was determined to have a look at Sousse, so we halted by the roadside to let the convoy get well ahead. Whilst we were waiting a native gendarme, on a beautifully caparisoned horse, stopped for a match. He was dressed in a very smart blue uniform with a red cap, and wore a superb pair of riding boots. We had quite a chat with him and he gave a graphic description of the air raids on Sousse, which we gathered from his gestures had been pretty fierce.

After a suitable interval we moved on into Sousse; it was only 7.30 am, so there wasn't much stirring. We went straight downhill towards the docks and harbour, to be greeted by a scene of desolation which beggared description. The harbour was full of sunken and overturned ships, and several damaged ones still afloat; cars and railway trucks, twisted into grotesque nightmarish shapes by the blasts and fires, lay on the quays. Buildings on the quayside were all hit, and some had been reduced to mere masses of rubble. Neighbouring streets were littered with broken glass, rubble, slates and tiles, and steel girders. A nude female plaster dummy from a costumier's window added the last hysterical note to the scene. The damage was tremendous, and though I knew it had been necessary my heart bled for the people whose property had been destroyed. The Germans had left only three days before, and no attempt had yet been made to clear up the mess. Over it all hung an uncanny silence, so that when we stopped the truck not a sound was to be heard except our own very small voices and the lap of water against the quay. A silence like the stillness of death hung over the area, and we were none of us sorry to move on. The bombing had been very accurate, and apart from the odd bomb here and there damage was confined to the immediate area of the docks and railway yard, where a train full of German ammunition, useful to us later, had been hit.

It was in a sober frame of mind that we left Sousse and set out to catch up the convoy. The road was good, though narrow, and all the way along it was the same story - broken down or shot up cars, trucks or tanks, demolitions (not very effective and obviously done in a hurry) and here and there a pathetic little roadside grave, freshly dug, with an improvised cross made out of wood from a ration box. The scene had become so usual that we hardly noticed it. We had a pleasant run, and caught up the convoy just as it was pulling off the road to camp at the little village of Sidi-Bou-Ali.

We camped in the usual grove of olive trees, and everybody wondered how long it would be before we saw action again. I had my usual sick parade of the local natives. While I was doing it a couple of planes flew over; the kids were terrified and ran for cover, though they were our planes. Whether the act was put on to excite our sympathy or not I cannot say, but they certainly looked frightened. Five minutes later they were happily playing the local version of our blind man's buff.

That day Germans were found in the village, living as natives; this news made us all very security minded. I fancy quite a bit of fifth column work went on, as it was obviously impossible to give every native a pass. I expect the Germans paid well in food for information given, and hunger knows no laws. The contrast to this was offered by one fellow who came up to my truck and showed me a letter of recommendation from his master, saying he was a good and trustworthy servant. This man, from what I could gather, wanted to join up there and then and fight with us; the French apparently wouldn't have him. I only got rid of him with the greatest difficulty.

Our camp life was now being made miserable by several new species of insect, notably a low flying fly with an irritating bite, which always went for one's ankles and calves. They were very persistent and took all the pleasure out of reading or sitting still; the only way to avoid them was to wear boots and slacks; they never came above knee level.

After a couple of days we left Sidi-Bou-Ali for our battle positions; as we pulled on to the road we were met by a most stimulating sight. Eighteen American Mitchell bombers flew by, right "on the deck", escorted by Lightning fighters, the first I'd ever seen.

As we went into battle, the situation on our front was that the Germans had taken a very strong position in the high hills just north of the town of Enfidaville. It was an ideal defensive position, and had been long prepared; we knew we had a hard nut to crack, and were once more, as at Mareth, in the unenviable position of being overlooked all the time by the enemy, while we were for the most part on a bare plain with little natural cover but small plantations, all of which were registered by the enemy guns and shelled from time to time. The date was the second week in April.

Our guns were located behind a low ridge which gave them some flash cover, and the command posts were in a couple of deep wadis. I put my R.A.P. in the wadi next to one battery, so that I was actually between the guns of the two batteries - not an enviable position to be in, for we had the noise from our own guns and the best chance of being hit by enemy shells replying. However, the wadi was twelve feet deep, so we felt pretty safe, and in fact it turned out to be the best R.A.P. of the whole campaign. We were in a good position as we never needed to go above ground even for our meals; we just walked up the wadi, which was just as well, as it turned out. We were overlooked by the enemy from a position just over four miles away, and had to keep our heads down after mid-day. Unfortunately, there wasn't room in the wadi for the truck, which had to be left in the open, hidden from the enemy only by a small hillock of rock. Of this, more anon.

The attack, as usual, opened with an artillery barrage. The noise was worse than that at Mareth, because we were between our own guns and in front of one battery in addition to having a lot of twenty-five pounders in the neighbourhood. It was amazing how many guns had been concealed on what had appeared to be a flat plain; every hillock, wadi and mound as far as the eye could see spouted flame. It was pitch dark; the flashes of our own guns lit up the scene almost continuously. After a bit we got used to the noise, and I turned in fully dressed and got a little sleep. The silence as the barrage ceased woke me, and I climbed up the side of the wadi to have a shufti, which doesn't mean what YOU think but means to have a look-see. I was standing blearyeyed looking at the scenery in the rising moon when there was a wheeeee-bang! and a cloud of black smoke appeared about a hundred yards in front of me. I was so sleepy it took me a second or two to realise it was an enemy shell, after which I fell backwards into the wadi. We all expected more shells to follow but all was quiet then and during the next day or so, so it must have been a shot at random. Our troops had attacked Djebl Garci, better known as Razorback Ridge, but had been unable to reach the top, so we were faced with a situation in which the enemy held the top half and we held the bottom. Our guns put smoke down on the top half to cover our troops attempts to advance, whilst the enemy was shelling the lower half in an attempt to dislodge them. We had a front seat view of this for the next two or three days. The Germans were so well dug in that our guns could do little to dislodge them; so much high explosive was thrown at the rock that we expected each day that its shape would have been altered. Our men had to contend with the crossfire, from the machine guns which they couldn't see, and the Germans were using scaling ladders to relieve their men in the higher positions. Away to our right, similar trouble was being experienced with Takrouna, a flat topped rocky hill with a mosque on top; it was eventually captured by a small party of Maoris and a sergeant, who scaled it at night. I went to see Takrouna after the fighting in Tunisia was over, and how it was ever taken I can't imagine. The enemy certainly considered it impregnable.

At about this time the enemy began to make his presence known personally to ourselves. We had been spotted, and for one day we had quite an unpleasant time. Harassing rounds were landing in the area at odd times throughout the day, and now and then the fire became quite concentrated. We kept our heads pretty low, and it all whined overhead, a few dead fragments only falling in the wadi. We made here the interesting discovery that a lot of the stuff which whines overhead or falls around with nasty thuds is clay and stones, and not dangerous metal at all, which was very cheering and comforting. A shell hit the hillock behind which my truck was parked and a splinter went through the body, hitting the medical comforts pannier and breaking two bottles of brandy inside it. This annoyed me very much, as I could have drunk the brandy first, and nobody will believe the bottles had any in when they got broken! My batman had a narrow escape. He was on the far side of the truck when the stuff started coming over; he was narrowly missed by the one that hit my truck, and instead of falling into our handy hole, he started to run. The shells chased him right across the area, and he was lucky not to be hit. Motto; don't panic and get below ground! When he had recovered his breath he said "I reckon we ought to open a tin of fruit!" We all concurred and we duly opened a tin of pears. The result of the shelling was as usual no damage to anybody or anything, except my truck, and we gave them back worse than they gave us.

Life now settled down to quite a humdrum existence, disturbed only by the odd bit of shelling at infrequent intervals and by our bombers going over day and night to pound the enemy positions. The opposing forces were so close together that our field guns put down smoke during each raid over the enemy area to be bombed, as a guide to our airmen. We passed the long hours in the R.A.P. reading and writing letters and having target practice with an Italian rifle we had picked up. We got so used to living below ground level in the wadi, that we had to force ourselves to climb up into the open when it was safe, so that we didn't become too funk hole minded. After some days, we moved our position and went over to the opposite flank, to a position in a wood south of Enfidaville and on a main road. Overlooked as usual all the time, we needed no encouragement to dig; we had our R.A.P. in an old gunpit, suitably altered, which saved us a good deal of time and labour. With regard to cover when overlooked, I feel sure in my own mind that it is far better to dig in and disperse in full view rather than to go into an obvious small wood which is a target in itself and can be ranged on by the enemy guns. This was borne out clearly by what happened to us. One battery, out in the open plain with no cover, never had a shell near it. The other in a small wood was shelled several times, fortunately without producing any casualties, but it was very unpleasant just the same.

On the evening of our arrival in this position we were joined by an ambulance from the American Field Service. This is an organisation of volunteer drivers in charge of cars provided by a Quaker philanthropic body in America. Our driver was an astronomer from Boston; he had been in the Middle East for eight months, in Syria most of the time. Before that he had been doing anti-malaria work in Mexico. We took to each other at sight, and have become firm friends since. I was more than glad to see the ambulance as I had not had one before, and had not been able to get about very well or get my casualties away. Now my worries in that direction were over. Two days later another driver joined us; he was the son of a cotton goods manufacturer in Cincinnati; and, together, the two Americans livened us up a great deal, which was a good thing, as we had begun to get rather irritable with each other after living in such cramped conditions for so long.

I had my bivvy in a nice deep hole, so we were very comfortable. A suspicious scuffling the first night made me wonder if I had rats as my companions, but on investigation I found the interlopers to be a pair of frogs, who renewed our acquaintance each evening until we moved. Even their somewhat clammy companionship was welcome during the noisy times. Sure enough these came in due season. Jerry had the front and back of the wood registered, and sent over a few now and then just to remind us. I was later forced to the conclusion that the enemy had so many targets to take on that he was unable to give any one objective a real pasting. One evening a complete squadron of tanks made its way down the road quite unmolested, and traffic was often nose to tail; just occasionally they got fired upon, but rarely for more than a few rounds. To complete the picture, one of the little reconnaissance planes used by the artillery came and parked itself at the corner of our wood. These little crates fly around at about a hundred feet, taking advantage of every bit of cover and spotting for our guns.

Our astronomer driver turned out to be a keen photographer; he had most of his apparatus with him, and did a few prints for me, the ambulance making a capital dark room. Every evening we had a get-together in the R.A.P. when over tea (laced occasionally with a little Canadian whisky) we argued about post war problems. It was interesting to have a fresh viewpoint on things, and to get the American viewpoint on such questions as war debts, etc. There is no doubt in my mind that the biggest barrier to improved Anglo American relations is just sheer prejudice, the blame being laid equally on both sides. All the Americans I have met have been very decent, and have a great respect for the British soldier, though they think him a bit slow. American truck drivers, who habitually drive flat out, can't understand our convoy speed of 15 miles in the hour, or rather couldn't; I think they are learning now! They do three journeys while we are doing one, and then they have to be laid off in hospital because they have overdone it! They are now learning that "more haste less speed" is as true in modern mechanised war as it ever was in standard trench warfare.

The Cincinnati American, Bob Orton, turned out to be entirely without nerves, which was very stimulating to one or two of the R.A.P. staff (NOT myself) who had become rather jumpy. We carried out a full scale barrage one afternoon, which he and I viewed through my binoculars from the top of my truck. Once again I was struck by the amazing use of every rise in the ground to provide cover for our guns. Some of the field guns were right up amongst the rear infantry. The sight of the shells falling made me feel almost sorry for any of the enemy in the area. We had a few rounds back after the barrage stopped but there was no damage or casualties except for a small tree in the wood.

Bill Cobb, one of our subalterns, hurt his foot rather badly when he fell into a slit trench in the dark, so I seized the chance for a day out, leaving the Regiment to the tender care of my medical orderly, Bombardier Jones. We put a day's rations in the ambulance and pushed off to Sousse, where I got Bill's ankle X-rayed (no fracture). We ate our lunch in the yard of the civilian hospital whilst waiting for the X-ray result, and then had a look round Sousse. They were making a very good job of clearing up the damage and many people could be seen re-entering the town, often driving an overladen donkey cart or lorry containing all their goods and chattels. I couldn't help wondering how many of them would find their homes bombed and uninhabitable. After a look round, we went back towards the front, and down to the beach near Army Headquarters, where we spent an enjoyable afternoon lazing and bathing and having a brew of tea; I read a bit from the autobiography of Benjamin Franklin. I remember very vividly one letter in which he recommends single young men to be chaste or, if this is impossible, to take a rather older woman as a mistress, for various good reasons which he gave in detail! All in all it was a very pleasant day, and we managed to forget the war for a few hours. After I had taken a photograph to commemorate the occasion we went back to our R.A.P. home to find that all was well and that the day had been uneventful.

All this time the Eighth Army had been hammering away at the Enfidaville positions without making much impression; Takrouna had been taken, but the upper part of Djebl Garci remained in enemy hands. It was now decided to shift the main effort inland to the left flank whilst leaving enough guns on the coast to give the Germans the impression that we were still all there. The Americans and First Army were making progress, and part of the Eighth Army went round to join them by forced night marches. The Regiment had to move over to the left flank by night to give concealment, so we packed up soon after dark ready to move. No lights were permitted, naturally, so we were unlucky that there was practically no moon either. Things went fairly well whilst we were on metalled roads but after about an hour we came to desert tracks, far from smooth and very dusty. I had the misfortune (as usual) to be travelling at the rear, and behind a truck which was very capably throwing out its own smoke screen from a worn engine. We none of us knew the route exactly, so had to stick fairly close to the vehicle in front for fear of being left behind. So we just had to drive into the smoke cloud and hope for the best, and it wasn't until we had finished the journey and were just about to pull into a field that we rammed the truck, doing little damage. We were all very fed up and bad tempered; it was 2.30 am, very cold, and as usual, our HQ, who were leading the column, had forgotten about me, and there was nobody to say where I should go. So we just pulled in beside a cactus hedge and kipped down in the truck; we were due to move early in the morning, so it wasn't worth putting up bivvies.

Came the cold and foul-tasting dawn, and we found ourselves in quite hilly country; it was a relief to be able to walk about without feeling one was constantly being watched by the enemy. We discovered the radiator of my truck was leaking very badly. It had been punctured when the truck was hit by shrapnel, but had been successfully repaired. It was now to get gradually worse until, by the end of the battle, we had to stop and fill up about every two hours.

Reconnaissance parties came back with the usual gloomy report about the battle positions "bare as your backside, old boy! All cramped up together. We are taking over from a Field Regiment, and Jerry's got the place taped". (This latter statement proved to be true, for once in a way). I went and had a look myself, and picked a handy spot in a rather wide wadi below one of the battery headquarters. It didn't look a bad spot to me, there was a nice deep hole for my bivvy, and for once I decided not to dig the R.A.P. in, but to use the truck and transfer a little stuff to a nearby hole if any metal started flying around. I also removed my tin trunk and sank it in level with the ground; I didn't want it damaged if the truck was hit again.

The usual period of waiting now ensued, whilst ammunition, etc, was brought up. We were now getting used to the sequence of events - a move, followed by a period of waiting, then a gun programme or barrage, followed by defensive fire or firing in support of local infantry attacks. Then a spot of enemy counter shelling, after they had spotted our guns, followed (soon, we always hoped) by another move. This time we were firing in support of an attack by the Fighting French and the New Zealanders under General Freyberg. We started off with a small barrage - quite a mild affair after what we'd been used to lately - and followed up with a defensive fire task designed to stop the enemy from counter-attacking. In this we were successful (when I say WE I mean all the Royal Artillery units engaged, and not only the 51st Medium

Regiment - we were only a drop in the bucket), and we drew little fire from Jerry, most of it inaccurate.

The next day we had what turned out to be our last air raid of the campaign; a mixed bunch of German and Italian fighters carrying bombs came out of the sun and caught everybody napping. The ack-ack opened up, but for once it was very poor, and the enemy got away unscathed, though their bombs fell wide of any possible target and just dug out a bit more soil from the long suffering Tunisian landscape. The next day our bomber boys started in; we had three waves of eighteen in an hour including some Marauders, which I hadn't seen before; we could see some of the bombs from them hitting the ground.

The next night we had to fire in support of another small attack, and this time we drew accurate, though not very heavy, return fire. The enemy planes must have photographed the gun positions during the raid two days earlier. Fortunately, we had finished firing and the men were all in slit trenches when the rounds began to fall; one of the first salvos hit a box of charges, which started to burn furiously; very fortunately, another round landed very close to the fire about thirty seconds later and the blast of it put the fire out.

We didn't do much more in this position. The next night we had a four hour thunderstorm, which caught everybody napping; I happened, by pure good luck, to have my bivvy fairly well up the side of the wadi, but all the command posts and most of the other living quarters were dug in at the bottom. The Wadi became a young river after about two hours, and most people spent a very wet and uncomfortable night. There was a sorry spectacle the next morning - everybody wringing out wet clothes and re-erecting collapsed tents and bivvies, whilst the smell of drying clothing and blankets pervaded the air. It was a warm and sunny morning, so all would have been well, but we suddenly got orders to move in one hour so everything had to be packed wet. We were off on our last move; the final phase had begun.

What will happen in the next instalment? You will hear about our last and worst position; about the Italian general who wanted to keep his sword; and about the last day, the surrender and what followed. Don't miss your copy! Place your order now!!!

BULLETIN SEVEN

"The End of the Beginning" (Winston Churchill) — April/May 1943

As I closed number six bulletin we had just come out of position at the western, or left flank, of the Enfidaville line, moving off at an hour's notice. The final phase in Tunisia had begun, and the position was roughly as follows. The Eighth Army had been pounding away at the Enfidaville position for three weeks, without making very great impression. It was known that jerry had a healthy respect for the Eighth Army, and would keep as many troops as possible on the front opposite us. In the meantime General Alexander, with units from the Eighth and First armies was pushing an attack in on the enemy's west flank, and the American and British First Army were advancing on Bizerta. Once Alexander's force broke through on the Tunisian plain the Enfidaville position would be menaced from the rear and General von Arnim, who had replaced Rommel, would either have to run for it, with little chance of getting through to Cape Bon and the sea, or else stand and be gradually surrounded, which was what eventually happened. Our task now was to press the enemy hard and demoralise him with a great weight of shells, bombs and missiles. To do this, we were to move to woods in front of Enfidaville, only three thousand yards from the enemy front line; in addition, the matter was so urgent that we had to move in broad daylight and fire a barrage at 6 pm. It was terribly short notice, but we did it, and moreover, we were the first Regiment to be ready, beating the field regiments, who have much lighter guns, to it. The Signals and Survey sections did a magnificent job; the former have to lay all the telephone lines, the latter to survey in the guns, so that their exact position on the map is known.

But all this is anticipating somewhat, so let us return to our wadi, where damp and dispirited at having to move so hurriedly, and knowing nothing about the facts I have mentioned above, we bitterly cursed the powers that be who ordered us about without regard to our own comfort. However, we cheered up as the morning wore on, and had quite a pleasant run back to our hide on the coast side of the main Enfidaville-Sousse road, where we were to await the arrival of reconnaissance parties who had gone forward earlier to select the gun position. Jast as I finished taking a photograph, I noticed our HQ were starting to move off, as usual without notifying me. I had to fill the radiator before we could go, by which time we were well behind. The roads were incredible sights - jammed nose to tail with field guns and lorries all going into forward positions in broad daylight under the eyes of the enemy, who must have rubbed his eyes in bewilderment before sending down the range to his guns. Nothing much happened until we got to a point on the road about a mile north of Enfidaville, where we were due to turn off along a track which by-passed the town. By the time we reached here, a good deal of traffic had passed and Jerry was getting the range pretty well taped; unfortunately, just as we arrived at the junction, there was a box-up somewhere ahead and we spent a very uncomfortable twenty minutes sitting their waiting for it to clear. Traffic coming from Enfidaville tore past us on its way south to safety, and we could see shells bursting in the town, further up the road we were on, and near the track up which we were due to go. So you may imagine that we weren't in exactly a peaceful frame of mind as we turned on to the track.

The ambulance had become separated from us in the mix-up, and was two or three places behind us. As we turned the first corner in the truck we could just see Jock Cobb turning off the main road, when a shell landed very close to him and the vehicle was completely hidden from view by dust and smoke. We all felt sure he had been hit, and when the smoke cleared the car remained stationary for what seemed ages; at last it began to move forward again and we all breathed sighs of relief. However, our troubles were not yet over. A salvo of three one-seventy millimetre shells burst across the track about thirty yards ahead of us, and quite a large amount of scrap whirred unpleasantly close. One of our three-ton trucks loaded with ammunition was in front of us; the driver panicked, jumped out of the truck, and hared off across the minefield. There was no room to get past, and none of the other fellows on the truck could drive, so we had to stop. I was literally yammering with fear inside, but managed to keep a fairly cool exterior, I was told later. The position was decidely sticky. George Blythe, my driver, jumped out and into the ammunition lorry and I took over my truck in his place; it was a good job we acted fairly quickly, as we had only just got moving when another salvo landed just behind us, one splinter going through the cover of my truck, but doing no damage. We did not stand upon the order of our going, and the rest of the trip was fairly quiet by comparison. We arrived at our HQ position to find it was only just off the main road, always a bad thing; they had already had three bursts in the area, one narrowly missing the cook's truck. I pushed off a bit further forward to one of the batteries, which was also just beside the main road; we were to curse that road many times in the next few days, but just at that moment we bent all our energies and backs to digging a really deep hole for the R.A.P. and our beds. The time was 6.30 pm, the date May 7th. An hour later a shell landed on one of the Bofors AA guns attached to us for protection, killing three of the crew and wounding two others. The day ended for us on a sober and gloomy note. As it grew dark we huddled in the R.A.P. and brewed tea, whilst the noise from our own guns shook the ground beneath and around us. There was no enemy fire after dark, and I turned in at about 10.30 pm.

The next day dawned bright and clear, and we all felt a lot more cheerful. We now discovered that we were camped a bit close to an olive oil refinery (the place is dotted with these) which made our lives miserable with a sour odour of fermented oil when the wind was in the wrong quarter, whilst the pool behind it bred voracious (but not malarial) mosquitos. It was baking hot, and as the day wore on the flies made us more and more irritable. There seemed to be little doing in the way of war; the artillery all around us, including our own guns, opened up two or three times an hour, but we had become so used to this that we hardly noticed it, though I imagine the enemy knew all about it at the receiving end! The Germans were pretty quiet on the whole but the trouble was that when they DID have a go the target was all too frequently on the main Enfidaville/Tunis road just east of our position. Fortunately, most of the shells burst on the far side of the road, but just now and then one fell short, when it came unpleasantly close to us. One landed in a pool behind the olive oil works and distributed it's contents in a fine spray all over us. However, the mosquitos got a lot less in number afterwards, so out of evil cometh good!

During the next few days our artillery activity on the Enfidaville front was on a prodigious scale, greater than anything seen since the last war. There were hundreds of guns packed into a wood a mile square and these pumped thousands of shells at the enemy positions, which were becoming more cramped and crowded as our net closed in on them. The flank attack which burst through on to the Tunisian plain from the west was preceded by a terrific barrage; there was a gun every ten yards and the attacking infantry found the enemy completely jellied with fear and incapable of any real resistance, so the guns must have saved many lives THAT night. During the last days our own guns were fired at three and four times their normal rate per minute; towards the end the men got pretty tired, but they saw it through and did a magnificent job.

During this period German aerial activity had completely ceased, and our own, as far as bombing went, was on a small scale; all the bombing effort had been switched to the west and Cape Bon, to stop enemy attempts at evacuation. Our Air Arm was really wonderfully flexible and the main effort could be placed anywhere at very short notice. We had the usual fighter patrols up and also did some "air-shoots". In an air-shoot the pilot of a patrolling fighter watches where the shells fall and tells the men on the guns by wireless how to correct the aim. Two Spitfires did the job for us, one keeping a look-out for enemy fighter interference, which never once appeared, for the enemy had no aerodrome left!

So we come to the 11th May, which date the wireless told us that all organised resistance in Tunisia had ceased. We laughed rather wryly, as if anything, fire from the enemy was rather better organised than our little bit of the front than heretofore, and we were shelled rather heavily several times, fortunately without casualties. Prisoners were now beginning to come down the main road in fair sized batches. On 12th May things reached a climax. The Italian general in command of our sector came across under a white flag to say that he would surrender if he were allowed to keep his sword. He was informed that the terms were unconditional surrender and that the bombers were coming, and returned to his own lines with his sword between his legs. In the afternoon the bombers came, fifty-four of them in three waves, all in ten minutes. The target area was very close to our own lines, so they had to be very careful.

In a few minutes the hill was covered with white flags waving in the early evening light. This was the last ground attack by aircraft on troops in North Africa. The 164th Division had now surrendered, but all was not yet over; the 90th Light Division, traditional enemy of the Eighth Army, still fought on, and the artillery got busy knocking them about. The same evening, the long procession of prisoners started to come in. They looked dirty, unshaven and glad to be out of it. I wondered what their thoughts would be as they passed the quiet groups of our men who were watching them go by without much comment. Our own chaps looked just as scruffy as the prisoners, who must have been annoyed to think that they had been beaten by such a crowd, for the British Tommy doesn't look the tough fellow he really is.

All that night we went on firing shells into the 90th Light Division positions; they were now completely surrounded, our tanks having met each other on the coast road and joined up. It was really futile of them to continue, as they were obviously done and it was an unecessary waste of life on both sides.

On the morning of 13th May the 90th Light Division were still holding out. I was just about to finish off my sick parade when a noise new to most of us was heard. It was like some gigantic beast with whooping cough. Whooooo-ooo, followed by a slowly deepening whine, getting nearer and nearer. Then crump-crump-crump-crump. Mortars! Now mortars have certain advantages over guns and bombs, for the shells fall slowly, there is plenty of time to get below ground and they take some time to change their aim. Against this is the one snag that shells fall almost vertically, and therefore one is a bit more likely to land in a slit trench than a shell which travels fairly horizontally. We got used to the noise after a bit, but they were dropping a bit too close for comfort. Finally our luck, which had been so good up till now, failed us. They found one of our gun positions and put two salvoes down on it. The first wounded one gunner, and the next salvo killed one of our officers and two men who were helping the wounded man, and wounded three others. So the 13th, up to now always a lucky date for the Regiment, provided our only officer casualty, and that ironically enough when according to the radio "all enemy resistance has ceased on the Eighth Army front". By the time we had done our duty for the wounded it was all over. 90th Light had surrendered to General Freyberg at mid-day, and soon afterwards our guns fired their last shots into the sea. On this melancholy note the fighting in Tunisia ended for us; most of us felt pretty downcast at the loss of our comrades. The officer concerned was one of our best subalterns, and I believe he could have saved himself if he had left the wounded man in time and run for cover.

That afternoon we took out the ambulance and went forward to see what we could of the front and the prisoners. Long lines of these were coming in, many of them in their own trucks; they should have burnt them or damaged them as we did at Dunkirk, and so prevented them falling into enemy hands, but they were too tired or lazy to walk, and so we captured many vehicles. Our Quartermaster found a Volkswagen or People's car which he ran for about six weeks. However, it proved to be poorly made and unreliable, and fell to pieces soon after we got back to Tripoli. We didn't see much that afternoon as the roads were crowded with prisoners and sightseers and there were too many minefields for comfort. We returned to camp with one article of spoil only - a very good football, found in the back of a German cookhouse lorry! That night the brew-up fires flared forth once more, as the victory was celebrated in tea, the only available beverage. Somehow, I couldn't work up much enthusiasm for the celebrations. Seeing all those prisoners made me realise how futile it all was, though I can imagine there was great rejoicing at home at what was our first major victory.

We lost no time the next day in getting out of our battle positions, and went down to a spot four miles south of Enfidaville. Everybody was now agog to get around and see a bit of the battlefield; here my ambulance came in as a godsend, for it made me independent. We paid several visits to the front line positions, including one to

Takrouna. I still cannot understand how that place fell. There was, of course, lots of loot to be had, but most of it seemed quite useless to me, and all I brought was a small tent for future use as an R.A.P. People were bringing in pistols and revolvers by the dozen, most of them burnt and useless. I had hoped for a camera, but here discipline had been good, and they had all been damaged beyond repair. The owners hearts must have bled at having to destroy them.

We decided that a visit to the Tunis area was essential, so we started at 6.30 am to be sure of a cool run, the distance being about sixty-five miles. Lots of other people had the same idea, and the road was pretty crowded. We stopped from time to time to view demolitions, crashed aircraft, etc, and we stayed quite a while at Grombalia, a little town on the main road. Here there was a camp of at least 3,000 prisoners, mostly Italian but some Germans. The latter were very pleasant and friendly; it seems a pity that such a pleasant people should have the peculiar kink that they have. Most of them were fairly young, about 23 or 24, and looked pretty fit. The typical Italian prisoner is a miserable being indeed. He is an undersized, runty little man, about 5 ft 4 ins tall; he is always at least two days away from a clean shave and is dressed in a bluey-green uniform of inferior material, shapeless and with baggy knickerbockers. When marching, he has with him a cheap little fibreboard suitcase, in which he carried lots of letters and photographs of his family, a rusty razor and a gap-toothed comb, the latter rarely used to judge by his dirty and unkempt hair. It is quite impossible to treat this little man as a serious enemy. His looks remind me of how our dog used to look when he had been ticked off or been refused a walk!

At Grombalia we also saw that always tragic sight - a bombed cemetry. Beside the elaborate vaults of the Italian families, the graves of soldiers, Allied and enemy, stood out by reason of their stark simplicity. Even the Germans had, by this time, given up using the elaborate black crosses I spoke of in a previous bulletin. What a pity it took a war to make British and Germans find common ground.

We had lunch at quite a nice farmhouse, in whose outbuildings we found an entire Italian advanced motor workshops, complete with everything necessary for repairing engines of all types. It had been pretty thoroughly wrecked, but we found one or two useful things. The place was defended by three German eighty-eight millimetre guns all in perfect condition.

After lunch we pushed on into Tunis. This is a big town, somewhat like Cairo but on a larger scale. It was only five days since the place had fallen so there were no shops open. The town was crammed with troops of all ranks and nationalities; it was pleasant to see a few really smartly dressed French women about. We were able to buy one of the first copies of the Tunis Telegraph, which was a single page news sheet on sale for the first time that day. There was little to see, but we investigated the dock area where most of the fighting took place. Our bombers had knocked it about pretty badly but there was little sign of the fighting. We decided to push on and have a look at Carthage. The road out from Tunis is a magnificent highway, fifty feet wide and lined with trees on either side. We passed El Aouina airfield, where there was a terrific scrap dump of damaged Axis aircraft, including a six-engined giant Messerchmitt 323 and several fighters almost in flying trim. The airport buildings had all been wrecked by our bombers, but it must have been a fine place in peacetime.

Carthage is a really delightful spot situated on a peninsula east of Tunis. The only remaining sign of ancient civilisation is the amphitheatre, the ruins of which are well preserved, though somewhat marred by the wreckage of several burnt-out German lorries. There were lots of them all over the town, Jerry having to some extent imitated Dido. A pity they didn't chuck themselves on the burning vehicles, so making the comparison complete and ridding us of a few more Nazis. Later on, Churchill addressed a large crowd in the amphitheatre, and I dare say he is the greatest man who ever graced that stage. Modern Carthage consists of beautiful white villas, set on a hillside sloping down to the sea with a magnificent view across the bay to the mountains beyond. On the other side of the peninsula is Sidi-bou-Said, where a formation had set up its HQ in a villa, the property of one of the Jewish barons I believe, and one of the show places of Tunisia. Time was now getting short, so we turned for home, leaving quite the nicest place I have ever seen in the Middle East to doze in the light of the sinking afternoon sun.

The next few days were spent loafing around. On the first Sunday out of action we had a full dress parade and thanksgiving service, of which I have some excellent photographs. The CO made a fairly typical speech boosting the Regiment and saying how proud he was to command us. A lesson was taken from Isaiah 25. The relevant parts were as follows "For thou hast made of a city an heap; of a defence city a ruin. Thou shalt bring down the noise of strangers as the heat in a dry place, even the heat with the shadow of a cloud; a branch of the terrible one shall be brought low. And in this mountain shall the Lord of Hosts make unto all people a feast of fat things, of fat things full of marrow, of wine on the lees well refined".

Soon we moved our position in an attempt to get rid of the mosquitoes, which were somewhat troublesome, and pitched camp on the side of a green hill overlooking a small salt lake. Naturally, as soon as we had left the mosquito area, we were all issued with nets! We were certainly in a lovely spot; every evening flocks of flamingo flew over towards the lake, their pink plumage making a picture in the rays of the setting sun. My thoughts went often those evenings to the lovely Duke Ellington tune of the same name, "Flamingo".

We knew we were due to leave for Tripoli soon so everbody was bent on seeing as much of Tunisia as possible. Once again, the ambulance was a godsend, though I knew I wouldn't have it for much longer. We made several trips into Sousse, and one day went out to Monastir, an old walled town on the peninsula just south of Sousse. This was quite a resort in peacetime, with a very fine bathing beach. Here we saw the first lemons since leaving England. Price one shilling each! It's an ill war that blows nobody any good.

Finally, the sad day came when we knew our good friends the Americans had to leave us. The evening before they left I gave a farewell party for them in the ambulance car. There were nine of us, and we drank some concoction of gin, water, sugar and lemon, mixed by Bob Orton. Anyhow, we got through three bottles of gin between us; I retired to bed at about 11.30 pm and fell asleep straight away. I heard next morning that the CO broke up the party at midnight. It seems he didn't like Bombardier Jones, (who had crept in somehow) playing his bugle at that hour! The next day we said good-bye to Jock and Bob, who went off to join their own American Field Service Ambulance Company for the move down to Tripoli. We promised to look them up when we got down there ourselves. In a day or two, on the first of June, we set off on OUR journey to Tripoli. It was going to be a pleasant trip, and we were all feeling good about it.

That's all this time folks, more soon.

BULLETIN EIGHT

"Tripoli Travelogue"

On June 1st we turned our bonnets south for Tripoli, leave and recreation. Our camp site, when we left, was fairly well covered with articles of loot which even this early on had been found useless and not worth carrying further. Motor cycles (often with only a chain missing), tables, chairs, tents and boxes of all shapes and sizes were there.

We were all in fine fettle as we left camp at 7.30. We had behind us the knowledge of a job well done and now we were ready to collect a bit of the rest and relaxation that we felt we had earned. It was lucky that our first day's run was only a short distance of 60 miles to Kairouan, for we were held up for well over an hour at the start by a long column of prisoners marching from Sousse to new camps by the sea. It was an amazing sight, this column of dusty, sweating, dishevelled men laden with all manner of paraphernalia and personal possessions. Many had fallen out by the wayside; they were mostly Italian and were begging for cigarettes and our soft-hearted fellows were, of course, giving theirs away! This made me very angry. Our sailors risked their lives to bring us the cigarettes and I remembered the experience our soldiers had when in the hands of the Italians. Even the Germans used to apologise to our men when they had to hand them over to the "care" of the Italians. Now we were told that the Italians didn't want the war and loved the British!

We had a brew up stop at M'Saken, an Arab town lying in the bend of a mile long loop of the main Sfax-Sousse road. Here we turned off to the west along the road to Kairouan, for we were to bypass Sfax and rejoin the main road again at Mahares. The roads were crammed, for everybody was on the move back and the whole thing had to be organised very carefully. That night we camped on open ground on the side of a hill six miles east of Kairouan. The next morning I set off early in my truck with the intention of dropping a sick man off at hospital and waiting for the Regiment to catch up. When I got to Kairouan, however, the road was jammed solid with vehicles. Plans had miscarried somewhere, and it was pretty obvious that it would be some hours before the Regiment arrived. We had a look round Kairouan, a fairly typical Tunisian town with tree lined streets, white buildings and the usual wog smells. The mosque there is one of the oldest Muslim places of worship in the east; we didn't think we would have time to get the necessary pass to see inside it, and so didn't try, which was a pity as things turned out. We went on down the road, and parked ourselves to wait for the Regiment. It was lunchtime before the column on the road even began to move. We saw our friends from the Light Anti-aircraft Regiment go by and gave them a wave to speed them on their way. It didn't bear much fruit, for about a mile after passing us the officer's car, a veteran Ford V8 of some sixteen thousand miles, threw all its big ends out on to the main road and gave up the ghost. The American Field Service ambulances also passed, but we saw no sign of Jock or Bob; we heard later that they broke a spring just after the start and had a week's holiday at Sousse and a pleasure trip down by themselves. Trust them!

We watched the stream of vehicles go by for an hour, after which time it stopped moving again. It was now nearly 3 pm and it seemed doubtful at this rate whether the Regiment would reach us at all that day, so we decided to go back through Kairouan and see what plans were being made. We found them by the side of the road very browned off, having moved exactly three miles in small fits and starts since 9.30 am! The Regiment's leading jeep had stopped near the entrance to an American airfield so we pulled off the road there and had a brew up whilst we watched the flying. They were trying out a captured Italian Macchi 202 fighter against a Kittyhawk and a Mustang. Judging from what I saw the Mustang had the Macchi licked all round, whilst the Kittyhawk was slightly slower but definitely more manoeuvreable. The aerobatics passed a pleasant hour, and about 5 pm the column at last started to move. This was unfortunate for the 51st Medium Regiment, who had just received permission to brew up (they had been doing it unofficially most of the day). There was a lot of bad language and many burnt fingers as red hot brew cans were removed hastily from the fires and scalding tea spilled from the mugs as the trucks got going. The delay had caused the column to open up a good bit when starting, and by the time we fell in at the tail we were doing a steady forty miles an hour to keep up with the truck in front, and we kept on at this rate, except for negotiating the town, until we were well on the other side of Kairouan. The road surface was now getting steadily worse, and as it grew dark we turned off on what was little better than a desert track, full of awful ruts and potholes. Everybody was getting pretty fed up and hungry, and it was a relief when we once more came onto a good tarmac road. There was no moon, and the truck in front had no tail light, so driving was a bit tricky. We were glad when we made camp in the inevitable olive grove at about 10.30 pm.

We were off early next day, and the journey was uneventful; we rejoined the main road at Mahares and towards evening passed the Regiment's battle positions during the fight for Wadi Akarit. That night was spent just south of Gabes, and the next day's run took as far as Ben Gardane. The day after that we covered in brilliant sunshine a stretch of road between Ben Gardane and Tripoli, which we had traversed by night on the way up. For a long way, the road was now resurfaced and beautifully smooth and ran within a mile of the sea. One or two planes wheeled lazily in the sky, but otherwise there was no sign of the war except for our convoy. At one halt somebody passing us waved to me, but it wasn't until he raised his hat and showed his bald pate that I recognised an officer who had been with me in my Field Ambulance days. He couldn't stop and neither could I, so that was all we saw of each other.

We entered Tripoli that evening, but were diverted round the town to our camp area. A lot of us expected our camp would be beside the sea but it was obvious that the whole Eighth Army couldn't have a seaside billet, and we were in an area of soft sand three miles inland. It wasn't too pleasant an area really, but I suppose it might have been a lot worse. All sorts of latrine rumours were flying around, "Tripoli is out of bounds to troops", etc, etc. However, we soon got organised, and parties of men were despatched to a reserved area of beach for three days at a time. There was also a stretch of beach reserved for officers, where we could go for a few days. I decided to wait and see, and spent some time putting walls on a new bivouac I had scrounged. When I had it finished it was tall enough for me to stand up in, which was a great comfort. The camp area didn't improve with aquaintance; it was very hot, and the prevailing breeze from the sea blew loose sand over everything. It was like living in a miniature sandstorm all the time. My job of running the mess now entailed a lot of work too. There were plentiful supplies of melon, tomatoes and other fresh vegetables to be bought, and I also managed to arrange for a daily supply of ice, which made life a lot more comfortable.

My chance for leave came after about a week; I pushed off down to the beach with my looted Italian tent, plenty of sweets (we had a canteen issue a day or two before) and lots of books and magazines, which had arrived from home just at the right moment in an absolute flood. I think the Post Office had been saving up sea mail, knowing we were coming back to the Tripoli area, for some of the letters and parcels were three months old. Amongst other things, I received a still edible portion of my daughter's christening cake! It was delightful to lie on my bed at night, looking out at the stars and hearing the waves break on the shore at the foot of the cliffs (all of six feet high) just outside my tent. We were reminded of the war fairly often, as there was an anti aircraft school near to us, and the guns fired most days; there were also a few aircraft about. The water was very salt, and too warm to make a bathe stimulating, except very early in the morning. The rising sun and the flies generally woke me for a dip about 6 am. One morning I saw a perfect picture, and wished I had been a painter to record it. Flying out of the heart of the rising sun straight towards me came a homing Beaufighter, skimming the wave tops like a graceful seabird. It flew right over my tent at about fifty feet, and the pilot gave me a cheery wave. I also saw another phenomenon - a perfect sand ring in the sky, like a smoke ring blown by some giant pipe smoker. It was a perfect circle and remained for nearly fifteen minutes before dispersing gradually in the wind.

Soon after returning from the rest camp we were summoned to hear Monty speak. He had just flown back from England the day before. He spoke in the Miramare theatre in Tripoli, the home of opera before the war. All officers had to be in their places ten minutes before the advertised time, and there was no smoking or coughing, except at stated intervals. Montgomery arrived prompt to time - a thin, wiry man dressed in khaki drill slacks, battledress blouse and Tank Corps beret. He had adopted the beret as his standard headgear when he assumed command of the Eighth Army, to remind him as he said, that it was a tank war that he had to fight. His favourite alternative headgear is an Australian hat, decorated with the badges of all the units serving in Eighth Army.

Monty has a magnetic personality and a good opinion of himself and the Eighth Army. He spoke of future operations, reviewed the campaign from Alamein to Tunis, and compared the British, Italians and Germans as soldiers. He handed out a terrific line which did us all good. Many of his prophecies about future operations have already come true; it is to be hoped that they all will in due time.

We now settled down again into a routine. The weather was very hot, so we rose at 6 am, had an hour's training, then breakfast and another hour. Work ceased at about 10.30 am. I ran a course of first aid lectures. The rest of the day was spent in bathing and visits to Tripoli and other places. It was too hot during the day to do anything but laze on the beach and bathe.

Tripoli is, superficially at least, a fine modern town, with tall white buildings and wide tree lined streets. I am told, however, that the drainage is bad, and that the streets flood regularly during the rainy season. The old walled town is out of bounds, so I was unable to explore it. The Fascist symbol - the bundle of rods and an axe - is everywhere. There are two theatres convertible for films and one cinema, all very hot and stuffy. The buildings LOOK good but are really rather badly made; much of the plaster is cracked and broken, revealing the poor quality brickwork beneath. The Roman Catholic cathedral, built in 1922, will look well in another twenty years but has not yet lost its new odeon-like appearance. The RA Army Chaplains department has converted a small private theatre into an excellent Parish Church, where recitals of gramophone records are held as well as church services. This building was used by Rommel as his planning centre, and an outline map of Cyrenaica and Libya is still visible on the wooden floor.

Amenities for the brutal and licentious soldiery were poor, but they improved as time went on, which was more than one could say for the officers' establishment. This was a sort of pavement cafe, where ices could be obtained made of water and rice at a bob a time; coffee (essence) was five pence a cup, and a cake cost sixpence. Across the road was a superb cafe with shady awnings and brightly painted chairs and tables; this was given over to the sergeants, but after a couple of months was reserved for officers, the other establishment being closed down. Amusements in the way of cinemas and ENSA shows were really well organised; it must have been a difficult task, for the numbers of troops to be catered for were enormous. The high spot of the ENSA shows was "Spring Party" which brought to us Leslie Henson, Dorothy Dickson, Beatrice Lillie, Vivien Leigh, and Richard Haydn and several others. We also had a chance to see the film "Desert Victory", which was very good but a bit strung together.

Shopping in Tripoli was a doleful experience. None of us had seen a shop for four months, and were all anxious to spend a little money, but there was very little to be had except trashy "souvenirs" at fantastic prices, and some fair dress material, also terribly expensive. After some time an attempt was made to introduce some sort of price control, but it failed simply through lack of co-operation on the part of the troops, who paid whatever they were asked. The locals must have thought us very soft and simple. Examples of prices are - cloth, of inferior cotton quality, twelve shillings a yard; sandals one pound thirty; combs (sixpence at Woolworths) three shillings, etc. Another annoying thing was the absence of any metal coinage or small change generally. The lowest note in British Military Authority currency is one shilling; below that sum, change is given in Italian lire notes, each worth a halfpenny. The natives soon got on to the racket of saying "no change, George"; the position has improved lately with the issue of British Military Authority lire notes.

Tripoli has a fine harbour, about a mile square, but much of it is now obstructed by the hulks of burnt out and bombed ships, including an Italian hospital ship; this had been camouflaged, so the Italians had only themselves to blame when it was bombed.

Bomb damage in the town is not severe.

The King had arrived in North Africa, and in due course the great day came when he inspected our Regiment, amongst many others. I felt sorry for him; it was a broiling day, and he had thousands of troops to inspect. We later discovered that he was suffering from a bad dose of Tripoli Tummy. Owing to the heat he was in a closed car, so we didn't get a very good view of him. The heat was terrific, and several men in the ranks passed out and had to be spirited quietly away to recover in the shade. I saw an amusing side light on the Royal visit - a squad of Basutoland native pioneers being taught to cheer "Hip, hip, oolah!"

My medical work during this time was becoming more and more heavy. There was little serious illness, but there were large numbers of men with mild desert sores. The heat and the sand and sun combine to devitalise the skin, so that every little scratch or knock becomes septic, and sometimes takes weeks to heal. The fair haired are most affected, and sick parade became one depressing procession of these sores, varied with an occasional attack of Tripoli Tummy - diarrhoea which brings with it a terrible feeling of weakness and lassitude. I had a sharp attack of this myself, and was fit for very little for about a week. There was also a bit of a scare about malaria, but to date there has only been one case in the Regiment, and the men are basically very fit.

In the middle of July (actually, the day before the invasion of Sicily began) we went off to practice camp in the mountains at Garian, sixty miles or so south of Tripoli. News of the invasion came as a complete surprise to us, for we had seen little sign of any preparations for it. Most of the effort, according to the news, came from Algerian and Tunisian ports.

It was a pleasant change to be up in the mountains, and to wake up cool in the mornings. It got very hot in the middle of the day, but it was a dry heat, much pleasanter than the damp and muggy atmosphere of Tripoli, which reminded me of Torquay in the middle of the summer. We were at practice camp to learn how to shoot in mountainous country, after so long in the desert and on flat plains. The difference is quite marked; in the desert you see every round fall and can mark it and correct the range easily. In mountainous country there are dozens of unsuspected wadis and valleys, so that it is quite possible to fire several rounds without seeing one land. At the end of the first day the CO pointed out a prominent target, and fifteen officers each had one shot at it; twelve of the rounds were never seen to land. This gives some idea of the difficulties.

On the second day the Signals Officer and I did a combined shoot; we were without the services of the Padre, and were on our mettle; some people had been unkind enough to suggest our success at Tmimi had been beginners luck. To cut a long story short, we were given a small hill as a target, and allowed sixteen rounds to hit the top. We landed plumb on the target with our eighth round, in spite of not seeing the first two rounds fall. The CO was in fits of laughter, as two officers, unknown to us, had been given the target the previous day and had failed to hit it at all. So we earned a glass of gin that evening in the mess, and are looking forward to our next attempt.

We were all thrilled to hear about the invasion of Sicily, especially as an officer attached to us for the camp had been in on the planning of the job, and was able to tell us a good deal about it. It is now safe to say that the whole show went incomparably better than anybody had anticipated. The start of the invasion took us by surprise; we knew nothing about it, so the security must have been very well handled. There is no doubt that we caught the enemy completely on the wrong foot; many of his units simply walked in and surrendered.

On our return from the mountains we moved the whole Regiment down to the sea, near the place where our officers leave camp had been. We found it terribly stuffy and relaxing after being in the mountains, and the salt water didn't improve the men's sores; in the end I had to forbid bathing for all men who were being treated by me. Now that we were living in more or less peacetime conditions, the question of the mess catering became larger and larger, and I at last attained my dream of having a sergeant to run things for me. Up till now I had only had a useless Lance Bombardier, incapable of carrying out an order or supervising anybody! The sergeant appointed proved keen on the job, and now things are done properly. I am responsible for the catering and discipline in the mess, whilst the Padre handles the accounts side. Soon after our return from the mountains we gave a cocktail party. The whole thing was done in style, and the Royal Artillery Band, who were visiting us at the time, played suitable selections from their repertoire. It really went with a swing.

Life now dropped back into the usual routine, with one or two notable differences. If one was not awakened at 6 am by the local ack-ack school firing their morning practice, the melodious sound of our bugle did the job nicely at 6.30. The bugler is a dance band trumpeter in peacetime and gives us a new "swinging" version of reveille these days. After sick parade a bathe was necessary to get rid of the sweat of toil. After an early lunch I generally slept for a couple of hours under a mosquito net - the only way to keep off the flies. At 4 pm a nice fresh water wash down, followed by tea preceded a visit in the evening to a local cinema or ENSA show, or to the pictures or a gramophone recital of classical music in Tripoli. We had managed to link up again with our American friends, Jock and Bob, and I usually spent at least one evening a week up at the Field Service camp where I met a lot of very nice fellows. We used to just sit around and discuss Anglo-American post-war co-operation and affairs in general. At other times we would go off and see a picture together.

Soon the opportunity came for me to have a little more leave, this time at an hotel in Tripoli. The place had obviously been a sort of high class brothel in peacetime; all the rooms were in pairs with a common bathroom connecting. The baths were rather ducky - only about three and a half feet long and you sit up in them instead of lying down. The weather was rather hot and sticky, so I appreciated the bathing facilities and it was nice to get away from the sand. I did a good deal of reading and letter-writing, and went to the pictures once or twice. After nearly a year out here, during which time I had seen nobody I really knew well, I ran into two peacetime friends within five minutes of each other on the last evening of my leave! They had both been out here over two years, so we didn't find much to talk about.

The question of malaria prevention was looming large when I

returned to the Regiment; we knew we were bound for Italy or Sicily eventually, and we now started to take a couple of little yellow pills each week, with the idea of warding off malaria when the danger eventually arose. The British soldier is as stubborn as a mule when invited to take anything new for his own benefit. During the first week or two, the most amazing properties were attributed to these harmless little pills. They were said to be ralxing, constipating, and indigestible. They made you sleep heavily, they gave you insomnia, etc. After a month everybody just took them as a matter of routine, and no more grumbles were heard.

We had captured and tamed a chameleon, Champagne Charlie, who lived in the truck and had a daily blow-out on flies. He got quite friendly, and would crawl all over us exploring. He went off one day after about a month, and we never saw him again. Incidentally, we discovered that chameleons don't actually change colour with their background, but only deepen or lighten their prevailing brown-green colour.

We had another two or three weeks of dull routine and then went back to the mountains again for some more gunnery. It was all Regimental work this time so I didn't have another chance to see what I could do in the way of shooting. We were working in with another regiment; they went out on a night scheme and their medical officer fell over a thirty foot precipice in his truck. Nobody was seriously hurt, and the truck was later recovered and driven away under its own power; however, I wasn't too happy about the whole thing, as we were due to do an indentical scheme two nights later. During the shooting the other regiment had a slight accident; two men were wounded, one in the back, and I had to deal with them as the other medical officer had no truck. Neither fellow was really badly hurt, but the road was so bumpy that it was a bottom gear job all the way, and it took three and a half hours to take them nine miles to the advanced dressing station at Garian. They both stood the journey remarkably well, but I was a bit anxious about the one casualty, who had lost rather a lot of blood. Apart from this, the practice camp went very well; the Regiment is certainly well trained for war and there is a real feeling of satisfaction at working in your own job and knowing that you are a vital cog in the machine.

Three days after our return to Tripoli, the armistice with Italy was announced. Unfortunately, a Regimental Dinner was scheduled for the next night, so we couldn't celebrate the event really fully, but we toured the camp in jeeps and had a drink at each of the battery messes. The Regimental Dinner was really good, though I do say it myself. It was the first one for two years; we put two of the big tents together to make a dining hall, and the whole show went with a swing. For those interested, the menu was soup, roast lamb with green peas, roast potatoes and cauliflower, melon a la Tripoli, biscuits, cheese and coffee. I felt really very nervous as it was the first time I had supervised such an undertaking but all went well and everybody was pleased.

The fall of Italy had little effect on the local inhabitants. Some of the prisoners working at the hospital were inclined to take liberties, but the town life went on as usual, except the prices of everything became even higher than before.

Rumours as to the future of the Regiment now became rife, and the most fantastic theories were advanced. Last minute preparations were being made, and there was much head scratching over the question of kit. People with small trucks had to leave a good deal behind, but as I had plenty of room I decided to take all mine, as I didn't fancy leaving it to the tender mercies of the army.

After all had been done that could be done in the way of preparations, we settled down to a time of tedious waiting. The invasion of Italy had begun on September 3rd, so we were wondering when our turn would come. We knew all about the Salerno plan, too, except the actual date.

On this note of expectancy I will end, very annoyingly. Next issue will tell all about our landing on new soil, and of what befell us.

BULLETIN NINE

"Exploring the Soft Underbelly" — September 1943

The last edition closed on a note of expectancy; the Regiment was "tooled up", as it were, and waiting to go "over there". The Salerno landing had just taken place.

To ease the period of waiting leave was reopened, and I went again to the same hotel as before. It was a lot emptier of men than last time but there were many more women, mostly nurses leavened with a few ENSA concert party people including Avril Angers.

I wish I could give you a clear idea of the reaction of men, long away from their company, to the presence of white women. You just can't help following them with your eyes when they walk across a room; even the sound of their footsteps on the stairs or their voices in the passage makes you attentive. I am sure the women themselves, most of whom were new to the Middle East, hated all the attention they got, except for a certain type which revels in it. I would have given a lot just to have sat and talked with one or two, but I felt certain they must be fed up with male company, and never had the courage to approach any of them.

I did little of note during my leave, and returned to the Regiment out of sorts and anxious for a change of climate; the weather was hotter and more relaxing than ever, and nobody had any energy or initiative. Our wise CO saw how things were, and to get us mobile and fit again, he arranged for us to go once more to the mountains between Jeffren and Garian. We had a week up there in the mountain air, which did everybody the world of good. We never stayed more than thirty-six hours in one place for the last few days, and often moved at short notice, and twice at night, which got us fully mobile again. On the Saturday we had a gala holiday. The morning was devoted to regimental sports; driving and wheel changing competitions for the drivers, a slow motor cycle race for the despatch riders, and a hoop race, using gun wheels as hoops, for the gun teams; it really went off very well. The afternoon was free for all to do as they wished (you're right - most of us slept). In the evening we had a bonfire, an issue of tea and rum all round, and an impromptu sing-song. I played my mouth organ, and for the first time in my life (and probably the last!) I had an appreciative audience; they wouldn't let me go until I had played three encores; ain't rum grand! The party broke up at about 10.30 after a good time had been had by all.

The next day we moved on again, and pitched our camp on a disused Axis airfield, which had been ploughed up by the Germans before they left. In the afternoon we all went off to take a look at the countryside. We had a look over a tobacco factory (a good deal of tobacco is grown in these parts) and a very new community centre consisting of school, hospital, and church, all built in quite a pleasant modern style. Our most interesting time was spent at a village of troglodytes (cave dwellers to you). These people are debased Jews who fled from Spain in the days of the Inquisition and settled in North Africa. They live in caves, thirty feet or so below ground level, so that they can be cool in the summer and warm in winter. They showed us over one of their dwellings; the elaboration of tunnels and passages is amazing, and it was certainly very cool and free from flies down there. All the chief rooms opened off a deep area about forty feet square, open to the sky at the top so that they lived in the bottom of a wide shallow well, as it were. The amount of earth they had to shift must have been enormous. The women of marriageable age are kept carefully out of sight but we saw one or two very handsome young girls weaving and making baskets, and the older women were all very striking, with that carriage and dignity seen rarely except in women who are used to carrying burdens on their heads. The sole remaining sign of Jewish origin with these people is their religion. They still keep this up, and showed us their synagogue, with a separate room for the women who worship behind a thick grille, away from the prying eyes of young and lusty males. These people have kept themselves a close community and there has been practically no intermarriage with the Arabs.

Three days after our interesting visit to the troglodytes, we returned to Tripoli to await embarkation. We had hoped to embark within a couple of days of our return from the mountains, but this was not to be, so we returnd to our old spot on the sea shore. The locals had been busy during our absence, and had dug up every single tin or piece of waste paper we had buried. It was still very hot, so of course the flies were terrible.

It was at this time that I came into possession of my motor cycle, a venerable BSA with much service to its credit at the hands of the famous Fourth Indian Division. It was in a pretty poor state when I got it, not having felt the touch of a spanner or a grease gun for some considerable time. However, George (my driver) and I set about it and soon had it in good running order, though the engine was so worn as to be past praying for. I was fortunate enough to get a brand new engine for it, but didn't fit it to the bike until we arrived in Italy.

During this time the harbour had been full of transport ships taking units over to Italy. A few of them showed signs of having been in a fight, but none showed signs of serious damage. During our stay in Tripoli heated discussions had been going on about what units should be allowed to wear the Eighth Army flash - a crusader's shield - on their shoulders, and what units should not. It was really all very silly and childish, but I was amused to see the shield painted on the funnels of several of the assault craft in the harbour. Apparently even the navy considered themselves part of the Eighth Army, and they certainly played a great part in the two invasions.

I can't think why I forgot to say so before, but our seashore camp at Tripoli was close to the Mellaha road circuit, on which the Tripoli Grand Prix car race was run in peacetime. There is a very fine grandstand, scoreboards and pits; the road circuit is very fine, set in an oasis of palms and native buildings.

We left our seaside billet for the last time at the end of September, and went to a concentration area near the docks to await embarkation. This period of waiting became exceedingly tedious; we were all keyed up to go and were kept waiting for days; all the trucks had to stay packed, and living conditions were very rough, especially as the area had been left absolutely filthy by the troops who had previously occupied it. This latter fact nearly landed me in a first class row with the local medical brass hats, for when the CO complained they pointed out a few minor defects in our own sanitation and tried to pin them on me; however, I had a clear conscience and a good sanitary diary and was able to stand up for myself in this matter. We were all heartily glad when at last the time came for us to leave this atmosphere of bumph and boloney and get on with the war.

We rose at a hideous hour and took our transport down to the LST (Landing Ship, Transport). This is a ship with a door in the bows and is specially designed to carry trucks across and land them directly onto the beaches. They also have sleeping accommodation for a certain number of troops. They are wonderfully designed for the job they have to do, and after I had made my tour of inspection, I was left with the comfortable feeling that Germans are not the only people who can do an efficient job at designing equipment for war. Everything seems to have been thought of, which is a wonderful thing when you remember that these and other invasion craft are planned and put into production in a hurry. The one on which we travelled was manned by an American crew, and it was interesting to compare their idea of discipline with that of the British. To our eyes their discipline seemed easy going to the point of laxness, but during the voyage we discovered that every man, from the Captain to the stewards in the ward room, knew their jobs from A to Z and were extremely competent. The accommodation for officers being somewhat cramped, I elected to sleep on deck, and was glad I did so, as the cabins were very hot and stuffy at night. Needless to say, the old bogey of seasickness was uppermost in my mind. I took a new drug, however, which prevented my being sick, though I felt a bit queasy for the first few hours. This was good, for LSTs are flat-bottomed, and therefore tend to roll very badly in anything but a flat calm.

We lay at anchor that night in Tripoli harbour, and set sail the next day at 8.30. As our diesel engines took us past the wrecks and through the gap in the breakwater, we gazed our last, we hoped, on Tripoli. We were all heartily sick of the place, its profiteers, touts and flies. We all hoped devoutly that we should never have cause to set foot there again.

We were escorted by small American patrol craft, very fast and well armed, but for all the enemy we saw, we might just as well have sailed unescorted; the voyage was quite uneventful. As soon as we sailed it became known that our destination was Salerno, and I think we all felt a thrill to know that we were to enter Europe again at such a famous spot. In the meantime we all relaxed, wrote letters and slept.

The weather was rather bad for the first thirty-six hours, with rainstorms and clouds. Fortunately the rain wasn't too bad at night, so I was still able to sleep on deck. After so long on British Army rations, the American food was our chief topic of conversation. Unlike British officers, who draw their rations in kind, American officers, at least in the navy, receive a certain sum of money as ration allowance, and buy their food from the ship's quartermaster. In practice they have nearly the same food as the men and forego their money allowance. Our messing cost us five shillings a day, but was well worth it. We had lots of spam, hamburgers, frankfurters, etc. Americans are great at mixing sweet things with meat, and our most interesting dish was hot cakes (scotch pikelets), spam and molasses (syrup). Sounds like a horrible mixture, but tasted grand. Then, of course, there was coffee, the best since leaving home.

The officers were very young, between 21 and 25 years; most of them were ardent "swing" fans, and had quite a few records. They made me feel very old; they knew nothing of jazz prior to Benny Goodman; most of them had heard of Louis Armstrong, but few knew even the names of the great ones of jazz, and enthused over performances which were mediocre compared with the average jazz record of ten years ago. Ah me! Tempus fugit.

One morning we awoke to find that the convoy was approaching the Straits of Messina. It was a perfect day, and as we approached the narrows we were able to get a good view of both Sicily and the mainland through our binoculars. The convoy halted whilst the ships got into line astern, so we had time for a good look round. Etna had a nice little cloud of smoke at the summit, and we could see Catania at the foot of it. The narrowest part of the Strait is less than two miles in width. We could see Messina on the Sicilian side and Reggio, on the mainland. Messina didn't seem too badly damaged, except for the waterfront, where there was hardly a serviceable building left. A large passenger ferry boat, lying on its side in the shallows, bore eloquent testimony to the accuracy of our bombing. We passed very close to Reggio, where the rail ferry terminus showed severe damage. There wasn't a single whole building left in the town except, oddly enough, the church, which seemed to be intact except for broken windows. The damage will take some time to repair.

After passing through the Straits, the convoy reformed and steamed on; later in the afternoon we came abreast of Stromboli, a sugar loaf island sticking straight up out of the sea, with a white cap of smoke from the crater of its volcano. As darkness fell we saw the fires reflected in the low cloud which preceded a heavy rainstorm. We were due to disembark the next morning, so we were all very excited, and I couldn't sleep very well anyway, owing to the rain. However, the excitements of the voyage were not yet over, for in the middle of the night, which was pitch black because of the rain clouds, a destroyer going the opposite way steamed right down the middle of our convoy, and a collision with one of our LSTs was only just averted. The rain became too heavy for sleeping on deck, and I had to retire to the ward room in dudgeon and damp pyjamas and sleep there.

Naturally, everybody was up early the next day, though we might have spared ourselves the effort, for the rain came down in torrents and it was quite impossible to see anything of the shore. Fortunately, it cleared up about 8.30, and as we arrived at the lower border of the Gulf of Salerno the town and beaches came into view. Then we realised for the first time what a bold decision had been taken when Salerno was selected as the place for a seaborne landing. From the beaches, a plain of about half a mile in depth and three miles in length, cliffs five hundred feet high towered over the sea, giving the Germans a perfect view of the beaches and for many miles out to sea. I shall never cease to be amazed that we even got a real foothold here, let alone chased the Germans out. Invasion across the Channel should be easy compared with this. As we drew closer in shore, the weather cleared and we could see some of the cleverly camouflaged German gun positions. They had the beach enfiladed from end to end with eighty-eight millimetre guns, and no doubt there were many other defences which we couldn't see. I take off my hat to the brave men who fought and won these beaches. It must have been the toughest job yet in this war. We later heard that one of the medium regiments was engaging tanks over open sights at a range of only five hundred yards! I wish I could compare Salerno with some well known English place to give you some idea of the task our forces had to face, but I can't think of anywhere at home that would be as difficult to assault.

We had to wait a good while for our chance to close the shore and disembark, and to make matters worse, it started to rain again. Some irresponsible body gave the orders to unshackle the trucks on the top deck (all vehicles had been chained to the decks during the voyage to prevent them sliding about). The result was that when we did hit the beach (at about fifteen miles an hour) all the back rows of trucks skidded forward on the wet decks; mine sustained a badly bent mudguard, its first scar for a long time. But before we actually ran ashore, there was some delay whilst they tried to start the bulldozer, which every LST carries to keep its head to shore and push it off if necessary. There was nearly half an hour of sweat and swearing before it could be persuaded to budge.

Finally, the great moment came; at full speed our Captain headed the ship for the shore. We struck with a dull thud and ran aground dead opposite a prepared wooden runway. We had arrived on European soil once more. A new chapter in the Regiment's history was about to open.

That's all this time. Next time read all about Italy, and our experiences of European fighting.

BULLETIN TEN

"Sunny Italy" — October to November 1943

Thud! The crash of crockery in the ward room of our LST proclaimed that we had more than touched Italian soil at last. A dismal drizzle of rain almost hid the town of Salerno as we began the tedious task of getting the vehicles disembarked. Our skipper had beached us dead opposite a wooden runway on the shore, so we didn't have any trouble with vehicles getting stuck in the sand. Once on terra firma we were directed to a marshalling area on the sea front. Here we had a natter with the crew of an American Ack Ack gun who showed us the local army newspaper. In this we read that the editors of several English papers were pressing for a Third Front and more vigorous action against Germany! Will these people NEVER be satisfied? They were made to look pretty silly in 1942, after raising hell about a Second Front, but they don't seem to have learned the lesson. We all thought it colossal cheek, and voted that all the editors concerned be sent at once to fight in Italy! We admired the Americans' gun, and they had a good laugh at "Enema Ernie", the gremlin I have had painted on the side of my truck. He is depicted enjoying a shower bath with the aid of a Higginson enema syringe.

Considering that it had been the scene of several days hard fighting, Salerno did not seem very badly damaged. However, it was three weeks since the landing, and I suppose a lot of the mess had been cleared up. The most amazing contrasts in poverty and wealth were to be seen in the streets; children and grown-ups in rags begged for "biscuits and bully", and yet many of the people, especially the women, were turned out in the height of fashion and ignored the brutal and licentious soldiery completely. We were to find this contrast almost everywhere we went; abject poverty marching hand in hand with finery and good living.

We were afraid we were due to camp for the night on the sea front, but fortunately we got orders to move inland at about 2.30 pm. We were getting a bit anxious as our clocks had been advanced an hour on the way over, and we were now on ordinary British summer time, the same as you are at home. That meant that we had lost a precious hour of daylight at the end of the day.

Our route inland lay along a first class main road, which climbed the cliffs and ran inland through a deep valley; we were soon involved in a severe traffic jam, and realised that the days of desert warfare and "make your own way" were indeed things of the past. We passed through village after village, climbing all the time; the streets were lined with people of all ages, begging for cigarettes and sweets and biscuits. This constant begging got very irritating after a time, and we later found that it was a racket, for their was little real shortage of food. There wasn't much sign of damage in the villages, but at various points along the road were very thorough enemy demolitions, which had been very cleverly bridged by our engineers. In this country a good demolition is worth a lot to the enemy; some of the "blown" bridges spanned gorges a hundred feet deep, and no vehicle could pass until engineers had built a bridge, often under shell and mortar fire. I think these Royal Engineers have one of the worst possible jobs; they have all the hazards of front line fighting with no excitement to offset the danger and no chance to hit back.

The convoy gradually got more and more split up, and we found ourselves travelling just in front of two American soldiers in a "duck" - a large amphibious truck. At the frequent halts they gave us gum and cigarettes, and told us harrowing tales of the first days at Salerno - grossly exagerrated, as we later found out. They were very amusing and in great spirits, and we looked forward to meeting many more like them and fighting in their company.

At last we stopped climbing and emerged into the sunlight again, after being buried in a deep valley most of the time. However, it didn't last long. Clouds closed in and heavy rain began to fall; we splashed our way along over flooded roads and through muddy village streets, where the bad weather offered one compensation - no local populace begging for food.

We were bound for Scafati, a village near Pompeii and right at the foot of Mount Vesuvius, a romantic spot at which to spend our first night on Italian soil. Looking up after dark, we could see the fire in the crater of the volcano reflected in the clouds above it. Being "sand happies", we gaily pitched our tentage and tightened the guy ropes right up. In the middle of the night there was a terrific thunderstorm, the ropes shrank, and nearly every bivvy fell down. The camp was a sight the next morning, and the air was blue with bad language. We had learned our first lesson; never trust the Italian climate.

We awoke to a watery sunrise and our first clear view of the peak of Vesuvius, which had been covered by low cloud the day before; we were all suitably awed by the crown of smoke, and then got down to the job of digging drainage ditches for our tents and drying out all our bedding. Everybody was laughing and retailing there version of the night's disasters, but I couldn't help feeling that if the bad weather went on tempers would become correspondingly frayed.

Before we landed we had read in a Soldier's Guide to Italy that we would see many "warm looking women". This phrase we found a masterpiece of understatement; it was certainly a sight for eyes weary of blanket clothed Arab women. Aldous Huxley would have called them "pneumatic" (vide Brave New World). I'm afraid some of them must have been punctured by the time we arrived! Like Eastern women, however, Italian women age rapidly, which is no wonder when you consider that they have a child every year and do most of the manual work on the land as well. But more of this in later bulletins.

We were quite near Pompeii, and naturally seized the first opportunity to take a look at the ruins. These had been used as a camp by the Germans and had been bombed by us, so the scars of modern war were added to those of time and lava. Unfortunately, one of the bombs hit the museum, which I am told held most of the really interesting relics. The Padre, the Adjutant and I did the sights together under a guide who spoke tolerably good English. Some of the ruined houses were quite interesting and many of the paintings on the walls were in an excellent state of preservation - embarrassingly so, in some cases! Our guide left nothing to the imagination, and the joke was that every time he had what he considered a particularly fruity piece of information to impart about the debauches of the ancient Pompeians, he always buttonholed the Padre (who wasn't wearing his dog collar), and made quite sure by over emphasis that he understood! All in all, I came to the conclusion that ancient Pompeii couldn't have had a juster fate; Sodom and Gommorrah weren't in it! To get a real idea of what the city must have looked like, one would need several days spent looking at the ruins and also a look from the air; I don't think it was possible to get more than a hazy idea of the place from the three hours we spent there.

After one more night spent in the same camp, during which there was a small air raid on Naples, which was fifteen miles away, we moved off to go into action for the first time (for me) on European soil. It was a brilliantly clear morning as we rolled along the main road to Naples. We passed through Torre Annunziata, a great resort in peace time, now badly knocked about by our bombing. Our route bypassed the centre of Naples but fortunately I lost my way, and saw rather more of the town than most people. Naples has been severely damaged, though not as severely as some of the earlier reports made out. We passed the main railway marshalling yards and if anybody doubts the efficacy of bombing raids as a method of disorganising rail transport, what we saw should convince them. Practically all the railways of importance were electrified, which made them easier than ever to put out of action. There were few undamaged trucks to be seen in the yards we passed; you could see where whole trains had been set on fire and burned from end to end. Apart from railway damage, many of the streets were almost blocked by huge bomb craters or the debris from bombed buildings. Sewers beneath the streets had been opened up, as had gas and water mains in places. Being a stranger to Naples I was unable to even guess the true extent of the bomb damage, but I wouldn't care to be a citizen of Cologne or Berlin, if this is the damage caused by a small number of medium sized raids.

From Naples we went north along the main road to Rome; guns were to go into action north of the town of Aversa, and about four miles south of the Volturno river. I, as usual, was at the rear of the regimental column, and didn't find Regimental Headquarters until dusk. They were in quite a comfortable house, and had a harrowing tale to tell of the difficulties of the terrain. We were in hemp growing country which is rather like flax; the place was riddled with pools for rotting the hemp, and as a result mosquitoes abounded. In addition, though the ground looked and felt firm underfoot, it would not bear even a jeep without giving way. Nearly every vehicle in the regiment got hopelessly bogged down and had to be pulled out onto the road again by a breakdown wagon. It took many hours to get the guns winched and heaved into position and we realised more clearly than ever that the old game of driving up and getting into action (as practised in the desert) was gone for good and all.

That night I slept in a house on a camp bed for the first time for a long while. We had to have mosquito nets up, and gave the rooms a good spray with Flit before kipping down. This was unwise, as it brought down on us thousands of minute flies who had gone into winter quarters in the ceilings. They could be heard dropping onto the stone floor all through the night, and crunched under our feet when we got up next morning. After so long out of action we were all a bit jumpy, and started now and then when nearby guns fired. However, we soon got used to the noise.

The next day I left HQ to find a regimental aid post handy to the guns; after careful reconaissance, I had to settle down beside the main road, as everywhere else was either waterlogged or occupied. In theory we were always taught to avoid main roads because of bombing and shelling, but I really doubt if there is much in this, especially now that we have air superiority. At Wadi Akarit our roadside position had been a bit sticky, but otherwise we found there was nothing to choose between a roadside position and any other, as far as shelling and bombing went. After all, they don't often hit the road even when they are aiming at it! One other snag about a roadside RAP is that you get a lot of casual customers for dressings, as well as a lot of people enquiring the way; this gets very irksome at times.

Having selected my position, the great question was to dig or not to dig. In any case it was no good digging down more than three feet, as the hole soon flooded with water. However, Jerry very kindly made up my mind for me by shelling the place pretty thoroughly; shells landed very close to some of the guns, but they buried themselves in the soft ground and inflicted no damage or casualties. My place was in no immediate danger, being well to a flank of the line of fire, but our excavations proceeded very rapidly when the shelling had ceased! We put up our tent and my bivvy, by which time it was nearly dark. A horrible dank mist comes off this marshy area at dusk, and we found it very cold because we were still in thin tropical uniform. The mosquitoes got pretty active too, though our anti-mosquito cream kept them at bay. That night Jerry repeated his shelling performance, this time with a few air bursts (like shrapnel) - more frightening than dangerous, but very unpleasant all the same. RHQ came out of their house at a smart double, I heard later, but it was all over in a couple of minutes. The Germans seemed to have the guns pretty well bracketed, and we all wondered what would happen when the time came for us to open fire, always assuming that the guns would stay above ground for more than a couple of shots. Some of them were already sinking up to their axles in the soft ground under the pressure of their own weight.

The next day was quiet, and we watched Italian civilians passing on the roads. Many of them were going up towards the front, only to be turned back by Military Police. They were carrying on with harvesting the hemp and ploughing the land all around us and some had been killed by shellfire a few days before. The families returning to their homes travelled on carts loaded high with bedding and furniture, drawn by one or two mules, which the driver encouraged with a whip and a long drawn-out cry of "A-a-ah!", rather like a woman in labour; it was an interesting contrast to the staccato "Brrrh!" used by the Arabs in Africa. In the afternoon I went forward three or four miles to Caserta, to collect an ambulance. The railway here had been well and truly bombed and the station was full of burnt-out freight cars containing aero engines and spare parts. At Caserta is a royal palace which belonged to the King of Naples. It was a terrific edifice about the size and shape of the Queen Elizabeth hospital at Birmingham, with a very fine set of ornamental gardens in the grounds. Next to it was an officers training unit of the Italian Air Force, and nearby was a prisoner of war camp in which our men had been incarcerated. This looked a pretty primitive place to me, and must have been very miserable in the winter. There was a first class hospital attached to the Air Force school, and the nurses and orderlies were working under the command of a British Field Ambulance. Later the place became a British General Hospital.

The road we travelled to Caserta and back was typical of many roads in Southern Italy; the surface is of tarmac, very skiddy when wet, and about thirty-six feet wide; there are few curves and the road is lined with small plane trees or poplars, very dangerous if one runs off the road at speed. It's only advantage over the average British main road was that it was dead straight for miles, which made driving monotonous but safe. Of course, the Germans had blown every bridge and, as these were numerous, hold-ups at diversions were common. After all the trouble we had gone to, we were fated not to fire a shot from our first position. After a couple of days we had orders to move nearer to the coast. Remembering one spot of shelling, I thought it was just as well!

The roads we had to move on were vile. It had rained heavily, and trucks coming from the fields had covered the main roads with a thick layer of gooey mud which was dynamite to anyone riding a motor cycle or the driver of a tractor and gun, the total weight of which is fifteen tons. The by-roads were beyond words; they were ankle deep in slushy mud and full of hidden potholes. The mud was so thick that it jammed solid between the tyres and mudguards of motor cycles and either stalled the engine or brought the unfortunate rider crashing to the ground. As I was riding a motor cycle I had full experience of this! Added to all this were the narrow village streets with sharp bends, each a new problem for our tractor drivers and crammed with gossiping Italians; no wonder tempers were a trifle frayed towards the end of the move. It took us all day, going in fits and starts for about fourteen miles, and we were all heartily sick of mud by the end of the day. One redeeming feature was a luncheon halt beside an apple orchard. Piles of fruit were lying rotting on the ground for lack of labour to gather them in, and everybody had a good tuck in. With the inevitable result that I was busy with the castor oil and Epsom salts for the next few days!

Well, I think this is a good place to end this issue. In the next one you will read of our first actions in Italy, and my personal reactions to the war in Italy, the local populace and things in general.

For the present "Good-bye".

BULLETIN ELEVEN

"The Rain it Raineth every day" — November 1943

At the end of the last bulletin we were en route to go into action near the west coast, and I take up the tale again towards dusk on the same evening when, very ill tempered and muddy, I was looking round for a suitable R.A.P. The move had occurred in such a flap that I hadn't had much time to go ahead of the guns and pick a good spot, as I generally like to do; so I was left with the miserable job of doing a reconnaissance on a motor cycle in the fading light with a fine but very wetting drizzle of rain falling.

I went first to Villa Literno, where one battery was to fire from the station yard area. Just to cheer me up, there was a chalked notice at the entrance to the village which said "Keep 100 yards interval between vehicles. Enemy shelling"! This first dismal note was echoed by the sight of some badly battered houses at the crossroads. The station and railway sidings were a dreadful sight. There was not a whole house in the area, which was pitted with bomb craters and strewn with rubble, wire, corrugated iron and other debris. The place had received a couple of daylight raids by Fortress bombers, just before the Salerno landing, and the goods yard was a tangled mass of wagons, rails and signal wires. In the half light and rain it made the most dismal war scene I had yet come across, and reminded me of some of the scenes in pictures like "All Quiet on the Western Front" and "What Price Glory?". Over it all hung a dank smell compounded of burning and rotting refuse and dead animals. I vowed I would not have my R.A.P. there if it could be avoided, and fortunately found part of a Field Ambulance on the spot and glad to take care of the battery, so I heaved a sigh of relief and made off in the dusk to our other battery, a couple of miles away to the east.

The light was now at its trickiest, and I ground along in second gear, cursing the rain, the mud, the lousy road and the war in general. The road was covered with a slushy layer which effectively concealed all the potholes from view, without in any way cushioning the bumps when I rode through them. In this connection, I have often noticed that the side of the road YOU happen to be using always looks worse than the other side, until you are making the return journey, when all the bad bumps have moved over so that they can shake you up again.

Muddy and irritated, I arrived at the other battery position to find that George, our driver, had dropped my truck sideways into a ditch, effectively blocking the only driveway up to the farmhouse in which the command post was situated. Fortunately most of the trucks had already gone up, for we had to wait a couple of hours until the guns arrived before we could get a tractor to pull us out. We nearly got stuck again just inside the gate, and it was 10 pm before we had picked a place for the truck and settled down for the night.

We were due to fire at 4 am so it was lucky that pits had been dug ready for the guns, which rolled in like cars parking at a cinema. They were in a really good position, behind a six-foot bank at the side of the road; next day you could just see the muzzles poking over the top of the bank, like horses surveying the world from behind paddock railings. I expected the local inhabitants, and especially animals using the road, would run for dear life when we fired, but to my amazement nothing of the sort happened. The people looked a bit startled, but the mules and oxen just tossed their heads and plodded on; even at night, when a six-foot flash of white flame was added to the roar of the explosion, they rarely showed fright. The most scared people were Army depatch riders, who put their heads down and made a dash for it with throttles wide open hoping to get through between salvos. One of them hit a pothole one night and took a nasty toss.

The rain had cleared when we woke next morning, and we found ourselves in pleasant if somewhat muddy surroundings. The truck was parked in an avenue of walnut and plane trees fifty yards from the command post farmhouse. One row of tall trees served as supporting trellis for vines of red grapes which, unfortunately, were overripe and rotten owing to the lack of labour to gather them; however there were plenty of good walnuts on the trees; jolly good grub, the old walnut, especially fresh picked. We were glad to be able to sleep in a house, for the guns were only a hundred or so yards to our left and behind us, and the noise when they all let go was terrific; the house cut down the noise to a surprising degree, and I slept all through the first barrage which began at 4 am. Altogether, we were very pleasantly fixed, and I looked forward to a few days in these comfortable surroundings.

The weather stayed fine, and the next day I nipped over to Villa Literno again. It looked a lot better in the morning sunshine, and I was able to take a closer look at the wrecked goods yard. The Germans had systematically blown up every switch point and junction box and had booby trapped any of the trucks which were still habitable. Royal Engineers had cleared all the explosives away, however, and I was able to see the wrecked wagons which contained, amongst other things, eighty-eight millimetre ammunition, bombs, torpedos and aero engines. It was interesting to speculate how many allied soldiers owed their lives to the destruction of that vital war material and the blockage of the line by the raids.

Our guns were in the back gardens of houses, and one was so close that it removed a tile from the roof of the house in front every time it fired, much to the annoyance of the owner who came regularly each morning to see the latest damage. I am afraid he got little sympathy from our gunners.

It seems a good opportunity at this point to deal with the general attitude of the Italians I came across to the war and the presence of the British and Americans in Italy. It must not be thought that what follows is the result of very short acquaintance with the country, for the opinions I express now are formed after three months in Italy at the time of writing these words, and are not hastily put together after a week or so in the country. Moreover, I believe they sum up fairly well the experience of most allied troops when dealing with the natives of Southern Italy - that is the country as far up as Rome. I can only speak personally of dealings with the country folk, as we have been near few large towns; I have heard a good deal, however, from people who have been billeted in Naples and round it.

The Italian populace welcomed the invading Allied Forces with open arms (and mouths). This was a surprise, as we had been led to expect a much less cordial welcome in Italy than our troops had received in Sicily, which was never pro-fascist at any time and had been the scene of much unrest since Italy entered the war. What I often wonder is whether the Germans received a similar welcome when they came to Italy's rescue in 1941. Most Italians I have come into contact with are friendly in a passive sort of way, but few bestirred themselves or put themselves out to help us in any way, and many were resentful of our presence in their houses. Mind you, there WERE exceptions to this, but only a few; I shall mention them from time to time. But the attitude of most of the Italians I met was that they had backed the wrong horse and were now trying to get out of the deal as lightly as possible. Time and again I have been told of highly educated people in important posts in the cities, whose attitude could be summed up as follows; "the war was no affair of ours; Mussolini and his fascists are the culprits. They have gone so lets forget all about it". They seemed to think that the whole Abyssinian affair can be written off just like that, and they will feel unjustly treated if it isn't.

To revert to my own experiences with the country folk. I found them illiterate, ill clad, dirty and poverty stricken for the most part. The men are lazy and shiftless, and the women do most of the hard work. It is the commonest sight in the world to see a woman with a large bundle on her head and a heavy basket in each hand, whilst beside her walks her dandified man with his hands in his pockets. The children are filthy, inadequately clad in rags, and far too numerous. Most women seem to have a child regularly every year or so. The houses, built of stone, have large draughty rooms, devoid of fireplaces except the kitchen, in which the whole family seems to live during the winter months. These people seem to be in little better state than they were in mediaval times in England. What their future will be I am unable to conjecture. I am told that the "real Italians", whatever that may mean, live in Northern Italy; I hope to be in a position to find out for myself later whether this is so. One thing I forgot to mention is that the Southern Italians are damnably cruel and thoughtless in the treatment of animals, which would not be tolerated for one moment in Britain or, for that matter, in Germany.

After this somewhat vitriolic digression let me return to the matter in hand. On my return to the R.A.P. I found, to my joy, an American Field Service ambulance parked outside. Though I knew it was impossible, I hoped against hope our friends from the Tunisian days would be with it. Actually, the chaps turned out to be a couple of duds; one talked all day without saying anything, and the other read all day and never said a word, whilst neither was a really expert driver. However, I was grateful for the ambulance car, as I knew the British one I then had with me wouldn't have stayed long, whilst the American was permanently attached although the drivers would be changed each month or so. As a matter of fact, most of the American boys were great fellows, and these two were the only two duds I have had up to the date of writing.

We now settled down to a life of pleasant ease in fairly good weather; one of the chief diversions during daylight was watching people being taken by surprise when our guns opened fire. A mile or two in front of us the battle for the river Volturno crossings was going on, but apart from the gunfire and the traffic on the roads, much of it bridging material, there was little sign of fighting. We had no return fire, and never saw a German aircraft. In fact we were destined to be in Italy for three weeks before we saw an enemy plane in the sky.

The Volturno battle brought us our first casualties of the campaign. During a battle of this type the Regiment sends forward a Forward Observation Officer with a party including a wireless set and signaller. His job is to call down fire either on his own initiative or on request from neighbouring units of infantry, tanks, etc. The officer in charge of our party gave a magnificent performance, breaking up several counter attacks and damaging enemy tanks with gunfire which he controlled. Sometimes, enemy were within a few hundred yards of him, and he was under fire from mortars and machine guns. When night fell he could no longer see, and before the party could make their escape they were overrun and captured; we have heard that they are all quite safe and unwounded; it was extremely hard luck after such a magnificent show and the officer concerned was awarded the Military Cross for this action.

There were many setbacks before the Allies became firmly established on the northern bank of the Volturno river, but once that happened progress was rapid, and the Regiment moved up close to the river, to a small town a few miles east of the town of Capua. Here I had a hard time finding a suitable R.A.P., but finally moved into the courtyard of a house, much against the will of the occupants. The head man, via an interpreter, told a harrowing tale of overcrowding etc, but when I made it clear that I was coming willy nilly as it were, the people became quite friendly and gave us a very nice room on the ground floor to sleep in. As it turned out the whole family slept in the cellar, but came up topside when our guns, only two hundred and fifty yards away, fired. In vain we tried to explain that they would be safer below; they cowered in one corner whilst the father stood at the doorway and shouted every time he saw the flash from our guns, so that the rest of the family could brace themselves for the bang. The noise was terrific, and shook the house to its foundations, breaking several windows.

It was one afternoon whilst we were in this billet that I came in to find one of my chaps sitting on one side of the room, and the family plus three RC priests on the other, exchanging compliments in English and Italian respectively, neither speaking a word of the other's language. To the onlooker the sight was too funny for words, but I believe the scene pointed a moral and was good propaganda for a universal language, basic English or otherwise. Whilst we were in this position the weather became worse again, and we were warned by the locals to expect bad weather for a couple of months. How right they were!

We moved on after a few days, and at long last crossed the Volturno river at Capua, using a very fine floating bridge, the first of its kind in that theatre of war. The town of Capua was badly knocked about, and both the bridges had been demolished. American engineers were already at work rebuilding the bridge and they had it up and open to traffic within three weeks - a wonderful achievement. These American combat engineer battalions have the most elaborate equipment, and they certainly know how to use it. As we awaited our turn to cross, we could see the spirals of brown smoke from twenty-five pounder smoke shells streaking the sky a few miles in front of us. The queue of trucks waiting to cross the bridge stretched for a mile on each side of the river, with the vehicles nose to tail. What a glorious thing is air supremacy!

Our position across the river was ankle deep in mud and the roads were terrible. We found an ideal R.A.P. in a house with a bombproof cellar and lived in real comfort for a few days. We had a roaring fire going, and all took a hot bath in front of it on our first night in the billet. Our stay was uneventful except for a couple of episodes with mines; neither of which involved me personally. In a few days we moved further up the Appian Way (Route Seven to the modern army). I wonder how many of the men who tore up and down in army transport gave a thought to the history of the road they were traversing. From my conversations with our own soldiers, I judged that very few even realised they were on a road which went back to the days before Christ.

We set up our R.A.P. in the barn of a farmhouse, and my sick parade was conducted in the down-to-earth company of chickens, sheep and pigs. The tenant of the farm was an old soldier with a hatred of the "Sporco Tedesco" (dirty German) which would have been funny had it not been tragic. I don't know how German travellers will fare after this war for Germany must be the best hated nation that there has ever been in world history. They seem to have an absolute genius for making themselves disliked. The farmer used to greet me each morning with "Buon Giorno, Signor Capitano" accompanied by a cracking salute, and nothing he or his wife could do for us was too much trouble. We all got severe indigestion from eating the roast chestnuts they literally showered on us. We were shown a cunningly concealed cave in which chickens had been hidden whilst the Germans were about, and also the donkey with two festering bullet wounds in its buttock. The Germans had become trigger mad, and had shot at anything which moved. Many were the carcasses of cattle and horses we saw in the fields and beside the roads; some had clearly been killed by shellfire, but many had obviously been killed by bullets. Their stench made life unpleasant for men living in the nearby houses and we burnt as many as we could with petrol. It was whilst we were here that I gleaned first hand knowledge of German atrocities inflicted on harmless civilians. We are not allowed to say anything on this subject at present, but I believe now a lot of the tales I had previously heard with scepticism.

My daughter Geraldine's first birthday came round whilst we were still at the farm and was duly celebrated with a little Scotch; the Germans provided the fireworks by staging a raid on Naples. The planes passed right overhead, and the flak patterns in the sky were terrific. To crown the display, one of our night fighters bagged a raider, which burst into flames and fell about a mile away from us. One of the ambulance drivers was stupid enough to strike a match in the open to light a cigarette. I don't think he'll do it again!

On this joyous note, I will end this bulletin; I fear the next one will contain more tales of rain and mud. Ta-ta for now.

BULLETIN TWELVE

"Mud, mud, inglorious mud" — still November 1943!

At the end of the last bulletin we were in the middle of an air raid on Geraldine's birthday. Nothing more of note happened whilst we were in residence at the farm except for a terrific influx of surface mail. All our surface mail posted between June 1st and September 1st arrived within the space of a few days, and we were inundated with bundles of magazines and papers, which were very welcome though it was difficult to know where to put them all.

Everybody at the farm turned out to give us a royal send-off, and the old farmer obliged with a final salute and an "A Riverdici, Signor Capitano" as we drove out of the yard. We moved up to the little town of Sparanise, only recently vacated by the Germans and within an uncomfortably short distance of the front; however, we had good gun positions behind a ridge of hills. The Germans had wrought havoc in the town, demolishing houses indiscriminately to block the streets and wrecking the already inadequate and primitive water supply system. I went ahead to spy out an R.A.P. and was waiting at a corner in the town for the convoy to appear when a most embarrassing interlude occurred. A dear old lady came up and started talking to me. My knowledge of Italian being somewhat limited, I could not understand what she was on about, but as she was almost weeping I knew it must be something sad, so I shook my head and made suitable noises which I hoped were indicative of sympathy. Suddenly, with absolutely no warning, the old dear siezed one of my hands and covered it with kisses - and round the corner came our first gun tractor, with the gun crew hooting in derision when they saw what was happening. Was MY face red! The locals were delighted to see our big guns, and there were many cries of "Ah, molto buono. Canone - boom! Tedesce - finito!" The Germans had taken all the food they could lay their hands on in the town and the people were pathetically grateful for any spare biscuits, etc, that we had.

There is little of note about our stay in this area but our existence was livened up a bit by the occasional appearance of bomb-dropping enemy fighters. The recognition of some of these was very tricky, and led to a few heated arguments. The AA gunners had my sympathy, for it was extremely difficult at times to distinguish friend from foe, and as a result the guns often opened up late or not at all, thus earning the scorn of all in the vicinity. But it is very difficult to make a snap decision when you know the odds are heavily in favour of the planes being friendly. Our R.A.P. was in the town, and I couldn't help being struck by the incredible laziness of the Italian men. Their main task of the day is to stand at the street corners with their hands in their pockets gossiping; the women do all the work including fetching all the water; this they carry in huge bottles or jars balanced on their heads. When I read of women at home agitating for fairer treatment and equal pay for equal work, I think of the lot of the women out here and friends, I laugh; how I laugh.

One of our gun positions was situated in an orange grove; the fruit was still yellow on the trees, but I sent some home packed in straw, and it survived the journey, arriving in excellent time to grace the Christmas table. I fancy a lot of families of men in the Regiment benefited in the same way. It is hard for us out here to realise how monotonous civilian food is these days, for the army rations are really quite good, despite complaints to the contrary.

Progress in the local war was fairly rapid, and in about ten days the enemy had once more retreated so far that he was out of range of our guns. For various reasons we could not take them further forward for a few days, so a period of "stand easy" was declared, though we had to be ready to fire "just in case". I siezed the opportunity for a trip back to Capua where some shops were now open, in the hopes of being able to buy some Christmas presents, but the journey was a complete waste of time. The shops were full of cheap junk at fancy prices - Tripoli all over again. I am glad to say that since that time price control has been instituted, with the usual result that everything worth buying has gone from the shops. The only answer appears to be pay up and look pleasant or do without, and the soldier abroad wants to send home something to his people.

Our next move took us up Route Six - the Via Casilina - the other road to Rome, where our task was to support the great attack on Monastery Hill (the first of several hills ro bear that name) or, to give its Italian name, Monte Camino. The Germans had done their usual thorough demolitions, and there were dozens of diversions round blown bridges. The biggest, called "S--- Creek", was particularly well named I thought. The road had a grand tarmac surface and ran through open pasture land, over hill and dale. It was a pleasant change from the dead-flat roads we had recently been travelling on, and there were delightful views of little fairy-like villages perched on or at the foot of small sugar loaf hills and overlooked by small forts or castles. I may say that the fairy-like appearance disappeared on closer inspection, for the houses were cramped and dark and the streets smelly and dirty. The hills were covered with low dark green scrub, trees or short grass. The whole scene stood out crisply in the afternoon sun, for the day was fine after a night of heavy rain, which had made all the diversions muddy and a problem for the drivers of our heavy ammunition lorries. The main roads were also covered with sticky mud which made it awkward for trucks and extremely dangerous for motor cyclists, who stood a fair chance of being run down from behind if they fell off. The roads were crowded with American trucks, all with skid chains on and driven like bats out of hell.

I had the greatest difficulty finding a suitable place for my R.A.P., and had to be content with a muddy cul de sac twenty yards from the main road. The fields were fortunately fairly firm, but even so some of our guns were got into position with the greatest difficulty. It poured with rain the second night we were there, and some of the fellows who had been silly enough to pitch their bivvies in a small valley nearly got washed away in the resulting cataract. The R.A.P. staff were all sleeping in houses and managed to keep fairly dry, though we found the roof a bit leaky in places. The weather gradually got colder and colder, so we changed from our tropical kit into battledress, and not before it was time. The cold weather also did away with the danger of malaria, and we were thankful to be able to hand in our mosquito nets, and to say good-bye to the gooey anti-mosquito cream we had been rubbing into our exposed areas of skin each evening. We all devoutly hoped that by the time the malaria season came around next April we would be out of the malarious part of Italy.

We were now near some American troops, and had an opportunity of comparing some of their methods and ways of life with ours. We found their food much more interesting than ours, though they grumbled about it even more than we did about ours. They were glad to exchange Spam for Bully beef any time, much to our surprise at first; but we soon realised that Spam is Spam, whether it is fried or eaten cold, whereas you CAN try and disguise Bully a little by stewing, frying, mincing, etc. Their best ration is called five in one; it is a pack containing enough rations for five men for a day or one man for five days. One case we sampled contained the following menu. Breakfast: fried ham and egg pate (and it really TASTED like fried ham and eggs), cereal, biscuits, apple butter and jam. Lunch consisted of cold pressed meat and baked beans, with biscuits and sweets to follow. The evening meal consisted of pea soup, Vienna sausages, boiled potatoes and string beans, canned peaches, sweets and biscuits. There was coffee for every meal, and five cigarettes per man per day. This is the top American ration, issued to the front line troops. Other packs exist which are less luxurious and elaborate but still miles better than our food - or so WE thought! But I have come to the conclusion that every army thinks their allies are better equipped than they themselves are, for it was the same with clothing and equipment. The Americans were delighted to exchange one of their Grenfell cloth zipper jackets (rather like a golfing jacket) for a battledress tunic; the result was that our fellows were soon turning out in the most motley collections of clothes imaginable, and it finally got to such a pitch that orders on the subject had to be made. In common with most other British soldiers, I found much about the American army to criticise, and much more to admire. In the interests of censorship I will skip the criticism, but I must express my admiration for the Engineers and Signal Corps people who are magnificently equipped and do a wonderful job of work. I am glad that the bridge they most commonly used, the Bailey bridge, is a British invention. Their medical people were very good too, though it seemed to me that there was an even greater wastage of doctors than there is in the British Army. Their equipment is simply superb, and their people were very good to any of our chaps they had to deal with.

I must now explain a little about our OP (observation post) parties, whose job it is when in mountainous country to go forward to the top of the nearest peak in order to observe the fall of shots and correct the range, etc, using wireless. In order to traverse the mountainous country our OP parties were equipped with mules, three in number, called respectively Ma, Pa, and the Little Bastard; this last was well named, for I had to treat several people who had got too close to his rear hooves. These animals carry an amazing amount of equipment, and are a godsend on the rough ground; there is an art in getting the load balanced exactly, and we had one or two amusing mishaps before everybody got the right idea.

News was coming through about strikes at home, especially among the miners, and they caused great ill-feeling in the Regiment, one battery of which contains quite a high percentage of miners. The strikers were reviled right, left and centre, and their pay and living and working conditions were compared with those of men in the Armed Forces. I felt pretty bitter myself, but couldn't help feeling that the men must have had some very great provocation to make them strike at such a critical time. I knew that in peacetime everybody made money out of coal except the men who hewed it, and I imagine that the miners accept that they will be forgotten again after the war. I don't suppose that they compare their pay with men in the Forces, but rather with that of other war workers. After all, five pounds doesn't seem much money for the work a miner does when you hear of aircraft workers earning ten pounds punching holes in sheets of metal. I think the men were wrong to strike, but I believe that they SHOULD get better wages. The blame really lies with the Government, who should have conscripted all labour at the beginning of the war.

At about this time my two American ambulance drivers were relieved by two more, who turned out to be a couple of the finest chaps imaginable. One, Jerry Addoms, was a doctor's son from New York, who was studying international law before the war, and the other, Johnnie Armstrong, was from a family in Pennsylvania. They both "mucked in" wonderfully on any odd jobs there were to do, and we had a happy time whilst they were with us. The day they arrived we were motoring down the main road, deserted for once, when we got involved in a small German ground-strafe by aircraft. We couldn't see what was happening so all jumped out. John and I took refuge in one ditch, whilst Jerry dived into an iron pipe at the other side of the road. Just as things were at their noisiest, John and I saw the ambulance start to move slowly forward. I was just thinking what a cool customer Jerry was to move the ambulance off the road in the middle of a raid when I suddenly realised that there was no driver! The car was just running away, as in our haste to evacuate it we had forgotten to put the hand brake on. Fortunately the car ran gently into the ditch and stopped itself, but it was a nasty moment; we none of us fancied dashing out to put the brakes on just then.

By this time we were all getting a bit bored with the war; the weather was steadily getting wetter and colder, and this naturally slowed down progress, which had been slow anyway by the standards of desert fighting. I never fought in the desert during the hot weather, but people who have agree that it's definitely the best place for war. There are no civilians to get in the way, and no battle-scarred towns and villages; the sand covers all the signs of war very quickly. The flies aren't any worse than they will be here (they COULDN'T be). Best of all you really DO advance when you've won a battle and not just move forward a mile or two. I suppose the converse holds true and you have to run a hell of a way if you're beaten in the desert, but for a winning army, give me the desert every time.

We did have a little air activity to keep us on our toes, though it was never on a large scale. Our biggest raid was by a dozen or so FW190's which tried to bomb a diversion; they missed hopelessly and then flew down the road at zero feet, machine gunning all the way. I am pleased to say that with my own eyes I saw them all cease fire and lift up over an American hospital about a mile in front of us, continuing their firing after they had passed it by.

Just as we were getting unbearably fed up, the opportunity came for a complete change. It all happened very suddenly; I was awakened one evening at 11 pm and told to be ready to move at 6 am the next morning; fortunately the hour of readiness was later changed to 8, which made things a little easier. However, we didn't get very far the next day. We were bound for the other side of Italy and the battle of the River Sangro under the command of General Montgomery. Officially, I should have returned my ambulance car and got one when I arrived at the other end but our two Americans were so anxious to come with us that I took them along. I knew we would not be away long; I sent a note to their OC telling him what I had done, and decided to face his wrath when we returned.

On the first day of the journey proper we started at the hideous hour of 3 am. It was pitch dark and pouring with rain, and very cold as well. I had volunteered for the first trip on the motor cycle, and put on everything I had in the way of warm clothing, topping off with a gas cape and my steel helmet. I managed to keep quite dry and warm, but must have looked rather like a Michelin man. Soon after the start the read became very cut up and muddy, with plenty of large potholes to keep me on the qui-vive. About 5.30 am the rain cleared and the countryside was bathed in a watery light from a half moon; soon after dawn, however, the rain started again, but by this time we were on main roads once more and climbing steadily across the Appenines. The road was wide and well surfaced with tarmac. It ran through deep gorges and valleys, whose slopes were planted with tall plane trees. These were barren of leaves at the time, but must have been a picture in summer. At times the road ran alongside a railway or mountain torrent, and dipped, twisted and turned in its efforts to avoid insurmountable peaks. All along the road were little hamlets, sometimes only a dozen houses or so, with here and there, where there was room, a largish town. Everywhere one saw buildings plastered with inscriptions, "Viva il Re" "Viva il Duce" (sometimes hurriedly erased!) but never "Viva Badoglio" the present leader of Italy. There were also on some of the houses inscriptions of Mussolini's sayings; I think they reflect the Italian mentality pretty well. An oft repeated one was "Believe, Obey and Fight", and one that particularly caught my notice was this gem "War is Man's Destiny as Motherhood is Woman's". What a philosophy!

The weather cleared as the day wore on, and I sent Harold Jones, my medical orderly, on ahead to find a place for the night. He contacted us again just outside Foggia with the details of the camping site. We surged joyously ahead, for it was getting dark, and had gone about five miles before we realised that Harold was no longer with us. We pulled up and waited, but in vain; no motor bike appeared. After a while I sent my truck on ahead and went back in the ambulance to find Harold on the side of the road near Foggia - punctured! We flung the bike in the back of the ambulance and made for the camp area, where there was no sign of my truck. Nobody knew anything about it, and it was hopeless to go searching for it in the dark so we just wrote it off, had an evening meal and kipped down in the ambulance, very cosy! About 10.30 we were woken by voices in altercation, to find my truck had arrived, complete with very cheesed-off driver and batman. They had gone too far up the road and instead of realising it and coming back, they had just sat their waiting to be found. For their lack of initiative they got no dinner or sympathy and retired to bed in great dudgeon in the truck.

We started off again at 8 the next morning, with the bike now in the back of my truck, and made fairly good time up to Vasto, where we had lunch. The roads were much poorer, on this side of Italy than on the west coast; they were narrower, and the surface very broken up. The countryside was similar however, though more undulating. At Vasto I came across our old friends Jock Cobb and Bob Orton from the American Field Service whom I had last met in Tripoli, and we swapped experiences over lunch. After a tiresome afternoon spent on a very dusty roadside waiting for orders we moved on up, and were directed by mistake into a cul de sac. We had to get off the track to turn, and got badly stuck in some soft ground, for it had been raining heavily the day before. By the time things sorted themselves out and we got moving again darkness had fallen, and we crawled along in the half moonlight, lights being verboten and the road a strange one. We were directed up a very muddy lane, and found when we got to the top that we were in the wrong place; I must admit to some blame for this error, but the orders were very vague. However, I made matters worse by trying to turn the truck round in a very muddy farmyard. Here it got hopelessly stuck, and defied all our efforts to move it. By this time it was 10.30, and we called a halt for something to eat. We finally got the truck out at 11.45 pm, and were glad to call it a day, sleeping once more in the ambulance.

It was beautifully fine next morning, with a clear blue sky above the snow capped mountains from which Jerry (as usual) had a perfect view of our gun positions. After an early breakfast we had a look round and found ourselves an R.A.P. at Castel Bardino beside the main road, about a hundred yards from a crossroads, hardly the textbook ideal position, but the best we could manage. We knew it was bound to rain again, and were glad of the shelter of some disused and quite clean pigsties. Down to earth with a vengeance! We were right about the rain; it poured down all that night and all the next day, turning our area into a quagmire ankle deep in liquid mud. It was the worst mud we had been in; even our four-wheeled drive ambulance got stuck. We spent an uncomfortable hour during the middle of the second night, when Jerry shelled the crossroads. Most of the shells went miles over, but one or two were a bit too close for absolute comfort; a surprising number of them were duds, which failed to explode. Almost as soon as the guns had arrived in this area Monty (General Montgomery) visited some of the gun positions in his famous staff car, handing out cigarettes to the troops and explaining that he had asked for the 51st Medium Regiment because he knew of our reputation and he wanted an extra regiment's fire to help in the crossing of the River Sangro. He never went near the officers mess but spoke to the men on the guns, who had been moaning like Billy-oh till he arrived, but after a few minutes they were eating out of his hand. That's leadership!

We moved the R.A.P. later to a brickyard, where we had a pleasant little house. We had one more noisy night of Jerry strafing, but that was all. The weather got worse and worse, and when orders came to pack up and get going we were all delighted. We had a fine day to start our journey back; I went ahead to try and rescue some of our chaps who had been admitted to hospital, and spent quite a pleasant day. We had lunch on the shore of the little port of Termoli, scene of the Eighth Army's landing behind the German lines. We lost my truck again, owing to a change of plan, and didn't find it again intil 10 pm that night, by which time it had started to rain again! Next day we started at 8, and the road was very bad until mid-day, when we struck the main east-west road again. The scenery was even more lovely than on the way up, the valleys glowing in the afternoon sun. It was pretty cold on the bike though, and I took over the truck for the last stage of the journey, which lay over very steep hills and was very tedious, as we had to halt at every hill whilst our heavy vehicles crawled up in bottom gear.

Our last night on the road was a very disturbed one for me. First of all somebody set himself on fire and got pretty badly burned, and later one of our vehicles coming in late went over a bank and down a twenty foot drop, fortunately without serious injury to any of the occupants!

This ends the saga of our trip over to the Eighth Army and back and it seems a good point to end this bulletin. I will send you another one fairly soon.

BULLETIN THIRTEEN

"Christmas in the mud" — December 1943

When we returned from our trip to the Eighth Army it was to discover that practically no progress had been made since we left; in fact, one of our batteries went back into the same position they had occupied previously. Unfortunately, our old R.A.P. position was occupied, and the only spot we could find was a small cutting near a culvert beside the main Route Six road. It was safe enough, but we had our doubts about whether or not it would remain dry when the rains came, as we knew they were bound to before long. However, there was nothing to do but make the best of it; I pitched my bivvy on the highest bit of ground available, and it JUST survived the worst of the floods, though at one time it was surrounded on three sides by an ankle deep lake of water.

We were too far from any cookhouse for convenience, so decided to cook our own food; we were glad later that we did this, as we should have got soaked to the skin if we had tried to go over for our meals. Home cooking proved a pleasant change, besides helping to pass the time and keeping us warm. The weather got worse from day to day, though we had one day in every three fine, which helped to dry things out a bit. We noticed this redeeming feature of the climate all through the winter.

Whilst in this position we fired a big barrage in support of the attack which made Monastery Hill (Monte Camino) finally and irrevocably ours. For purposes of description this hill had been divided into three parts, Monastery Hill, Razorback Ridge and Barearse Ridge. The BBC couldn't face the last name, and it was variously bowdlerised as Barebottom, Bareback, etc, Ridge - much to our amusement. When the barrage started we found we had picked a very noisy spot, surrounded by well-concealed but very noisy guns. The barrage stopped at dawn and was followed by a large number of air raids by medium and dive bombers. The weather men had guessed well, for it was a perfect day, with hardly a cloud in the sky. The whole job was over in a few days, we were out of range, and another move was in prospect.

During our stay on Route Six, I couldn't help contrasting

American methods of mechanised movement by road with British methods, though I've no wish to criticise the former. The Americans drive very fast all the time, but keep their interval of thirty yards between vehicles religiously. The British drive more slowly, but often close up bonnet to tail whilst in motion. American trucks often wait in a queue for half an hour without switching off their engines, whilst our drivers tend to be more economical; just the difference between a people who have never had to think of petrol supplies and one which used to have to consider every drop. The Americans are extravagant with all warlike stores, but with this extravagance goes an open-handed generosity and a genuine wish to share their good things with their less well-provided allies. They dished out sweets and cigarettes galore to many of our fellows who were living near them.

Our move took us up into the hills, over vile roads shoe deep in slush and water, to a wooded hillside near the little town of Roccamonfina. The gun positions were very cramped and in the usual quagmire; every gun had to be pulled into position by a bulldozer, and even THAT got stuck on one occasion. Everybody was crammed into a small area, and I had my R.A.P. near a Main Dressing Station of the Field Ambulance in which my old batman, Kenneth Day, was serving. Sure enough, there he was, so large as life and just the same as he was two and a quarter years before, when I had to admit him to hospital with pneumonia. He came across to the truck several times for a brew of tea and a chat and we had some good times yarning about the old days in England.

Our camp was pitched on the side of a tall cone-shaped hill, whose slopes were thickly wooded with chestnuts; in autumn it must have been a picture, but now it was very dreary, the ground covered with mouldering leaves and broken twigs. However, the weather was reasonably kind to us, and though it rained heavily, there were plenty of dry days as well. The weather made the roads awkward; when wet they were covered with liquid mud, when completely dry it formed a fine dust, which covered everybody and everything on or near the road.

The Regiment by this time boasted a thriving canine population. A few strays joined us as soon as we landed, and we had brought several dogs with us. Once a thing like this starts it grows by geometrical progression; we are at the moment of writing sharing our our third generation of puppies. Lord knows where it will all end.

At last the time came, as I knew it must, when my two American ambulance drivers had to be changed. They had been with us for over five weeks, instead of the usual three, so I couldn't really grumble, but we were extremely sorry to see them go, especially as they were replaced by the talkative gentlemen who had been with us before. Soon after this relief took place, we moved down towards the coast, to the town of Sessa Aurunca. Here the Regiment was to have a partial rest and spend Christmas. The rest turned out to be very partial, for we always had guns in action. However, the men had a break of four days each at a leave hostel which we set up well out of shelling range; they deserved it, for we had been within shelling range continuously for two and a half months, except for the four days we spent travelling to the Eighth Army and back.

I set up my R.A.P. in a big cave below a farmhouse; it looked pretty good to me when I first inspected it, but there was a fault in the roof which dripped badly after a heavy rain, of which we had plenty in due course. Fortunately, troops billeted in the farmhouse moved out after a few days, and we had the use of two rooms. These were in the usual Italian style with stone floors, whitewashed walls and wallpaper on the ceiling; very cool in summer, but absolutely perishing in the winter. We left the R.A.P. in the cave, preferring safety to comfort, and used the rooms only for sleeping accommodation.

Soon, thank goodness, we had another change of ambulance drivers; this time the boys were a New York socialite (a very nice fellow) and a chap of indefinite profession (we never found out what he really did) from Philadelphia. We were still doing our own cooking, and the new boys brought quite a lot of American food with them. Charlie, the New Yorker, was something of a fancy cook, and made us several tomato and other omelettes, using egg powder which he made indistinguishable from fresh eggs. The first evening they were with us we had tinned fried chicken, which went down pretty well after weeks of bully beef and meat and vegetable stew. We also had plenty of Spam and other similar delicacies.

As I had suspected, there wasn't much rest for me. In fact, thank goodness, I am generally busier when the Regiment is resting than when we are in action. This time it was Typhus innoculations. Every man in the whole Regiment had to have three injections at intervals of ten days, and the task was made more difficult by the fact that we were scattered over a large area, and men were constantly away on leave, courses, or in hospital, etc. I just had to chase round everywhere on my motor cycle, appearing suddenly on gun positions at all hours, like an evil genie. It got so bad in the end that the fellows started to run away as soon as they saw me coming. However, the herculean task was finally completed, and I don't think there were more than twenty men out of six hundred who weren't fully protected against typhus. As a matter of fact we didn't have a single case, and I don't believe there were more than fifty in the whole of the Allied troops in Italy - a good record when you realise that Naples was a hotbed of disease, and was closed to all troops not on duty for nearly three months.

Preparations for Christmas had been going on for weeks, and a good programme was lined up when the day at last arrived. The weather was kinder to us than it had been last year, and the sky was blue, with a few white clouds and clear sunshine. After a late breakfast (no sick parade!) I set off to visit the various gun positions, partaking of refreshments (mostly liquid and alcoholic) at each. By about 11.30 I was feeling just nicely, thank you, which is just as well as it turned out. One of our guns had been used by an officer from another regiment for some form of target practice which he seemed to be enjoying; it was after all Christmas Day and it was the only gun in the area firing, and naturally this annoyed the Germans very much. Just before I reached the position the Germans started to reply and, unfortunately, they had a pretty good idea where we were, and put down a good deal of pretty heavy stuff which fell a lot too close for comfort. I was scared stiff, and felt absolutely helpless as I had no medical kit with me - the first time for months I had come away from the R.A.P. without it. Fortunately we had no casualties on our gun position but the neighbouring tank regiment had a direct hit on their cookhouse. Besides ruining their Christmas dinner, this killed one man and injured another pretty badly; by the time I had done my poor best and the mess had been cleared up it was past lunch time, though I would have eaten little anyway. Because of this incident I missed seeing the men's dinner and helping to serve them. They had turkey, pork, potatoes, cauliflower, Christmas pudding, mince pies, sweets and a pint of beer each; they all voted it a good show, as well they might. In the afternoon I slept for a couple of hours in view of the late night which was in prospect. About 5 pm we were invited to a glass of wine with the old farmer and his family; all the children were girls, most of them very plain, but one very pretty. We were used to seeing them in their working clothes, and were amazed when they turned out in outfits more suitable for the hotels of Naples than an Italian village. With great difficulty and violent evasive action I dodged an enormous meal of macaroni, though I couldn't avoid eating a few cakes and drinking some wine for fear of seeming stand-offish. We finished off with an excellent cup of thick black coffee.

By this time I was ready for another couple of hours sleep! However, it was time to go down to the mess, where Charlie (the ambulance driver) and I had been invited to dinner. I forgot to mention that the army had for once timed things right, and issued us with our Africa Star ribbons as a Christmas present. For most of us it was our very first campaign ribbon, and it was quite a thrill to sew it on though I don't feel we really deserve it, as we only fought with the Eighth Army in Africa for so short a time, and never knew anything but victorious advance. However, plenty of units who just happened to be in the delta at the time and never saw fighting at all got it, so perhaps we have a case after all. We had a quiet and very pleasant Christmas dinner but things petered out early and we were in bed by 11.30. So ended Christmas 1943; we wondered where 1944 would find us.

We weren't left very long to enjoy our period of Christmas peace. In a few days the whole outfit moved down onto the plain to fire in support of a small attack, which, we found later, was a rehearsal for bigger things. However, WE didn't see it that way at all. The whole area was as bare as your - well, I mean, there was no cover at all, except for a couple of villages, very obvious, and a few hedges. It didn't add to our peace of mind when we heard that the German patrols had penetrated to the village a mile behind our positions only two nights before we moved in!

We moved in by night; it was pitch dark, hellish cold and the roads thick with dust, just to make driving a bit more difficult. The roads were very narrow, and we were constantly running into trucks coming in the opposite direction, carrying rations for the forward infantry, who were only a couple of miles in front of us at some points. I had left my driver behind to hold on to our billets, to which we were returning after the job was over, so I was driving the three ton truck myself. I was anxious not to make a mess of the job, and did all right until we reached the entrance to our farmhouse, where the R.A.P. was to be, when the engine just died on me. Fortunately the truck in front got stuck in some mud, and by the time it was clear I had remedied the trouble and so kept my sheet clean. I tried to sleep in the ambulance that night in my clothes, but didn't do very well, as it was too cold.

Next day we spent digging slit trenches which we felt pretty sure would be required. We started by crawling about on hands and knees and being careful about camouflage, but another regiment just across the road had a queue half a mile long at their cookhouse for breakfast, so we gave it up after that, on the theory that Jerry couldn't shoot at all of us all the time anyway. I slept most of the afternoon; the barrage opened up at 11 pm, and was pretty dense for so small an operation. Nothing came back whilst we were shooting, but plenty of heavy stuff fell later, though most of it was in front of us; it was pleasanter when day-light came and we could judge better where it was falling. The Germans had a very big gun very close to their front line and well hidden, and with this they systematically searched the area, especially the village in front and to our right, in which we had a troop of guns. As a result there was a lot of civilian panic, several more houses were hit, and one of our drivers had his thumb skinned by half the base plate of a shell which cut his cap in two and would have removed his head if he hadn't ducked at the very last moment. About 11 am a dozen

ME109's got in a very nicely timed sneak raid, just when our fighters weren't looking. The accuracy of their bombing, fortunately for us, left much to be desired. The raid was directed at some of our guns, but the nearest bomb fell nearly half a mile away. That afternoon enemy gunfire became more intense, but we had no casualties in the Regiment, and nothing nearer than half a mile of the R.A.P. We had a sound night's sleep and returned to our cave at first light on New Year's Eve.

We had a small party in the R.A.P. to celebrate the arrival of what we all hoped would be a victory year, but retired, very mellow, well before midnight. We noticed the wind was a bit brisk, and it suddenly rose to gale force in the middle of the night. When we got up the next morning it was still blowing heavens hard and snow and sleet were falling. A horrible sight awaited us at our R.A.P. cave. The tent sheet covering the entrance had been torn down by the wind, pulling with it about half a ton of mixed solids, mostly large stone blocks and cactus, from the cliff above. Most of the stuff fell on the cab of my poor old truck. The roof was stove in, and so was the bonnet, but fortunately no glass was broken. The rain had reduced all the soil to a semi-solid squidgy ooze, ankle deep and very adherent to boots and battledress. It took us most of the day to clear up the mess; fortunately, though the wind remained high, the sun came out and helped to dry things out a bit.

This seems a good point at which to end this bulletin and start the New Year with a new one. So that is all for this time folks. Next time I will tell you about leave in Naples, etc.

"It's my leg, Doc!"
Morning Sick Parade.

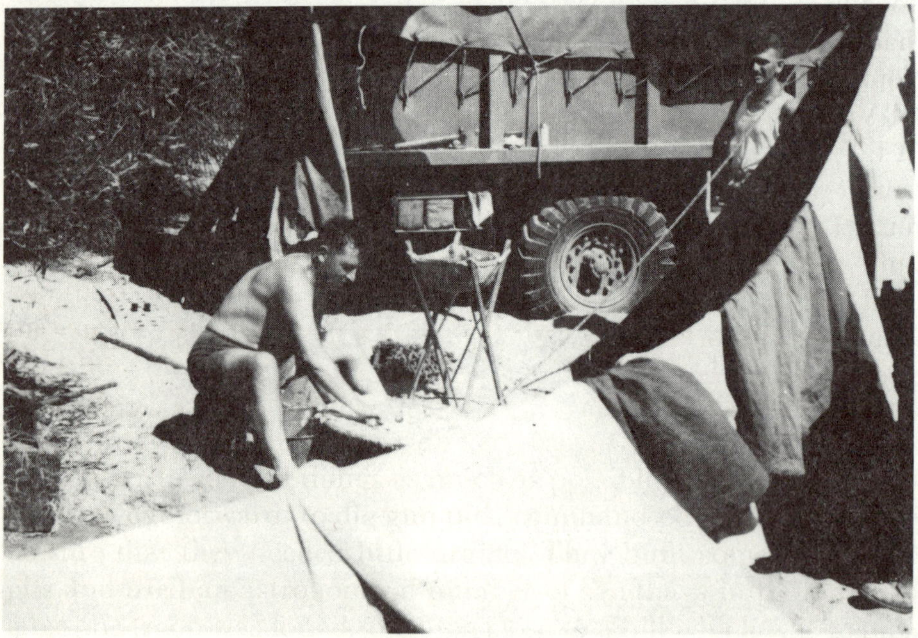

Open air laundry. Harold Jones in action.

BULLETIN FOURTEEN

"Leave, glorious leave" — January 1944

With the arrival of the New Year, life was dismal indeed. The war was "stuck", the weather was foul, and we were all bored; just the time for a spot of leave, you would have said, and the leave duly appeared. The Adjutant and I jumped into a jeep, and shot off to Amalfi, that Italian resort of the English. It sounds easy, put like that, but some preparation and a good deal of dressing up was needed before we could set off. From the skin up I was wearing: vests, woollen, one; pants, woollen, one; shirts, poplin, one; pullovers, jersey, one; jackets, battledress, one; coats trench, fleece lining for, one; greatcoats, dismounted, one; and jerkins, leather, lamb-skinned, unauthorised pattern, one; topped off with scarf, khaki, one and gloves, dress, pairs two - to put it all in Quartermaster's language. The Adjutant was similarly dressed, and we looked like a couple of transatlantic ferry pilots, but we were still cold before our luncheon stop on the autostrada at the foot of Vesuvius. Fortunately the day was beautifully fine and it had rained a little in the night, which helped to lay the dust. Our route lay through Naples and along the autostrada round the foot of Vesuvius to Pompeii. The autostrada is about 80 feet wide, and it takes four lanes of traffic at a pinch, and has no crossroads. The surface is tarmaced, and looked as though it might get a bit tricky in wet weather. The scenery, apart from Vesuvius, is very uninspiring; mostly old disused factories on the outskirts of Naples and market gardening country further out. Vesuvius had on her usual lace mobcap of clouds, and wasn't looking her best, and the view over the bay of Naples was poor owing to misty weather.

We had lunch at the end of the autostrada, and then pushed on to Salerno through very drab and uninspiring country, but once we hit the coast road all this changed. The weather was now warm and the sun shone brilliantly from a blue sky; each curve on the corniche road (and there were plenty) brought into view a new vista. Every little inlet harboured a few houses and lemon groves, and all along the coast there were little villages, the white houses like pieces of stamp paper, so closely did they cling to the face of the cliffs. We passed Vietri, where the commandos landed during the Salerno battle, and dozens of other little villages each, it seemed, prettier than the last. The corniche road is a wonderful engineering job. From hundreds of feet above the sea it swoops down to sea level at each village in a bewildering series of spirals and hairpin bends, reversing the process again after winding through the village. Driving was a bit tricky, as each bend might conceal anything from an enormous motor bus to a sort of roller coaster effort made up of a plank and four wheels, and much used by the locals. These latter nearly always occupied the crown of the road, and were rarely under full control. In addition, convoys of carts returning from market or lemon picking (the lemons were ripe already!) added to the driver's confusion. The road seemed to go on and on through village after village - Cervaro, Maiori, Minori, and then at last, Amalfi. The village came suddenly into sight as we rounded a promontory, and we looked down on a lovely view. The town starts at the water's edge and rises against the cliff in tier after tier of little white houses, and high above the rest was the Cappuccini Hotel, our home for the next four days.

Almost as soon as we arrived we discovered one of the major snags of this romantic coast - steps! There were a couple of hundred at least from the road to our hotel; there was a lift as well, but this had suffered from the war and was out of order. By the time our leave was over, our calves were stiff; coming down was even harder on the feet than going up.

The hotel was originally an old monastery; it was very popular before the war with the English intelligentsia and there is a plaque on the terrace commemorating the fact that the poets Longfellow and Osbert Sitwell and the composer William Walton often stayed there. The hotel stands high on the cliff, and there is a lovely view over the town. We had a front room, and the view from it after dark was simply breathtaking. There was a full moon, and the harbour was dotted with the bright lights of dozens of fishing boats. Nearly all the fishing here takes place at night; a bright light attracts the fish, which are then caught in a very large net which is towed round to enclose the whole area.

The hotel was reserved for Army officers on leave, and we came across one or two old acquaintances, one of whom we hadn't seen since our journey out together on the ship which brought us to the Middle East. One of the regular evening "features" was a couple of hours of music by a local band, composed of two mandolins, two banjos, a guitar and a "jug" bass. This last consisted of a down-at-heel gent with a very large walrus moustache, which gave his face a hangdog air too ludicrous to describe. This gentleman blew into a large size in water jugs, which he held on his knees. The vocal numbers were in the hands of three fifteen-year-old girls, all with rather piercing voices. They sang the Italian equivalents of "Ferry Boat Serenade" and "The Woodpecker Song" ad nauseam, besides several charming Italian folk songs.

Of course, we knew it was bound to happen in the end! One evening a well-oiled officer had a go at playing "jug" bass, and dropped the jug which shattered on the stone floor. What lamentations! Oh, it was the finest jug on the coast. The tone, so mellow. The weight, just right. The disconsolate owner was finally comforted with much money and turned up the next evening, amid roars of laughter and applause, with a new instrument; but somehow the new jug never had QUITE the tone of the old one.

Our first day was a Saturday; it was fine but there was a very cold wind. We went over to Sorrento to see our CO, who was on leave there. We couldn't travel round the coast, unfortunately as several bridges had been demolished and we had a rather tedious journey by the inland route over roads we already knew and thoroughly disliked. We found the CO in good form, but weren't very impressed with Sorrento. It is supposed to be a great beauty spot, but it is rather remote from the sea, being at the top of a steep cliff. At one hotel we came across a number of American officers, all pretty well-oiled at 11.30 in the morning. I must say that I have been struck all along by the intemperance of the American troops as compared with our own. One frequently sees American soldiers helplessly drunk in the streets at mid-day. I don't mean to suggest that our own chaps don't get drunk, but they seem to do it in a more gentlemanly way. Possibly the fact that the American troops get no ration of beer, or in the case of officers whisky, may have something to do with it. I have heard of bottles of Scotch fetching

£10 easily. The result is that the troops booze an awful lot of the local vino, much of it pure methyl alcohol suitably bottled and labelled! I once saw an American sergeant in a Naples street pay a pound for a bottle of Scotch which, of course, turned out to be a bottle of vino when he opened it. In this matter, at least, the Yanks are very soft. I can't imagine many British Tommies being caught out like that!

It was nearly teatime when we reached Salerno on our way home, but there was no tea to be had. Two very nice nurses asked us for a lift but, unfortunately, we weren't going their way, and we had a beautiful but cold drive back to Amalfi for dinner. For once, we were glad of the climb up to the hotel to get our blood circulating again, especially as it had begun to rain.

The next day, Sunday, was a stinker. It poured with rain outside, and inside the place was thick with padres, who were holding a sort of Old Home Week there. We sat in most of the day reading and writing. Fortunately, an excellent jazz pianist turned up in the afternoon, and we kept him hard at it. He could play anything you asked and his recital made me long for a gramophone and some of my favourite records. Altogether, a wasted day.

Monday really wasn't much better. The weather was dull and looked very uncertain. After breakfast we set off by boat to visit the Emerald Grotto. We hadn't been on the briny for more than half-an-hour before it started to drizzle, later changing to a steady downpour. We sheltered in a small bay for a short time but the rain showed no signs of stopping so we decided to pay off our boatman and return home by road; we arrived back for lunch very fed up after a three mile walk in the rain. The Adjutant got a speck of cinder in his eye which made it water very badly, and my feet were wet, so we made a happy pair. It was still raining after lunch, so we went into Salerno to the pictures, returning wet and fed up; there is little or no protection from the elements in a jeep!

On Tuesday, as a result of Sunday's fug and Monday's rain, I developed a streaming cold and felt like death warmed up; every time I had to climb those ruddy steps my breath came and went in indecently short pants, and my heart thudded like a sledge hammer. There was an old lady living at the hotel who spent her time doing paintings; I bought one which took my fancy. She was talking with some of the officers one day, and had the cheek to say that the Allies should have landed at Salerno a month before they actually did; "many of our fine Italian young men would have been saved if that had happened" The officers forebore, being gentlemen as well, to point out that many of those same fine Italian young men were now strutting the streets of Naples STILL in uniform and STILL wearing the campaign ribbons they had won in Albania, Abyssinia, Greece and Libya. With very few exceptions, the Italian armed forces have been conspicuous by their absence from every battlefield. The Italian nation seems to have no sense of pride; within three months of the Allied landings one could buy on the streets of Naples for half-a-crown a brass medal commemorating the Allied landings in Italy. Thus did a nation make money even out of its own defeat! Now there is talk of paying them for the railway wagons and engines the Allies used to transport their troops. Truly it is an insane world when, in an Italian city, one sees a Greek walking arm-in-arm with two Italian girls; yet we were ALL so mad that few are struck by the incongruity of such a situation!

We were due to return to the Regiment on Wednesday, but before doing so we went as far round the coast as the demolitions would permit, and also (at last!) visited the Emerald Grotto. This place really justifies its reputation. Like the Cheddar caves on a very small scale, it has not been ruined by a lot of multi-coloured lights. In fact, when we visited the place, even the small amount of electric illuminations normally laid on wouldn't function, and we saw the place by natural light only, which I believe was an advantage. The Grotto is a large cave, which communicates with the tidal sea by an opening in its outer wall about twelve feet beneath the surface of the water. Because of this, all the illumination enters it indirectly, through the water, and this fact is responsible for some wonderful and freakish light effects. Nothing abnormal is noticeable until the water is disturbed by a stone or the blade of an oar; when this happens, every drop of water becomes incandescent, and glitters like a brilliant green jewel. Near the point at which the cave communicates with the sea it is possible to see down to a depth of many feet, so clear is the water. We were lucky in that the sun was shining on the water outside, so enhancing many of the beautiful effects of the light. In addition to these effects, the walls of the Grotto bear the most beautiful tracery of stalactites I have ever seen; some had the fragility of lace, so that one had to touch them to convince oneself they were in fact made of hard calcium, patterned by limestone-laden water which had run in just that tracery for centuries. Altogether it was a beautiful spot, and we were both glad we had persevered in our efforts to see it.

We had an uneventful ride home, and found all well when we got there; a new ambulance driver had arrived in my absence, but he didn't stay long, and was replaced in a few days by John Armstrong, one of the grand pair of chaps who had been with us for five weeks before Christmas. He was as delighted to be back with us as we were to have him; we celebrated by making him a bew of his favourite cocoa á la 51 Medium Regiment!

Whilst we were living in our cave under the farmhouse we had occasional visitors, who came to try out their English on us. There was one girl who came occasionally; she had been to the University at Naples and said so every few minutes. She always brought her family with her, and they stood around in a semi-circle while she did her stuff; maybe I'm over-sensitive, but I think I know now how the animals feel at the zoo. Any minute I expected one of them to reach out and poke me with his stick with the 'orses 'ead 'andle!

I had visited Naples several times during our stay in winter quarters. From many aspects it looks a beautiful city, but it is a whited sepulchre, hiding the most dreadful slum conditions in Italy, or so I am told. I saw a good deal of air raid damage near the docks and railways, but the main parts of the city were hardly touched. The Germans burned the University library and blew up the post office with a time bomb which exploded one morning some time after they had left the city, killing and injuring many civilians. Many of the finer buildings were closed for the duration, including, unfortunately, the art museum containing some of the finest (and incidentally the rudest) statues in Europe. There were really very few spots worth visiting though I did go to the opera, and saw

Madame Butterfly very well done indeed. Shopping, the chief pastime, was both expensive and unsatisfactory, until price control was instituted in March, when of course most things disappeared from the shops!

I think this is a good time to end this bulletin and next time I shall be dealing with our part in the first great assault in 1944 on the Gustav Line. Order your copy well in advance! Cheerio!

BULLETIN FIFTEEN

"Fight on the Bald mountain"
mid-January to mid-March 1944

For some time big things had been in the air; recce parties had been out and new gun positions had been dug. Everything was very thick on the ground, and after so long in the protection of our cave, we were naturally a bit windy about sticking our heads out in the open air again. Fortunately, I found what was practically the ideal R.A.P. site. It consisted of a deep sunk lane, into which my truck just fitted. It had a good drive-in for the ambulance car, and communicated directly via a sunk track with one of the gun positions half a mile away. In the sides of the lane several good dry caves had been hewn out of the sandstone; these we used as sleeping accommodation, whilst a small one-roomed shack served us as living accommodation and cookhouse. It was surrounded by olive trees, and we got to know quite well the people who came there, war or no war, to till the land and wash their clothes.

Our guns, along with many others, were positioned on either side of the road leading down towards the Garigliano river, opposite Castelforte, a town on the hill and on the enemy side of the river. Once the battle started it was torture to ride down that road, so terrific was the noise and blast from all the medium and heavy guns. The ground was so bad that it was quite impossible to get any gun more than a hundred yards off the road. Most of our positions were pretty good, though one of the batteries was a bit close to the village of Lauro for the comfort either of our gunners (from enemy shelling) or the inhabitants (from the noise and blast of our guns, which must have loosened a good many tiles in the roofs). I was amazed by the fatalistic attitude of the Italian populace to the war. Here they were in a village less than three miles from the river, a nest of artillery, bound to be heavily shelled and probably bombed too. Yet they never made even a token attempt at evacuation, but remained put all through the battle. Some even attempted to return from villages further back, where they had been staying with relatives during the winter.

When we left our cave to move to the new R.A.P. the family in the farmhouse were all very downcast; the girls had done all our odd sewing and laundry for a month, and they had all been very kind to us. We left with many promises to return, and in fact we went back several times to see them, always receiving a delightful welcome from the young ladies. (Now I know what you are thinking, but it simply isn't true!)

Just before the battle began, and to our consternation, they moved a very heavy gun into a position about a hundred and fifty yards from our R.A.P. and just across the road. This gun fired a two hundred pound shell with a terrific thump, and we had visions of the roof of our shack descending on our heads; fortunately, it stood the strain but we watched it anxiously, and every time the gun fired a shower of dirt fell from the roof down our necks or into whatever food we were eating.

The battle plan was that the British infantry were to cross the Garigliano river and form up on the other side under cover of our barrage. They were then to advance up the hills on the right bank and dislodge the Germans. The attack was linked with an attack by the Americans across the Rapido river below Cassino. It was hoped that Cassino could then be outflanked and taken from the rear, the Americans having failed in an expensive attempt to take it by frontal assault.

The night of the attack was perfectly clear and cold, and I had a superb view of the barrage and of our shells bursting in enemy territory. The whole area was lit by the flashes from our guns, and the sky was criss-crossed by the sausage-like strings of tracer shells being fired by the light AA guns. We could see our shells bursting in a thin line a couple of hundred yards from the German bank of the river, and also on some of his gun and mortar positions. Within the first half-hour a couple of first-class fires were raging on the wooded slopes of the hills opposite. I have never seen anything like it before and shall never forget the sight as long as I live. We were even able to see and report flashes of German guns returning our fire, but most of it at that time was falling further forward; OUR turn came later.

After viewing this firework display we returned to the R.A.P. for our usual "barrage brew", a cup of tea with a spot of whisky in it, to warm and soothe us. There had been no German return fire by eleven so we went to bed. The noise was terrific; AA guns behind us assaulted our eardrums with their sharp cracking report, and the "heavy" across the road shook the ground every time it fired. And yet we slept; I awoke occasionally, but heard nothing unusual above the roar of the guns, though I DID think one crash was a bit heavier than usual, and it seemed to be followed by the sound of earth falling in our sunken lane.

The first intimation that all had not gone well came from Johnnie Ellard, my batman, when he came to wake me in the morning. He was unshaven and had forgotten to put his teeth in and was shivering in every limb. I was terribly sorry for him, but had the greatest difficulty in suppressing my laughter.

His opening enquiry "bit of a rough night, wanna it?" (Wasn't it?) was a fitting prelude to a tale of the night's woes. He, foolish fellow, had preferred the comforts of home to the safety of the cave-dweller, and had set up his abode for the night in the shack. It seems he had managed to get to sleep even in this building, and was awakened about 1.30 am by an extra loud crash, which shook plaster from the walls and brought the roof in. Now when you are in an unprotected building and something like THAT happens you just HAVE to get up and see what is what. He had just got outside the door, dressed only in vest and pants, when a large and explosive missile of unquestionably hostile origin landed about thirty yards away from him, on the edge of the road. Several boxes of ammunition and about a hundredweight of mixed solids took to the air and landed all round him. Ellard incontinently dived head first into our sunken road, where he encountered the only thorn bush in many yards. He then crawled to Harold Jones' cave, and spent a sleepless night shivering with cold. No wonder he looked a bit careworn the next morning. He was pretty jumpy for a couple of days, but soon recovered. Subsequent enquiries showed that several shells had fallen in the vicinity, one of which had hit the heavy gun position across the road, inflicting some casualties.

The first morning after a barrage is always an interesting time. One hangs around the command post, waiting for the first situation report. Have they got there? Did they have a tough time? Was the barrage OK? Did they catch Jerry napping? This morning followed orthodox lines. It was a lovely spring day, but the whole of the front was shrouded in the smoke of battle; the attack had gone well on our immediate front, but friends on our right had failed to cross the river, so that our right flank was left hanging in the air. Some of the battalions on our front had reached their objectives and were digging-in ready to meet the inevitable enemy counter attack. Others were on the slopes of Suja and Damiano, two hills which were to become well known to us. Our barrage had caught the enemy by surprise, and our leading groups found half-finished suppers on the tables in many of the houses. On our left near the sea, another formation had got across the river, and the bridge was up, protected by a smoke screen. Standing offshore we could see a couple of cruisers adding their weight to the fire of our guns. We wondered how the Americans had fared in their effort to cross the Rapido river, higher up the valley. Later we found the Germans had been waiting for them; they managed to cross the river, but found that Jerry had all the crossings and roads "taped" with withering fire (what did they expect?), and so they had to come back. They had terribly heavy casualties.

Here I feel I must digress a little, to contrast the British and American methods of war reporting for their army newspapers. The American method uses an intensely personal touch; the actual words of the man are quoted verbatim, together with his name and home address, and a story is built up from several such statements. The result is that when things go wrong, an hysterical note is apt to creep in, while if all goes well the impression is one of bumptious cocksureness which is offensive to British ways of thinking. Our method on the other hand is to play down the personal factor and concentrate on the regiments and other units, though they are rarely referred to by name. So that when our friends failed to cross the river, the general impression given was that the opposition was stiffer than had been expected and the river rather fast flowing. The Americans accounts of THEIR failure were full of such exclamations as "gee, it was murder!", "the Krauts could see every foxhole". "We were up to our waists in water for twelve hours" etc, etc. I don't want anyone to think I'm criticising the bravery of the American combat troops; I saw their front later, and they must have gone through hell. But I do feel that their method of reporting tends to lower them in the estimation of their British allies.

But to return to the battle. The expected German counter attacks materialised that afternoon, and our men were forced off some of the heights they had seized; from then on until darkness bitter hand-to-hand fighting went on for these commanding positions, with heavy casualties on both sides. Our artillery, helped by the spotter planes, did great execution among enemy infantry massing for counter attacks. The haze over the battle area cleared in the afternoon, and we could see our shells bursting on the wooded hills and in the town of Castelforte, still in enemy hands. We never really held this town, although for several days it became a no man's land, the hunting ground of Allied and German patrols.

The medical services had a tremendous job on their hands in this battle; for some days it was impossible to get ambulance cars nearer than one mile this side of the river. The wounded had to be carried down the hillsides (all terraced) under heavy mortar fire at times, and placed on jeeps, which were then ferried across the river on pontoons. A dressing station was soon set up on the enemy side of the river, but proved unworkable for some days owing to enemy sniping. I regret to say that the usual German respect for the Red Cross went by the board in this battle, and its protection was most flagrantly abused. In many cases only a couple of hundred yards separated the opposing troops. Under these conditions the Germans often sent out parties under the protection of a Red Cross flag, ostensibly to pick up their wounded. These parties came right up to our forward defence posts. Later in the day an enemy attack developed, nearly always aimed at the weakest points in our defence, proving that the stretcher parties were doing a pretty efficient job of reconnaissance.

For a couple of days the battle settled down to a slogging match between the opposing infantry, with our artillery chiefly engaged in destroying enemy guns and a few tanks and breaking up enemy infantry forming up for counter attacks. It was all hill fighting, and the most fantastic situations arose. For a long time our troops encircled the hill called Damiano, but they never got nearer than a hundred yards to the flat top, on which German infantry, completely cut off, were able to hold out because they could see every move we made. Similar situations occurred all along the front; we had observation officers right forward with the infantry so that they could bring down fire at short notice. At times they were able to throw grenades at the enemy, and three of our men were wounded, one fairly seriously, though he has now recovered and is back in England. The Regiment earned further laurels in this battle. We were the first unit to get a telephone line and exchange working across the river. We also had a party ferrying anti-tank guns across the river; they were badly mortared on several occasions and one man earned the MM for carrying on while wounded. Finally, one of our troop commanders, already mentioned in despatched for his aggressive OP work during the Enfidaville battle in Tunisia, was awarded the MC for outstanding coolness and devotion to duty in the present battle.

After three days we were all delighted to hear of the Allied landings at Anzio, and great hopes were entertained that Jerry would have to remove himself with some speed. This did not happen, and looking back one can see that such a result was not likely. We now know that General Alexander's task throughout the winter was to contain in Italy as many German divisions as possible. The Anzio beachead brought down from Northern Italy a large number of fresh divisions, and probably eased the burden of the partisans there and in Yugoslavia.

A little time after the Anzio landings, the troops who had failed to cross the river on our right were brought round by night and sent across the bridges which had been put up on our front, in the hope that they might be able to advance through our own holding infantry and push the Germans back. In this they succeeded, but only partially.

With the failure to make good the crossing of the Garigliano river, things developed into a stalemate on the west of the Italian front. We continued to hold some heights round Castleforte, whilst the enemy held others, and our artillery battered away every night at the enemy's routes of supply, which we got to know pretty accurately after a short time. In this position, we shot off more shells per gun than we did at Enfidaville in Tunisia; so much so that when our turn came to go to Anzio we were unable to do so; our guns were all worn out, and we had to wait for the barrels to be changed. On the whole, I think we had a lucky escape, though I suppose it would have been an interesting experience.

In order to reach further back into the German supply lines, one of our batteries was moved a couple of miles forward, down on the flat nearer the river; it was rather an exposed position, but we weren't very worried as there were so many guns about that Jerry couldn't pot at them all. Fortunately, another MO was handy, and I was able to stay in my old R.A.P. in the sunk lane. Ellard moved his bed back into the shack, and we were shelled again the same night! Jerry was harrassing the road, but most of his rounds were going over our heads and bursting about two hundred yards away. By a piece of miserable bad luck a stray piece of metal hit one of our men and killed him instantly; I had to go out and make sure there was nothing to be done for him, and didn't enjoy the trip much. The shelling wasn't severe, just three or four rounds each hour, but the snag was that you never knew when they might arrive. Altogether, rather a restless night. The Germans tried a sly fighter bomber raid the next evening; it was directed at some of our guns. Fortunately, the planes opened up with cannon fire first so our fellows all had their heads down when the bombs fell. One thousand-pounder landed near one of our guns and moved about half a cubic yard of earth, but no harm was done; rather a waste of time, really.

I now settled into a routine again. After sick parade was over at 9.30 I read until the mid-morning brew of tea. At about 11 I used to go for a walk calling in at RHQ on the way to see how the battle was going. After lunch, there was wood to be got in again for the evening fire, and it was pleasantly warm sitting out in the sun reading or talking to Johnnie Armstrong, the ambulance driver. After the evening meal I often used to slip up to the mess to listen to the wireless, or else we played draughts.

During our stay so long in one place, we got to know quite well some of the local people. Most of them were women, who came each day to wash clothes at the well near our R.A.P; this seems to be one of the main occupations of the women of rural Italy. They also do a considerable amount of the farm work. Amongst other characters, there are three or four that will always remain in our memories. There was "The Harridan", a widow woman, or so she said, who was (inexplicably) in a fairly advanced state of pregnancy! She used to stand and gossip for hours in a peculiar form of local patois which we found very hard to understand, even with our Italian/English dictionary. However, she brought us gifts of wine (terrible) and coffee (pretty fair), so she had her compensations. Then there was "Lana Turner"; we called her that for two very good reasons! Unfortunately, the resemblance ceased at waist level, and then Marie Dressler took over. Lana was a fairly typical Italian country girl; she said she was only eighteen, but she looked at least twenty-eight figuratively speaking. She had twinkling brown eyes, and the rosiest pair of cheeks I have seen since leaving England. She did our washing for us, and was terrifically strong and muscular; she could chop through a log of wood quicker than any of us. We had many talks with her, and found how Fascism had come to her village, which she had never left for longer than twenty-four hours in her life. Those who refused to acknowledge the Fascist regime were given only enough food for a bare subsistence, and were excluded from all schools and places of amusement. So, naturally, everybody became Fascists. Our quartet of characters was completed by a thin miserable-looking girl of twelve, called Maria, and "just the job" a small boy, so called because that phrase represented his total command of the English language, and he used it on every possible occasion. Sometimes, I regret to say, the phrase was elaborated to "just the blank-blank-blanking job!"

Meanwhile the stalemate war continued. Every afternoon with monotonous regularity the German guns would shell our supply lines and roads on our side of the river, and every night we harassed their supply routes; judging from prisoners' bitter complaints, our efforts certainly weren't wasted. Every one of their ration parties dreaded the trip to the forward areas, and they had many casualties. Activity in the air was slight on our immediate front, apart from our little artillery spotter-planes, but we often saw whole armadas of heavy bombers going to Anzio or Toulon or Genoa. One morning I counted a hundred-and-eighty Fortresses glinting in the bright morning sun. The noise form their motors as they slowly gained height was terrific. Even as I watched, one of them swung out of line and turned back; evidently something had gone wrong with it for it flew off in the opposite direction. Later the same afternoon we saw some of the same bunch returning; they came out of a big cotton wool cloud in the light of the westering sun, dragging white plumes of vapour with them. Higher still we could just make out their escorts of Lightning fighters.

It was about this time that the much discussed bombing of the Cassino monastery took place, during the American frontal assault on the town. At the time, no doubt, the bombing was justified, but in the light of what happened later it was really a fruitless operation. No doubt the Germans WERE using the place as an observation post, but they had just as good OPs in the ruins, and short of knocking down the whole of Monastery Hill, an obviously impossible task, it is difficult to see how we could have prevented the Germans seeing over the whole battlefield. However, it is easy to be wise after the event, and at that time we were not to know that the American attack would be a failure. Fighting in Cassino was very close, and led to the cracking of a few jokes in Army newspapers; in burlesque communiques it was said that "close fighting is going on for number six, Ciano Street; the Germans have been driven from the kitchen, but occupy firmly an important strategic position in the lavatory; our troops attacked this morning, and are making good progress; they have already reached their first objective, the wash basin". The real fighting can have been no joke, however, and I don't believe anything like it has occurred in the European theatre, with the possible exception of a day or so in Caen or Cherbourg.

At last the blow we had all been dreading fell; Johnnie Armstrong had to leave us. Altogether, he had been with us for two months, and he and I had formed a firm friendship. We had much in common, including ideas about world peace and the part Britain and America must play in ensuring it. We spent the hours discussing all sorts of topics. Johnnie was going home to the States, and was, of course, pleased on that account, but he was as downcast as any of us when he said good-bye and for two pins I believe he would have stayed. As soon as he reached home he wrote to us, and in his letter was very bitter about the home front in America. Apparently things over there are very similar to what they were in Britain during the last war; hysterical hero worship, a feeling that the war was already over, and no idea of the hardships of active service. He was very fed-up, and wanted to come back to Italy, but was unable to do so for family reasons. He was good enough to say that the weeks he spent with us were some of the happiest in his life, and we certainly missed him. I still hear from him regularly and he sends me copies of American magazines.

At this time I had been rather busier than usual, and amongst my patients were some negroes from Mauritius, whose camp was near my RA.P. They were the first native troops the local Italians had seen, and caused a great deal of gossip, besides inspiring terror; this solely on account of their appearance, for they were quite charming and better behaved than many white troops.

"Lana" simply couldn't fathom this, and kept well away from them during my sick parades. During one of our conversations she asked me, blushing rosily, whether they were "tutto nero" - black all over; when I replied in the affirmative, she wanted to know if their women were black too. When I said they were, she shuddered and then laughed and asked me how I knew! A bit of a facer, you must admit, and I don't think she really believed me when I said I had seen photographs of them. I had told her about my travels to Japan and Malaya, and she was open-mouthed with amazement. The height of her ambition was to go to Naples, all of thirty miles away!

During this period a couple of new officers arrived; they were very green, having recently left England, and I felt sorry for them. They were always very smartly turned out, with freshly scrubbed gaiters, etc, and their chief worry when they first arrived was to know whether we wore our web-equipment all the time! However, they settled in, and it wasn't long before we felt they had been with us for years.

All through the winter I had exulted in the possession of a three-ton truck, in which we were able to live during the bad weather, when we couldn't get a house. Now, alas, I had to give it up, owing to a reorganisation of the regimental transport, and I was given a fifteen hundredweight truck instead. As this was only a quarter of the size, drastic pruning of our kit was necessary in order to fit it in, though we managed to squeeze in a surprising amount by careful experiments in packing. I kept the canvas top from the three-tonner and had an extension made to act as an R.A.P. When the whole thing was finished, it resembled nothing so much as a side show in a fair, and we soon became known as "The Circus". As a matter of fact, we found the smaller truck much handier for tucking away in confined spaces, but I am afraid we may find it a bit damp next winter.

Our semi-static existence dragged on through February without much sign of a change in the war prospects. The Americans came out of the line at Cassino and the Indians and New Zealanders had a go. They got very little further than the Americans had done, and were held up by the same obstacles - strong points, dug in tanks, tunnels through which reinforcements could be got up in safety, etc, etc. One result of this new attack was that I saw Jock Cobb again. He had been my ambulance driver in Tunisia, and was working with the New Zealanders. I saw him for an hour one cold and windy day, and we had a lot to say to each other. He was due to return to the States in March, and had decided to study medicine, much to my delight; we had had many talks in which I had tried to persuade him that his brain was far too fine to be wasted on astronomy, on which he is something of an expert. His father is a very eminent surgeon, so I expect to hear great things from Jock in the near future. At about this time Leslie Henson, for whom I have a great respect, brought his "Gaieties" to the theatre at Capua, and I had the great good fortune to draw one of the few tickets issued to the Regiment. He had a first class company with him including Hermione Baddely. During one scene she lost the whole of the top of her dress accidentally, and showed remarkable presence of mind by whipping off a large picture hat she was wearing and using it to cover the devastated area while she took a bow!

The Garigliano battle had by this time reduced itself, on our side, to the holding of what ground we had gained on the far side of the river, and trying to kill as many Germans as possible with gunfire. At long last we got wind of a move, and I prepared to leave our R.A.P. which had sheltered us for almost two months - an all time record for me, I hope.

This seems a good point to end this bulletin and I will start the next one when we move to our new position.

BULLETIN SIXTEEN

"On the move again" — February to March 1944

Our move took us several miles inland, to the foot of Monte Camino, the ORIGINAL monastery hill, not the Monastery Hill above Cassino! We settled down in the small village of San Clemente, and I once more slept in a house, - first time in four months! We expected little opposition from Jerry, because he couldn't locate our guns accurately, owing to the screening effect of the mountains. Our chief job was to harass the German supply routes to a big stores dump which our aircraft had spotted. Our village was only a mile or two from the famous Pateley Bridge, which the enemy shelled regularly. He had the place taped, and generally managed to damage the bridge once or twice a week, in spite of our constant smoke-screens all round it.

It became the fashion to climb Monastery Hill, and I was inveigled into doing so one fine spring afternoon; it was a terrific climb, and it took us two hours to reach the first crest, but it was well worth the effort though I was stiff for days afterwards. I shall never cease to wonder how our infantry managed to fight their way to the top; no wonder it took the Guards to do it. The hillside is dotted with their graves, and there were a few German graves at the top - a disappointingly small number, I thought. However, they were probably multiple graves. It is a favourite and typically Hunnish trick to bury several bodies in one grave and put only one man's name on the cross, in order to conceal from us the magnitude of their casualties. There was one good sight, however; a multiple grave with six names on it, an officer and five German NCO's; probably killed by the same shell whilst holding a conference. There were a satisfying number of large shell-craters about.

It was a very clear afternoon, and the view from the top into enemy territory was superb. We could see for five miles clear up the Liri Valley - some wit had christened it "The Promised Land". This green area, ten miles long and narrowing from south to north, was the objective of all the attempts to breach the Cassino and Gustav Line defences; it was good tank country, and the Germans knew it; across the valley at the town of Pontecervo they had built another defensive line - the Adolf Hitler line. From our vantage-point we could clearly see Pignataro, a little town in the middle of the valley, and a first-class fire (probably a burning truck) on one of the roads. On our left was Monte Cairo, with Cassino and Monastery Hill at its foot. The sides of Monastery Hill were streaked with the screening smoke from our artillery, and a squadron of Mustangs was dive-bombing the town. On our right was the formidable barrier of the Aurunci mountains with the Garigliano River (formed by the junction of the Liri and the Rapido) running round their base on its way to the sea. Looking over our shoulders we could see what a task our troops must have had; observers on the hill could see every movement on the roads below for many miles around. During a last glance at the promised land we could see some of our air-bursts over the big enemy dump at Vallemaio.

A few days after our climb the New Zealanders opened a fresh assault on Cassino; this was preceded by the heaviest aerial bombardment of the war on such a small target. Unfortunately, the first heavies came over soon after 8 am, so we were unable to climb the mountain again, but we had a good view from the road overlooking Pateley Bridge. The attack was opened by Fortresses, and continued for four hours by Liberators, Bostons and Mitchells; the first formation were greeted with desultory anti-aircraft fire, but this soon died out. There was a fighter escort with each formation, but no German fighter pilots were in a mood for suicide that morning. All the planes bombed from about six thousand feet, definitely lower than the optimum height for the heavies. Possibly this accounts for some unfortunate incidents, which I cannot deal with here. There was also a slight ground-haze.

The bombing was a terrifying sight, and one not easily forgotten. I was physically sickened at the sight of so much destruction. The planes in each formation all released their bombs together, and the first salvo fell plumb in the centre of the target area. We were at least eight miles away, but we could see great gouts of reddish flame leap upwards as the bombs struck, to be followed by a pall of brownish-black smoke and dust which hid everything from view for a few minutes; by the time the slight wind had cleared this away the next formation was over, and the horrible spectacle was repeated. This went on for four hours, and the rain of death dripped all over the town and the slopes of Monastery Hill; our own troops had, of course, been withdrawn before the bombing started. So, unfortunately, had the enemy, as we later found out. The thunder of the bombardment reached us all morning as a dull intermittent rumble; after a time we ceased even to look up as formation after formation of bombers thundered overhead on their way to the target. As soon as the bombing ceased the guns took over and the rumble of the barrage lasted till five o'clock that evening, when it ceased as the infantry went in. By a miserable piece of bad luck the weather broke and heavy rain fell that evening, swelling the rivers and holding up bridging operations. In the end, this attack failed as had all the others - the Germans were still there and still fighting. The wonderful Ghurkas of the Indian Division got nearly to the top of Monastery Hill where they were cut off for nearly five days and had to be supplied by parachute.

The mass bombing of Cassino from the air was a new departure in warfare, and so experimental. On results, it must be judged a failure, and it is significant that this method has not been tried in France! Mass bombing has been used, but it was directed against personnel in open country, and not with a view to destroying buildings. The failure at Cassino was due to many factors. For one thing, the whole place was piled so high with rubble that it proved impassable to our tanks. What Germans were in the town were mostly killed or buried, but it seems that the enemy had a fair idea of what was coming, for the number of German dead was not great. Finally, the complicated system of underground tunnels gave bombproof shelter, and a route whereby the enemy returned to the town after the bombing and during the artillery barrage, so that they were waiting for our infantry when they arrived. Bombs which fell short of the town tore up the main road, which caused delay whilst the gaps were bridged. Cassino stopped Hannibal; in an Italian Military textbook of the last century it was considered impregnable. And so it proved, for in the end it was outflanked and cut off before being captured. Its capture will probably prove to have been the most expensive operation of the whole Italian campaign; its name should rank with Verdun.

As things were pretty slack on the Regiment's sector (we only played a small diversionary role in the Cassino attack) leave again became possible, and the Adjutant and I decided to try our luck on the Italian coast once more. We went this time to Ravello, beloved of English poets and American film-stars, and situated on the cliffs above Amalfi. Nine hundred feet above sea-level, it offers a wonderful view over the sea and the coast. We stayed at the Belvedere Hotel, run by the cousin of the great Caruso. The walls of the public room were covered with paintings of all shapes, sizes and styles, some of which appeared to my untutored eye to be extremely fine.

THIS leave hit a new low in my experience. It seemed as though the heavens had conspired with the infernal regions to ensure that we enjoyed the maximum of discomfort and inconvenience.

On our way down we had noticed that Vesuvius seemed rather more active than usual and there were several large fires. The next day we went to Naples to the opera and again noticed an increase in the smoke from the mountain. The opera was Carmen, and we didn't enjoy it much. The scenery and costumes were drab and the actors, I thought, third rate. The San Carlo Opera House, considered by some the finest in Europe, looked a bit faded, but must have been very beautiful when a bit newer. The Germans used it exclusively for propaganda meetings, but it is now the main centre of music and culture in liberated Italy; most of the audience was in uniform.

When we emerged from the Opera House it had just stopped raining. As we neared the outskirts of Naples I happened to look up at the sky, and saw a sight which was at once beautiful and terrible. The sky was clear, and above the crater of Vesuvius was a cloud of smoke and steam. It glistened pearly-white in the late afternoon sun and appeared to be solid and made of marble till one looked at it for a long time, when it was seen to be constantly billowing upward and changing its shape under the pressure of the hot gases inside it. When we got to the foot of the mountain we could see the streaks of molten lava, like re-hot icing on some gigantic sugar-cake, on the mountain side. The top had literally been blown off the cone by the force of some gigantic subterranean explosion, and the wooded slopes were burning fiercely. On the road we passed pathetic groups of refugees from the hillside villages and vineyards, carrying their portable possessions. It was as if war had returned again to people barely recovering from a hard autumn and winter. For most of them their means of livelihood - the vineyards - and their homes had gone, destroyed by the lava stream which, with the inexorable gait of a juggernaut, crawled down the mountain side, destroying whole townships which lay in its path. It was growing dark as we left, and the red-orange glow from the lava and the crater could be seen for miles. Near the mountain the ground shook and there was a continuous rumble as of some infernal artillery barrage. Every few minutes a fresh explosion threw an enormous cloud of dust and flames far into the sky.

We were puzzled because none of this dust had fallen around us, but as we journeyed south the puzzle was solved. Just as we entered Pompeii, three or four miles south of the mountain, the dust began to fall like fine rain; it got thicker as we went through the town, and covered everything with a black pall; the road looked as though it had been newly macadamed, and the grit crunched under our wheels. The dust had been flung so high in the air that a southerly wind high in the sky had seized it and carried it away from the mountain. By the time we got to Scafati the downfall became heavier, and quite large pebbles were clattering on the hood and bonnet of the jeep. We stopped to have a better look, and I picked up several pieces of the size of a golf ball, still warm after that long aerial journey; the dust was already an inch thick on the roofs of the houses and on the roads. It thinned out as we got further south, but was in evidence even at Ravello, twenty-five miles away. The next two days it got much worse; it was ankle-deep in the streets of Salerno, and was turned into a thick squishy mess by the rain which fell. The roofs of many houses in Pompeii and Scafati fell in under the weight of wet ashes; the road from Salerno to Naples was impassable for four days except for one-way traffic. Somebody in England suggested bombing Vesuvius to start an eruption when the Germans were still in Naples; I bet the Jerries were laughing during the eruption; it must have cost the allied war-effort a great deal, as we had to do all the rescue and relief work with Army Transport and Rations.

The eruption set the tone for the whole of the rest of our leave; it completely upset the weather, which was pretty unstable anyway, and in addition to ashes we had snow and rain! We took a guide who showed us round Ravello; we saw over the Villa Cimbrano (?), Lord Grimthorpe's place; the view from the gardens is world-famous, and in one grotto there was a beautiful half-size marble statue of Eve which I thought was one of the most beautiful pieces of sculpture I had ever seen. The unknown artist had caught the lady, finger-to-lip, starting at some sudden noise; the figure was full of movement, and the details quite incredible, every toe and finger was hewn out separately, and the waist-length hair was so life-like that one expected to see it wave in the breeze. The whole thing had been ruined by vandals, many of them English, who had scrawled their names all over the lady in the most obvious places. This applied to all the statues in the villa; to rest did not impress me very much. Garbo and Stokowski are said to have stayed there. The other show place is the Villa Ruffolo; at present graced by the King of Italy, it was naturally closed to sightseers. George Sand and Chopin stayed there. In addition, there is a cathedral founded in 1086 by the Normans; the coast is dotted with forts and towers built by the Saracens as look-outs. Many of the older houses in Ravello still show traces of the Norman builders in their door-posts and arches.

There is little more to relate about our leave; it rained or was about to rain every day till the last, which, characteristically enough, was brilliantly fine so that we were able to see what a nice time we would have had if the weather had been fine for us. The view from our bedroom balcony was superb and revealed the whole glorious sweep of the bay, with the terraced lemon-groves descending to meet the blue waters of the sea - blue with that peculiar tint which is characteristic of the Mediterranean on sunny days. We left Ravello with regret, determined to return in happier times. The road North from Salerno being impassable, we had to take the long way home inland and over the hills. The weather remained fine and sunny and we had a pleasant journey back to San Clemente.

When we arrived, it was to find the place swarming with Goums. These are hill men from French Morocco, and fight and live in their peculiar one piece garment; they wear turbans on their heads and looked strangely out of place in the postcard landscape of Italy, though their garb must have been magnificent from the camouflage point of view. The Goums (the singular is Goumier) carry their own women with them, and they have been trained to live off the land. As a result, they have no respect for Italian property; if they fancied a sheep they just killed one, and either roasted it whole or ate it raw (I SAW this with my own eyes). They tore down all the vine-poles for firewood, and when they left the place looked as though a swarm of locusts had passed over it. The Italian peasants were enraged but scared stiff. I felt sorry for them but, of course, you cannot repudiate your allies one minute and then make use of them in battle, and we had good cause to be grateful to the Goums later on, as you shall hear.

News of another move came through soon after we returned from leave. We were to take over from another medium regiment on the Cassino sector; they had been having rather a rough time, especially after being in a safe area for a bit. Recce parties went out and came back with the usual gloomy reports. The position was near a much shelled cross-roads, which we later came to know as Cox's Corner; Jerry harassed it regularly every afternoon with heavy guns. However, reprieve arrived at the last moment. Our move was cancelled, and instead we were promised a fortnight's rest in a rear area - the first time in six months in which the entire regiment had been right out of the battle-line; I believe this was a record at the time for any artillery unit in Italy; all the others had had rests before this.

Well, that's all this time, folks. Cheerio.

BULLETIN SEVENTEEN

"We take a breather" — April to May 1944

Unless my memory (failing owing to lack of use) plays me false, I left you in number sixteen just as the regiment was due to pull out of the line for its first complete rest in six months.

Our rest area was in two little villages, Grazzanise and Sparanise, just south of the Volturno river, whose crossing nearly six months previously had been the occasion of the Regiment's first barrage on Italian soil. The journey down from the front was quite pleasant, but very dusty, and billets didn't give a very favourable impression when we arrived. The village RHQ was in had been pretty thoroughly bombed - after the Germans had left, if the local populace was to be believed; as a result, the drains were all blocked up and the gutters running with sewage. The place stank like a cess-pit in the hot afternoon sun; I didn't fancy quartering troops in such a place, and said so, but there was nowhere else we could go, and we didn't expect to stay there long. The mess was located in a house which was already teeming with women and children; the latter rose with the dawn and settled down about 10 pm, and spent most of the day screaming and tearing each other's hair out in the courtyard; this told rather heavily on our nerves and some of us very soon began to yearn for the tranquillity of life in the front line!

I had my R.A.P. on the upper floor of a partially bombed house; the lower floor was inhabited by two old maids, one young one, a man and a little girl of four called Lucia, who soon endeared herself to everybody with her cute ways and amazing remarks. I must digress here to make a few remarks about the oddity of Italian ideas on morality. The cab of my truck is decorated with the finest collection of nude photographs in CMF, the outcome of two years careful hunting through Lilliput, London Opinion and Men Only. When the women saw these they were shocked to the core; yet any evening you can pass through a village and see women, many of them still in their teens, giving their babies the breast while they stand on the street corners and gossip with their acquaintances of both sexes. These people are full of such paradoxes. (I have a horrid feeling I've told you all this before; if so, excuse it, please).

We came out of the line just before Easter, and Easter week-end being the anniversary of the CO's assumption of command of the Regiment two years ago, it was decreed that fun and games were in order on Easter Saturday. The junketing took the form of a small dance, held in the near-by town of Capua. We even managed to get hold of a dance band, and everybody enjoyed themselves thoroughly. We got our dancing partners from among the nurses at the nearest hospitals. It was really jolly decent of them to come along; the dance broke up at 1 am and some of them had a fifty-mile car journey to face before going on duty at 6 am. They all entered into the spirit of the evening and made things go with a swing.

Next day being Easter Sunday, the CO had ordered a special parade in the main street of the village, followed by a thanksgiving service; this was a bit hard on the officers, not one of whom had gone to bed before 2 am. I had orders to stand by at the CO's bedroom at 9.30 with aspirins and chlorodyne, but these precautions turned out to be quite unnecessary; the CO turned up at 9 am as cheery as a cricket, wearing a new battledress and "ard 'at"; he even ate a soya-bean sausage, that abomination which has been described as Hitler's secret weapon; few of us could face it THAT morning!

The Regiment made a brave show, drawn up in the main street. Unfortunately, the sky was overcast, as it seems to be on all our ceremonial parades; however, I got some fair photographs of the troops as they marched past the saluting base after the parade, on the way to the service. All the village was en fete for the occasion, and some of the girls looked very attractive in their best rig-out. I noticed several costumes and coats which had only too obviously been made from American Army blankets, and very smart they looked too. Even today, you can get £2.10 for an army blanket; the thing finally became such a racket that the strictest penalties had to be enforced, and even now it has not entirely ceased. The Italian women, especially the younger ones in their teens, look very attractive till they open their mouths to talk. Then disillusion comes quickly; they speak very rapidly in shrill tones, and all together when they are in a group. It seems to be some sort of competition in which she who shouts loudest wins.

We now entered on a round of drinking parties which left everybody very much the worse for wear; practically the only booze available was the local "vino", compared to which rough cider is like soothing syrup. I gave up after the first night or two, out of respect for my stomach lining!

As I was the only doctor for miles around I built up quite a large civilian practice during our stay; it was really very unsatisfactory, as I could do little against the dirt and squalor which were to be seen everywhere. Practically every child had either impetigo or septic scabies and it was obvious that even if I managed to cure them they would at once relapse, which made everything seem rather futile. The only constructive thing I did was to wangle admission to hospital for an old lady with a horrible breast cancer. My fees (when I couldn't evade accepting them) generally consisted of eggs - priceless treasures, for an egg in that part of the country was worth a shilling. The land round the village was very fertile and had been drained and developed by Mussolini, so that the people (though they didn't say so openly) greatly fancied the Fascist regime, though it took a lot of the produce of their farms in taxes and levies. The ground was full of mines and unexploded mortar-bombs left from the Volturno battle, and we had to go out one evening and remove one that was in the way of a farmer's plough.

Whilst we were out of the line, leave to Naples was fairly easy. We went into KD here too, and I seized the chance to sort out all my kit and discard some of the worn-out stuff. Curious how one associates articles of clothing with places and events. I now have hardly anything left of the kit with which I left England, except a pair of boots and some pullovers and, of course, my service dress which, incidentally, I have hardly worn. We started a bridge school, and I found that I had a much clearer idea of the game than I had thought from my previous attempts to play it. (Are you listening, Pop?)

You might think that, with the finest medium regiment in the Army out of the line, the war in Italy would have stood still, but such was not the case. The fighting had died down all along the front to "patrol activity", which cloaked preparations on both sides. The Germans knew something was coming, but they weren't quite sure where, and as events turned out, they were caught napping. On the Allied side, the most tremendous troop movements were taking place. The Eighth Army was switched from the Adriatic Sector to the centre of the front near Cassino, and many new formations were brought into it. All this is said to have occurred without the enemy knowing, but I find this hard to believe; apart from recce by aircraft, he had highways under observation for at least six miles behind our lines from Mount Cairo, the mountain behind Cassino. The roads were jammed with traffic all day, and driving on them was purgatory because of the dust, pot-holes and petrol fumes.

The Regiment's position for the battle lay between Route Six (the via Casilina) and a road which had been made up on the embankment of a railway. I went up and had a look round, and didn't fancy the spot a great deal. Four of our guns were right out in the open, and there was very little flash cover for the others. Our guns have a muzzle-flash about six feet long, so they need to be well hidden when possible. However, in this case it just WASN'T possible; we were less than four miles from Jerry but some medium guns were even closer. The position was riddled with small streams, which we didn't like; the malaria season was upon us, and we were all anxious to keep up the Regiment's good record, for we had very few cases last year. Well, there it was. The position lay between two main routes of supply, and there was a hill in the area which the enemy used as a reference point and might shell at any time. On the other side of this hill was a quarry, which housed a divisional HQ. Fortunately, there were plenty of dressing-stations about, so my position was made very easy.

In order to conceal things as much as possible, only small parties of men went forward, to dig gun pits, command posts, etc; you may be sure that they needed little urging! They built some wonderful pits and used an astronomical number of sandbags in the process; later one troop was found to be too close to a hill which was to give them flash cover, and all their pits had to be re-dug three yards further back! We left our village rest camps about a week before our "D" day, though we didn't know the actual date of the attack until thirty-six hours before it was due to begin. In order to cut down movement in the area only the guns, command posts, etc, went forward; the rest of us stayed in an area about fifteen miles behind the position. This was a mixed blessing; it was more comfortable to be out of shelling range, and the blackout was relaxed, but I had to go forward nearly every day for one reason or another, and I and my motorbike knew every hump on that fifteen miles of road before very long.

At last the time came for us to go forward; we went by night and with no lights, so it was lucky that the moon was just past full; its light made our task easy. We hadn't been cheered up much by the news that Jerry had shelled the Divisional HQ in the quarry the night before and inflicted some casualties. My R.A.P. was beside a pleasant little stream, at the foot of the aforementioned hill, which was wooded. When we arrived the scene was one of surpassing beauty; the stream chattered away to itself as it ran over the stones, and a slight breeze stirred the trees from which, to complete the picture, came the song of nightingales. Four miles from the front and the eve of a great battle; yet the scene in the soft moonlight might have been the stage setting for some romantic opera, in the magic moment between the raising of the curtain and the entrance of the two lovers.

The next day was spent sandbagging and digging and as an extra precaution we drained the petrol tanks of the truck and sandbagged up the radiator and tyres. Our anti-malarial squads were busy clearing the area of stagnant pools, a herculean task, as the place was pitted with bomb and shell craters, each one of which had either to be filled in or covered with oil to prevent mosquito-breeding. We later got a very good chit from the staff-wallahs for this work, and for our antimalarial precautions in general which were adopted as standard drill by the formation (now in action) under which we were serving. We were the only battle-hardened (lovely word!) regiment in this formation, and as a result had to provide rather a large quota of officers to go with the forward infantry and tanks, so that they could bring down artillery fire when and where it was needed; we had four officers out on this job at one time, which made work very heavy for those officers left at the gun end, for we had our own OP as well.

Twenty-four hours before the battle begun the CO held a conference of officers and NCO's, at which he explained the whole plan to us and co-ordinated it with the grand strategy of the war. It was a peaceful scene, and it was hard to believe that in twenty-four hours the biggest barrage of the war would be let loose. The plan was grandiose in conception, and brought in every nationality then serving in Italy. The key point was that Cassino was to be by-passed and taken from the rear. To do this, the Poles were given the task of climbing Mount Cairo and coming down on top of Cassino; British and Indian troops, with tanks following up, were to cross the Liri and Rapido rivers and push up the Liri plain, and along Highway Six. The French were given the task of scaling the Aurunci mountains to the west of the valley and outflanking the enemy. The Americans were to attack across the lower Garigliano, the scene of our failure in January, and push up Highway Seven.

The plan envisaged the breaking of the Gustav Line, the Adolf Hitler line (ten miles further up the Liri Valley) the Unction Line below Rome, the capture of Rome and a final advance to the Line Pisa - Florence - Rimini. It was stimulating in its grandeur, but we had heard so many plans and had so many failures that we could be forgiven for being somewhat pessimistic as to the outcome.

The build-up for the attack had been going on for weeks, and our superiority in material was tremendous. We had a superiority of four to one in guns, about ten to one in tanks, and virtual supremacy in the air. A special part of the fighter-bomber force had been "laid on" to look after the enemy's guns. Matters were so arranged that there was always a squadron in the air laden with bombs; as soon as German guns or heavy mortars opened up, down came the bombs on the gun-positions. In addition there were a large number of light planes spotting for the artillery. American heavies had been out for days beforehand bombing all the roads and railways leading to the German front. Finally, much activity went on in ports in Southern Italy, and rumours circulated pretty freely that a new Allied seaborne landing was to deceive "Smiling

Albert" Kesselring and make him keep a few divisions up north for the first couple of days of the battle.

We got a great kick out of the conference, but the atmosphere was one of pious hope rather than expectation that all would go well; we were pessimistic after all our failures. As a final booster to morale we were told that this was really the opening of the Second Front, and that the Eighth Army had been given the honour of striking the first blow. This turned out to be pure hooey, for Churchill announced after the attack had begun, that the date of D day had no connection with operations in Italy or anywhere else!

Just before zero-hour the CO issued a special order of the day; it was so well phrased that I'm sure I shall be forgiven for repeating it verbatim here.

11th May 1944: "Tomorrow, May 12th, Is Enfidaville Day, and the anniversary of a resounding victory in which you all took no small part. I can think of no better way of celebrating it in wartime than the way that had been chosen for us - another Gunner's battle. You will win THIS battle too and we can have a double celebration next year - perhaps at home."

"Our Forward Observation Officers will be with the leading troops; see that when they ask, the guns speak true. Keep the drill steady and the lay accurate."

"Remember your comrades, struck down in that final hour (12th May 1943) and shoot to kill. Good luck to you all."

Could Monty have done better? I don't think so.

There I will leave you; I hope you can feel some of the tense excitement we all felt as zero-hour approached. I'll tell you about the battle next time. Cheerio.

BULLETIN EIGHTEEN

"Back to business" — May 1944

Our D-Day was gifted with perfect weather; the front was quiet with the uneasy stillness that often precedes a storm, and the sun shone down from a literally cloudless sky on our little green wood and stream. As if to mock the horrors of war, the most gorgeously coloured dragonflies flew around everywhere, ranged in colour from peacock blue to salmon pink. We spent the hours before zero (11.30 pm) putting the last touches to our passive defences, and dug and roofed-in a good slit trench; we did this as much to pass away the time as for any other reason. The sun was grilling, and as the afternoon wore on the tension mounted. Remember that we had been out of action for nearly a month, and were wondering what was in store! Our forward observation officers departed with our fervent good wishes; we none of us fancied their jobs, and hoped they would all pull through without any untoward incidents. We had two with the tanks and several with infantry.

We were all a bit jumpy when the barrage started, especially as one gun was within twenty yards of the R.A.P. and shook the whole place each time it fired, but we soon got used to the old familiar roar, and it was good to feel we were doing our job again. I climbed the hill at the back of the position and looked over the usual sea of gun flashes; twelve months ago such a sight would have been something to write home about, now it was merely commonplace, so plentiful was our artillery. All went uneventfully for about one and a half hours, after which the Germans got things organised. Their fire was remarkably accurate too; one round landed within fifty yards of our guns, and three more whistled overhead and exploded in soft ground between us and RHQ. That concluded the evening's performance as far as we were concerned.

I have come to the conclusion that the best place to be when stuff is flying around is on the guns; you are so deafened that you don't hear anything coming back unless it's extremely close, and so you don't worry. On the other hand, of course, you don't have the same incentive OR opportunity to duck! Our sole casualty that night was a fellow who got hit in the mouth with a ramrod during the heat of the barrage! I went to bed about 2 am, but was kept awake after the barrage finished, by a couple of German planes which kept stooging around dropping high explosives and anti-personnel bombs and machine-gunning the road. A waste of time, but very upsetting to the morale!

The next morning was fine again, but the gunfire had stirred up so much dust and smoke that visibility from the air was very bad; this curtailed the fighter-bomber programme on our immediate front, though there was plenty doing further back, as we heard later. Some FW190's came over and mixed it with some of our boys; in the course of the dog fight a Lightning of ours got damaged. The pilot tried to limp home, and I was watching the plane through my glasses when the tail came off; the plane spun down with its engines going flat out and crashed and burst into flames on the top of one of the hills nearby. The sight sickened me somewhat until somebody saw a parachute and I realised that the pilot had managed to bale out; he landed lower down on the same hill as his plane, and must have had a long walk home.

The battle was going more or less as planned, but was already distinctly behind schedule; bridge-building had been held up by extremely heavy enemy fire, and tanks had not been able to get over the river until much later than had been expected. Some of the tanks were on the same wireless frequency as ourselves, and one could get a good idea of what was happening by listening to the set in the battery command post. The tank men were Canadians, and they expressed themselves very vigorously at times, so we were amused as well as informed! We were glad to hear that casualties so far were lighter than had been anticipated though one brigade near Cassino had a very sticky time. The best news came from the French sector of the front. Here our old friends the Goums had been let loose, and were already swarming over the hills which had held us up through a weary winter; down on the coast the Americans were also beginning their drive up Route Seven, over the Garigliano bridgehead, gained at such great expense by the British in January. The Poles were held up in their efforts to encircle Monte Cairo and coming down behind Cassino and the monastery, and they were having very heavy casualties.

On our immediate front the tanks were across and exploiting a somewhat difficult valley, which was criss-crossed by many streams and hillocks - the latter good cover for anti-tank guns. The Regiment was heavily engaged all day in support of all this, and in the afternoon helped to break up a formation of enemy tanks massing to counter-attack. So the first day closed; as the sun set there was practically no sound of war, and the sole sign of hostile activity was an air-burst which blossomed in the sky like Dumas' black tulip, and hung for five minutes in the still air over Monte Trocchio, where our OAP was situated. That night was again noisy; the enemy sent over bombers, who went for the road with high explosives and anti-personnel bombs again.

The next day was notable for two things - the Rumour and the Fire. The first of these reached us soon after breakfast; allied troops had landed at Le Havre and Calais. Later this became elaborated and Marseilles was also mentioned. How this rumour started is a mystery, but it grew steadily as the day wore on. Military Police were said to be going up and down the roads giving out the news from loudspeaker vans. It was impossible to get any further news until that evening, when we listened to the BBC and found out the truth. I think even the most sceptical among us felt a pang when we knew that the time for the invasion was not yet come.

The Fire broke out in the afternoon in a haystack near one of our guns; it was probably started by a spark from the muzzle of the gun. The hay was dry as tinder, and burned accordingly. Some of the burning hay fell on some fused ammunition, and there were a few anxious moments while this was being moved. One isolated fuse went off, and somebody got a small splinter in the face, very near to his eye.

The next few days were dull as far as we were concerned; we continued to fire as required, but nothing came back, and we settled down to the usual hum-drum existence, with plenty of time for reading and writing. The French swarmed over the hills on the left, and it seems obvious that the enemy must fall back soon in order to prevent his right flank being turned. Signs of this withdrawal appeared in due course; the weather had cleared, and our fighter-bombers were out doing great execution on enemy transport making for the rear. The Ghurkas went into the little pocket containing the village of San Angelo, which had been left behind by the main attack, and the Poles were drawing closer to the monastery, where they were in heavy combat with men of a German parachute regiment. These thugs fought without quarter and used every dirty trick in the bag, including the hoisting of a white flag and then firing on the Poles when they showed themselves. Few German prisoners were taken on THIS sector.

The enemy was fighting a delaying action centred on the little town of Pignataro, five miles behind the Rapido river; meanwhile his main forces were withdrawing to the much-vaunted Adolf Hitler Line, the pivot of which was the town of Pontecorvo. Our bombers laid both these towns in ruins in due course, but there was a good deal of hard fighting ahead.

We were now out of range, and had to move forward, and our new position took us to the crest of the hill overlooking the Rapido river at the point where the Americans had tried to cross it early in February. As a result, the place was pretty heavily mined, and the gun areas had to be very carefully swept before we could occupy the position. I didn't fancy the position much; in addition to the mines, one of our bridges crossed the river at this point, and I had visions of the enemy shelling the area. In view of this, I was glad to get hold of a Field Service Ambulance car again; I forgot to mention that I had not been given one at the last position, owing to the nearness of the dressing station to my R.A.P.

Scenically, the new position was lovely; we were on the crest of the green hill, and got the full benefit of the evening breeze which rustled pleasantly through the leaves of several large trees. At the back the hill fell away into a steep little valley, in which all our tents were pitched and dug in to the sides. It was doubly pleasant on that first evening, for we had had a dreadful journey over very narrow roads choked with fine grey dust, which penetrated everywhere, even into our boots. Few of the tracks were shown on our maps, so that we lost our way several times; most of them had been bulldozed out of the fields to supplement the meagre supply of metalled lanes. As darkness fell we were treated to the most beautiful sight I had yet seen in Italy. The valley was inhabited by millions of fireflies, which twinkled away like Blackpool illuminations and turned the place into a fairy dell worthy of any pantomime. Unlike glow-worms, fireflies turn their lights on and off, thus adding to the effect; when you kill one it continues to glow for quite a time after death.

I turned in early, as it had been a tiring day, but was woken up about 11 pm to find that my foreboding about enemy action had been more than fulfilled. The place was as bright as day under a large moon, very ably assisted by flares dropped by enemy aircraft, who proceeded to smarten up the area for about ten minutes. I was more frightened than I had been for a very long time; there was nothing to do except to lie still and hope for the best. Some of the heavy bombs were uncomfortably close, and one fell about three yards from a gun, but fortunately failed to explode. Several fellows had narrow escapes from cannon-shells, and to add to the fun the enemy put air-bursts all over the area with the idea of keeping the A-A gunners' heads down. We later found out that six planes were involved, quite a large raid by present day standards, and the Bofors boys shot one down. I felt certain we were bound to have had some casualties, but once again we were lucky, thanks to our habit of digging well in. The narrowest escape was experienced by two men who had the nose-cap of a shell fall through their tent and land in a space three feet by one foot between their two bodies; they never knew what had happened until they saw the hole in their tent; then they felt amongst their clothes and found the nose-cap!

This was all that happened in this position, and quite enough too! We spent one more night there, but did very little firing, as the enemy moved back rapidly and was soon out of range. The morning before we moved I had a glance at a very interesting Intelligence report. From questioning of prisoners it emerged that when the attack on the Gustav Line started the Germans failed to appreciate the situation, and started to send reserves over towards the Adriatic sector; they were recalled hastily when half-way there, but soon ran out of petrol and were hopelessly delayed. Somehow, one always imagined the German war machine being run with ruthless efficiency, and it was amusing to find that they made the same mess of things as we often did, though I must say we have never run short of petrol yet.

Our next position was across the river, and it gave me a distinct thrill to ride across the bridge to the northern bank. I could not help thinking of the weary six months struggle and the many lives that had been sacrificed to make the crossing possible; it all seemed so futile, somehow. The route forward was over tracks and lanes a foot deep in fine dry dust; I was riding my motor bike and had the misfortune to get in with a column of tanks, and it was the nearest thing to hell I've ever experienced. Their exhaust gases fling up clouds of dust so that you can see nothing in front of you, and your mouth and nostrils become filled with the stuff; the only answer is to wear a scarf covering mouth and nose. On the way up I had a look at the little town of Pignataro; it had been completely smashed up and did not contain a single whole building that I could see.

The new position was about three miles south of Pontecorvo, key town of the Adolf Hitler Line; it was on territory which had only been cleared of Germans twenty-four hours before, and there wasn't a civilian to be seen. I set up my R.A.P. on the ground floor of a large tenement house, in which normally dwelt several families who farmed the state-controlled land in the district. The place was in terrible disorder, with property of every kind from bedroom china to cutlery and curtains strewn all over the place; the enemy had been cleared out the afternoon previous to our arrival, and we had a talk with some of the Canadian infantry who had done the job. The Germans had excavated an enormous air raid shelter beneath the floor of one of the rooms; it looked as though it would have stood up to anything. Now, however, the RAF have got this type of refuge taped; they drop a bomb with a delay-action fuse, which goes right through to the bottom before it explodes!

The guns were in a very poor position here, especially one battery, which was right out in the open, along one of the main tracks leading to the front; this track was crammed with vehicles bonnet-to-tail, and tanks amongst them. Everything was being rushed forward in a frantic hurry to try and break through the Adolf Hitler Line before the enemy had time to settle down and consolidate his position. Added to this it began to rain, and the tracks were stirred into muddy rivers by the heavy traffic; to add to the chaos a tank broke its track right on the principal crossroads, and traffic was held up nose-to-tail for an hour.

The next morning the civilians began to return to our billet, and some of them remained during all the shelling which followed, including some quite young children. The women all started sorting out the portable property lying around and several noisy quarrels developed in the process. The centre of the debate was, as usual, the well in the courtyard. One or two of the women were quite pretty, so there was always a group of male spectators, made up of men off duty, who hung around to see all there was to be seen of the said young women. (It's the same the whole world over!) In one or two cases there was plenty!

That evening we had the great flap. Just as dusk was falling, news came through from our forward officer that the Germans had counter-attacked. They were reported to have broken through our infantry and to be coming straight at the gun positions, being then only four thousand yards away. For the first time in this war I felt as the original "desert rats" must have felt when Rommel was coming their way; however, THEY at least could turn and run for it. That was quite out of the question for us, and it was a matter of fighting the guns to the last. Rarely have I seen a gloomier picture. A thin drizzle of rain was falling, it was nearly dark, and men were hastily being formed into squads.

Small-arms were being loaded and the bolts clicked and tested. Everybody's faces were as long as their arm, but even so the situation had its funny side. A certain officer from the rear area drove up on his usual evening visit, and all unconscious of the situation, walked into the command post. He was out again in a brace of shakes, and his car got off to a start which would have been no disgrace to pre-war Brooklands. Not that he was walking out on us, for his rightful place was back with the store wagons, but it was rather amusing just the same. At this critical moment too, my American ambulance left me, and was replaced by a Canadian one. It was a dramatic moment as the driver bade us farewell, and judging by his handshake, he thought we were as good as prisoners already!

I could take little part in the general panic, but we DID lay out the R.A.P. more carefully than usual, and we all put on our Red Cross armbands - the first time I have worn mine since Dunkirk. I may say that they were only found after a frantic search in the bottom of our deepest box, where they had been ever since we first came overseas! Having done all we could, we had a brew of tea, liberally laced with whisky, and settled down to an uneasy sleep. We were woken after an hour to be told that the whole scare was a mistake; French troops, in their odd steel helmets, had been mistaken for Germans by a rather nervous patrol, who raised the alarm!

The next day was an unlucky one for the Regiment. It was fine, clear and dry, and about 2 pm the Germans started to harass the road near our guns; probably he had seen the dust cloud kicked up by the traffic. Inevitably, some of the shells fell on our guns, and two of our boys had the miserable luck to be killed - our first fatal casualties for many months. In addition, several fellows from passing trucks were brought to me for attention, so I was kept pretty busy all the afternoon. I was in no personal danger, being in a good solid house, but I didn't like the shelling, and was jumpy for several days afterwards. It continued the next morning, fortunately without doing any more damage.

The next day the attack on the Adolf Hitler Line opened. We fired a barrage in support of the Canadians; it was slow, and advanced a few yards at a time. We started at about 6 am, but at 10 we had orders to cease firing about two hours and one mile before we had expected, and we all wondered what had happened. It transpired that the infantry had met unexpectedly tough opposition, and the attack had lost its momentum. The situation looked serious when, at 2 pm, the masterly decision was made to press on. The barrage opened up again and caught the enemy just as he was coming out of his dug-outs and preparing to counter-attack. There was a great slaughter of German infantry by the guns, and the way was opened for our infantry; in another twenty-four hours, the vaunted Adolf Hitler Line was ours; the enemy was making off to the north. The assault was not without cost to our side, but it was only by pressing on and giving the enemy no rest that even higher casualties were avoided.

There was a prisoner-of-war cage very near our billet, and it was interesting to study the contents. For the Master Race they made a very poor showing, and fifty per cent would have been considered unfit for any form of military service in the Allied army. Several had unmistakable signs of tuberculous disease of the spine, and almost all were under-sized and looked ill-nourished and weak. Part of this was possibly due to the fact that many of them had had no food or drink for forty-eight hours; our shelling had kept them pinned in their dug-outs. Our infantry paid the highest tribute to the effectiveness of our shellfire, and said that in many cases the enemy had no fight left in them, and surrendered on sight.

As a contrast to the above, I later saw two pukka German officers. They were sitting bolt upright in the back of a jeep, and might have stepped out of an American propaganda film. They were complete even to stuck up stiff hats, and one had the last detail - a monocle! They looked ready to spit on all who passed, and I kept well out of range!

Well, that's all this time, folks. In my next, the Regiment gets a surprise, and we prepare to depart for pastures new. Ta-ta for now.

BULLETIN NINETEEN

"Blessed relief" — May to June 1944

During the remainder of the battle for the Adolf Hitler Line we remained in our big tenement farmhouse, and it was a relief to know there would be no more shelling though we had a visit or two by German bombers after dark. The country was very flat and from the top floor of the house, where I had my bedroom, we could see the guns supporting the Poles "stonking" Piedemonte, a little village near the foot of Monte Cairo and a couple of miles up Route Six from Cassino. I later saw this town at close quarters (Piedemonte, I mean) and it was reduced to ruins. Shellfire could also be seen falling higher up on the mountain, where isolated bodies of Germans were cut off and still holding out, while on the extreme right could be seen the ruins of the monastery above Cassino; they had a certain grandeur when bathed in the golden light of the afternoon sun.

From another room we could see our fighter-bombers dive-bombing the retreating German traffic. This is a really thrilling sight; twelve planes stooge round till they see a suitable target or are directed to one by ground observers. Then they "peel off" and dive down vertically (literally) on their target; at a height of about 500 feet they aim with a burst of machine-gun fire; release their bomb, and flatten out and fly away at a very low altitude; plane after plane follows on, till a cloud of thick black smoke tells of another truck disabled and burning.

We soon had to move forward again, to a position north of the town of Pontecorvo, centre of the Adolf Hitler Line. The Germans had not left the new gun area long, and another regiment's recce party captured several prisoners, who were cowering in a dug-out. In this connection a most amusing incident occurred. The prisoners were put in charge of a young Canadian private, who was armed with one of the Germans' own rifles; he didn't know how to work it, so gave it to one of the prisoners. The latter showed him how to load it, fired a couple of shots into the air to show that the weapon really worked, and then handed it back to the Canadian, who marched the Germans off! After we occupied our position a couple of snipers started work (not near us) and gave quite a lot of trouble until they were hunted down and shot. The boys who finally got them left the bodies sitting bolt upright in the ditch beside the road; before long, the Italians had removed their boots and other serviceable clothing.

The route from the old to the new position was strewn with evidence of the recent battle including burnt-out tanks, knocked out anti-tank guns, and German dead. Pontecorvo itself was a terrible sight; the streets were ankle-deep in debris, and not a whole building was to be seen. I often wonder what sort of a winter the inhabitants of these destroyed towns are having in 1944. In Pontecorvo I saw my first German "beetle" tank; shaped like a last-war tank it was about six feet long, and controlled remotely by wires which unwound from the back end.

The new position for the Command Post was on the crest of a hill, with the guns in the small valley in front, and I managed to find a stable to use as an R.A.P. The area was thick with guns, as usual! We were near an old enemy gun area, where we had the satisfaction of discovering an enemy 105 mm field gun which had obviously received a direct hit; it may well have been one of the guns which had shelled us in our last position, so we were all the more delighted to see it. The whole area was pitted with shell craters, and the German gunners must have had a very shaking time. There was no sign of any graves, but from our knowledge of German methods we felt sure these were concealed somewhere, as it was impossible to conceive of everybody remaining alive in such a heavily shelled area.

That night we had another air-raid; it wasn't QUITE so close this time, but was still very unpleasant. A lot of us took refuge in an old enemy dug-out; we were grateful for this at the time, but regretted it later as we all got badly bitten by fleas. However, our regret was short lived, for two days later a bombshell of another sort arrived. The news came through that the Regiment was coming out of the line and going back to the Middle East for a rest.

I have come to the conclusion that one can never forecast the reactions of a body of men to a given item of news. The men were all paraded to be told about our coming out of action, and whilst they were falling in a conference was held for the officers. We were all afraid that the men would be browned off, and think our move to MEF was a prelude to service in the Far East, and we were all warned to be prepared to counter this fear in every way we could. Yet the chief reaction on the part of the men was "Great Stuff; we'll be able to get a bloody good feed at that place in Cairo" or words to that effect. SOME of them were uneasy about the future, but not many; I must admit that I had a few qualms myself, as did other officers.

However, I decided that every day out of range of the enemy was sheer profit and not to be decried; besides, we knew it was the "policy" to rest units in the Middle East. Our fears were pretty well allayed in the end by a personal letter to the CO from General Leese in which he said that he was looking forward to our return to Eighth Army after a well-earned rest. Nevertheless, we didn't feel we needed a rest, and were somewhat fed up at having to quit the field after six months weary static warfare, just when the great advance had started.

Though all this news was important to us, the war had to go on, and so had we until the Regiment that was to relieve us arrived. We were soon out of range, so rapidly was the enemy retreating, and our next move was literally a nightmare.

It's rotten being in a medium regiment in country where the roads are bad, because you get in everybody's way and so they make you move at night where possible. Our new position was only three miles up a perfectly straight road, but unfortunately this road was "one way" in the wrong direction, which involved us in a round trip of about ten miles, much of it on unmapped tracks. We started at 11 pm and ground and bumped our way forwards at a snail's pace, punctuated by mad dashes now and then, when the leading vehicles found the road good and increased speed, only to slow down abruptly after half a mile or so. Lights were verboten, so it was as well that the moon was high, otherwise I am sure there would have been some crashes. As it was, the tall hedges made many patches of the road into tunnels of darkness. Of course, the inevitable eventually happened; somebody near the end of the column stalled his engine on a steep hill and by the time we had re-started the rest of the convoy was miles away. As I was the only officer left I assumed a confident air and led the way on my bike; I had no map and had never been over the road before, so I hadn't much idea of the route. As usual when one wants to ask the way, the countryside was almost deserted, what people WERE visible had "only just arrived themselves" and could give no assistance. In the end I just followed my nose and, with my usual good luck, managed to catch the rest just as they reached the new position, by which time it was dawn. We could have been saved all the flurry, as we only fired a couple of salvos, by which time the enemy was out of range again. However, we were spared another panic move by the arrival of the unit that was to relieve us. Before they came, the CO held a little ceremony at which he pinned the MC and the MM on an officer and gunner who had recently been awarded them for gallantry.

We were to hand over every bit of our equipment, down to the last splint in my case, to the incoming regiment, who had left all their stuff in MEF for us to take over when we got there. This was a bitter blow to all of us. We had spent eighteen months "acquiring" stuff, most of it obtained when we cleaned up the battlefield after Alamein, and we knew we should never be able to pick up such stuff again; yet we couldn't take it away with us, as we were to have no transport except that needed for a limited quantity of heavy kit. In the change-over I lost some superb aluminium German water containers, far finer than anything the British Army provides, and lots of other buckshee stuff, as well as my famous walled bivvy, which had served me so well all through the winter. But we were to have one more taste of enemy action before we handed over. The night before the new people arrived, a German bomber came over and dropped bombs on a prisoner of war camp about a mile behind us. The pilot could not have done this by mistake, for the place was lit up as bright as day by whacking great arc lamps; why he did it heaven alone knows.

The next day the new regiment arrived, and the "opposite numbers" down to sergeants, came up to look round and start the process of taking over. The new unit was a regular regiment, and unfortunately they had the usual "regular" disrespect for our unit, which is "territorial"; they had been in the Middle East for two years, and thought they knew all about making war, having been on many exercises. We were laying ourselves out to be as helpful as possible, in view of our battle experience, but I am afraid our advice fell on deaf ears. Mind you, we must have looked a pretty awful shower to men coming from training areas where they had got used to polishing brass and scrubbing webbing. We had the Eighth Army style to the 9th degree, and everybody wore what suited them best during the hot weather. Doubtless we should have been the same in their place, but they had one or two expensive lessons. Even before we had left the area they had ditched two tractors and broken the axle of a three-tonner!

Their RMO proved to be an exception to all this; he was a very nice young fellow, and avid for every piece of advice and information I could give him. He had never been in battle before, and, with memories of my own initiation, I knew exactly how he must be feeling. He was far too conscientious for an RMO and stripped and examined thoroughly from top to toe every patient, even if he was only complaining of a sore eye; time, I felt, would alter this. I regretfully handed over my equipment, including motor-cycle, for which he was duly grateful, and from then onwards he took over. The next day we returned to our previous position in three-ton trucks; I had to carry all my luggage with the exception of my big tin trunk; this humping of baggage was to continue, on and off, for a month or so, by which time everybody was heartily sick of the whole business.

We had a couple of days to wait before we were taken to railhead to catch our troop-train down to Taranto. A delightful holiday atmosphere prevailed throughout the unit; the weather was brilliantly fine and warm, and everybody felt on top of the world. I took the opportunity of having a good look round the defences of the Adolf Hitler Line. They did not seem very formidable, and most of them had obviously been hastily flung up at the last minute. But one thing we noticed here as in all enemy defences - how they dug! Most of their dug-outs were twenty feet deep, and could withstand all but a direct hit from a very heavy bomb. I saw one six-barrelled mortar position which was covered with shell-craters; yet the crew were quite safe in their dug-out; near by was the remains of a house which had been used as an ammunition dump and had received a direct hit from one of our heavy shells. The whole area was covered with shell-holes, but these didn't show up well in photographs.

At this time I also managed to have a look at the ruins of Cassino, though how I did must remain a secret, as the area was out of bounds at the time. I really have difficulty in finding words to describe the scene of desolation. All trace of individual streets and houses had disappeared; the place was one vast heap of rubble in which here and there, some travesty of a building stood up. The centre of the town was marked by a green pool of stagnant water, out of which projected the upper hull and turret of a Sherman tank, like some prehistoric monster rearing itself out of a sea of slime. The stench of death and decay was everywhere, and the silence was broken only by the noise of traffic away on the far road, and the buzzing of hundreds of flies and insects who had found a superb breeding ground in this man-made charnel-house. I was unable to take any photographs at the time, but several were taken by somebody else at a later date, when the area had been cleaned up and the main Route Six reopened.

We were to have one more fright before we left, however. I was sitting having a mid-day gin with the CO when the house was racked by a tremendous explosion, which brought down some plaster on our innocent heads; we looked at each other with raised eyebrows and then made for the door and the outside air. There was an enormous cloud of black smoke about four fields away; we couldn't understand the cause of this, for we were well outside the range of even the heaviest guns; concluding that a mine had exploded, we returned to our drink, only to be startled again a couple of minutes later by an even larger explosion. As we left the room again, thoughts of secret weapons passed through my head. However, there were no more bangs, and we found out later that the cause of all the bother was a German dump of shells; these had been covered with hay for concealment The hay had caught fire, with the inevitable consequences.

This was the "Vale" (Latin) as it were, and next morning we crowded into three-tonners and left for the railhead at Vairano, only a couple of miles from one of our old gun positions of six months before. No doubt it was my childish fancy, but as we passed I thought I detected the image of a hand giving "thumbs up" in a cloud which was hovering over the top of Monte Cairo. After a very dusty journey, we arrived at Vairano at about 3 pm and had to sit on the ground in the sweltering sun for about five hours till the troop train arrived. This luxurious conveyance consisted of a string of cattle trucks, and I was reminded of the French trains (hommes 40 chevaux 8) of the last war, of which I had read so much in war novels. As a matter of fact, cattle-trucks are far more comfortable than carriages for night journeys, as you can put your bed on the floor and "get down" to it, instead of attempting to sleep in some impossible attitude on a seat. Whilst we were waiting to start, itinerant hawkers did a roaring trade in cherries (verree gooood!), which had just come into season. There were naturally no toilet arrangements on the train, so I refrained from eating cherries out of respect for my nether anatomy; I had no wish to skin it on some bridge or tunnel in the dark whilst the train was in motion!

I completely forgot to mention that just before we handed over, the men were all issued with new headgear. This was an abortion called a "Cap GS" (by beret out of fore-and-aft), and it looked like a cross between a tam-o'-shanter and a cook's cap suffering from some obscure wasting disease. Why the British Army can't design a respectable cap for its other ranks passes my comprehension. Why not just a plain khaki beret, as worn at present by our motorised infantry; much less material would have been required. But no! Another new design must be produced, which soon loses its shape, and is worn at a different angle by every fourth man.

The train started, without warning, at about 9 pm; there was a terrific jerk which flung us all off our feet, and away we went at a cracking pace - nearly 30 mph I should think. One interesting point I learnt before we left was that the Allied Armies PAY the Italians for every train they use - this after putting the ruddy railways in order after the Germans had wrecked them! I should very much like to know the reason for paying a conquered country (co-belligerent my eye) in this way, and I can only suppose that it is part of our policy of building the country up again as a market for our exports.

Troop train topics really deserve a special chapter to themselves. Our cattle trucks were four-wheeled, and the rails were definitely war time utility pattern, so that the trip was even bumpier than one would expect. The result was that, owing to the bumps as we crossed the joints of the rails, the person sitting opposite always appeared to be afflicted with some obscure form of nervous disease; he twitched convulsively in every limb at each bump. We all tried to stop this, but it was quite impossible; one just relaxed and twitched. Then, of course, there were the brakes; these proved rather poor in stopping power, but were grand at sticking on when the driver released them in order to start off again; the result was a bone-wrenching jerk each time we started. As we stopped on the average at least once every half hour, sleep during the night was not very sound; however, we were a lot more comfortable than we would have been in passenger coaches, and a spot of gin and lime made everybody happy.

We ground our way slowly down the east coast, and pulled in at Salerno at 5.30 am for breakfast and a shave. On leaving Salerno we turned inland just after passing through Battipaglia, destroyed by bombing during the landing last September, and for the rest of the day our journey took us through glorious mountain scenery, as we crossed the Appenines. For part of the journey, we were pulled by big American diesel-electric locomotives which whisked us along at a tremendous pace, up hill and down dale, over viaducts and through tunnels, in one of which a train had broken down a little while before and many people had been killed by the fumes from the engine. There were pauses en route to change engines and for meals, but we were getting pretty bored by the time the evening arrived. There was some doubt whether we would remain on the train all the next night; we were due to arrive at Taranto at 3 am and we devoutly hoped we would be allowed to sleep on the train and get off in the daylight. But, of course, we had no such luck, and were turned out in the middle of the night for a walk to the transit area - tents! We arrived to find that our good friends, the 69th Medium Regiment of whom we were to see a good deal in the next few weeks, had "laid on" a meal of stew and rice pudding, which was very welcome. By the time we had finished this and settled in our tents it was daylight, so we wrote off the night's sleep as a dead loss, and had a wash and a shave. After that, the problem of sick parades arose. I had brought very little stuff with me, and I didn't know how soon our ship would arrive. I tried treating everybody with my meagre stocks for a couple of days, but had to give it up very soon for an epidemic of "Taranto Tummy" broke out and I hadn't enough stuff to treat all the cases. By the time I had got hold of some mixtures and things, it was nearly time for is to embark, so I only had a proper MI room for about four days.

A few days after we arrived, the great "D" day occurred; Gordon Ellis and I were the first to hear the news, on his wireless. It got a very lukewarm reception from the chaps. "Oh, started at last, has it?" just about sums up the general reaction; they were all far more delighted at the news of the fall of Rome, received the day before.

I think this is a good point at which to break off. Next time I will tell you of our last few days in Italy, leave in Egypt, and the start of our pilgrimage to the Holy Land.

And so for the present, good-bye.

My flooded RAP.

Problems en route. Gun and tractor on Bailey Bridge.

BULLETIN TWENTY

"Middle-East merry-go-round" — mid-June to August 1944

Taranto is a magnificent Naval Base, with two big harbours separated by a swing bridge which opens at awkward hours of the day and makes you late for meals if you happen to be on the wrong side of it. Our camp was situated on sloping ground to the north of the town. The camp site was pretty dirty, but there was a pleasant breeze from the sea which made our tents cool; otherwise the heat would have been hard to bear.

As usual there was a great rush to get out of camp and see round the town which was three miles away; for the first (but not the last) time everybody realised what it meant to have plenty of transport readily available. You never miss it while it's there, but now we were indeed in a sorry state; all we had was one three-tonner to serve two medium regiments, so it was a matter of hanging round or trying to hitch-hike - a chancey business especially after dark. I stayed in camp on the first day. I'm afraid I lack the pioneering spirit, and prefer to let others explore the local entertainment possibilities and make any expensive mistakes that are to be made; in any case, I wanted to catch up with some lost sleep and write some letters. So my visit was delayed till the next day.

There is a marked contrast between the old town of Taranto, dirty, evil smelling, with narrow streets, and the new town, which owes most of its good points to the Fascist regime. The new town is laid out in geometrical pattern, rather like a modern American city, with the streets all parallel and of equal width. The seaport of the new town is quite imposing, and is fronted by some very fine buildings in white stone. The harbour smells; in it are still visible the torpedo nets and wreck buoys marking the warships sunk by the Fleet Air Arm in 1941. The streets are full of Italian Naval ratings and officers - a ropey looking crew if I ever saw one; they seem to do absolutely nothing except loaf about all day and make nasty noises at the girls, who struck me as being prettier than the average run of Italiennes I had seen elsewhere. There was little sign anywhere that the country had ever been at war, and the usual exorbitant prices prevailed in the shops, some of which had quite good materials for sale. The final note of ridicule was sounded by the sight of several Greek sailors, strolling arm-in-arm with Italian girls; it seems that Venus knows no barriers!

Amusement facilities in the town were remarkably few; there were three cinemas, in two of which the projection and sound were poor; the films at all three were old and very worn. There was one music hall which offered a third rate Italian variety show. The officers' club was housed in a garish restaurant; the food wasn't too bad, but was generally served half-cold. After the first evening I generally dined in camp.

When I had been in Taranto a couple of days I found that my brother's old regiment was still there, and went to see them. Otherwise I met nobody whom I knew at all outside the regiment. On the third night of our stay there was a small air-raid which frightened me, as I though I had said "Good-bye" to the noise of gunfire for a good long spell; one "dud" AA shell shrieked down and landed somewhere quite close to us.

The next day Gordon Ellis and I hitch-hiked our way to Brindisi, forty-five miles away. Here we saw "Blithe Spirit"; Emlyn Williams took the main part, and the play was very good. It was like a breath of home to see a West End play again, played by a West End cast. We had a capital lunch at the Brindisi Officers' Club, which was twice as pleasant as the Taranto place; Emlyn Williams was lunching at an adjacent table.

We left Taranto after six days; most of the Regiment had to march four and a half miles to the ship, but I managed to wangle a lift on one of the baggage lorries, on the grounds that I had too much first aid kit to carry! The ship the *Banfora,* was a very old packet, but turned out to be both seaworthy and comfortable. The cabins were rather cramped though; I shared one with four other officers, and as we had to keep the blackout up all night, the fug was something terrific, for it was the middle of June.

I found myself with plenty to do; the medical staff were a good crowd, and I got on vey well with them. Within three days of sailing I was offered a partnership after the war in the practice in Somerset from which the Ship's MO came! I seized the opportunity during the voyage to do a lot of vaccinations and inoculations that were outstanding, so a sore time was had by many; the rest of the time was spent sleeping, eating, playing cards and reading. The food was superb, and a pleasant contrast to Army rations. The other medium regiment wasn't so lucky; they had four hundred American WAACs on board. Women on a trooper are a menace; they disturb all the men and have to be given cabins, so the officers don't like them either! Other details are best not mentioned.

The voyage was uneventful, and we arrived at Port Said one sunny afternoon. I was forcibly reminded of September 1939, when I had to spend eight days in the place; it seemed to have changed little since then, save for a couple of burnt-out tanks at one wharf. As soon as we had docked, everybody was, of course, all agog to know what was going to happen to us and where we were going, and the usual ridiculous rumours were soon in circulation; the only concrete fact which emerged was that we weren't getting off that day, which was a relief; it was already fairly late in the afternoon, and we didn't fancy a panic pack-up and a night move. As it was, we spent an extremely pleasant evening; there is no black-out at Port Said, and it was like peace time again to see all the ships lit up after dark (by the way, I forgot to mention that there was no blackout in Taranto either). We slept a lot more comfortably too, owing to the better ventilation of the cabin.

We disembarked at 2 pm the next day, and got straight into an Egyptian state railway train on the quayside - a pleasant change from the usual sweaty march to the station. I must admit that it gave me a certain inner glow to be able to hold forth on the scenery along the canal and in Port Said harbour; I'm afraid the phrase "when I was out here in '39" occurred more than once! We were bound for Cairo (DEAR old place!) via Ismailia, and the first thirty miles or so of our journey lay along the banks of the Suez Canal; however, there was no shipping to be seen, so the view soon lost its novelty. I noticed the regularly spaced AA gun and searchlight and balloon positions, and wonder how on earth the men who manned them avoided going mad in those featureless surroundings. It must have been nearly a year since they had had a raid.

We stopped at various stations on our way to Ismailia, including El Kantara, the Crossing Place - where the caravan trail to Mecca used to cross the desert. We had a wait of ten minutes here during which we renewed acquaintance with that enemy of all British troops, the Arab hawker. I must say I found it a bit depressing to be listening to their chatter again and this depression increased during our stay in Egypt; I believe the others felt the same way. We had said good-bye with such relish and finality to the Arab world eight months before, when we none of us expected to set eyes on a wog again, except after many, many years, and then only of our own volition. And here we were again, and still at His Majesty's expense. Nothing was changed except for a few new catch phrases - "nice shoe shine, bags of bull" was one - and the same trashy "silver" jewellery and trinkets were for sale.

It got dark before we arrived at Ismailia, so we didn't see much of the place; we played bridge for a while, and then tried to sleep. I got up in one of the luggage racks and managed to get two or three hours quite sound kipping before we detrained at Mena Station at 3.30 am. From here we were taken by three-tonner to Mena Camp, in the desert, a couple of miles from Mena House Hotel and the Great Pyramids. Our advance party had a hot meal waiting for us and everything well organised, Even our mail had arrived, and I spent a joyous fifteen minutes round about sunrise reading all my letters; plans were also discussed. We were in Egypt for ten days only, during which everybody was to have four days leave; work was more or less forbidden.

After a wash and brush up, everybody who could manage it pushed off into Cairo for a look round. I had to go to a General Hospital to arrange for some medical supplies, which took up most of the morning. It was hellishly hot, so I returned to camp for lunch and stayed in for the rest of the day. The next day I went shopping, and got myself a pair of soft shoes and some new KD. There was penty of stuff in the shops - most of it American and at outrageous prices. I had my polyphoto taken, but the result didn't meet with general approval, largely due to the fact that it was too hot to look comfortable in front of a camera. I also renewed my acquaintance with Groppis - a paradise for us starved soldiers. You can get every variety of ice under the sun here, and it is the rendezvous for people with a luncheon engagement in Cairo. I met some of the chaps here, and we went out to the Gezira Club for lunch and tennis.

Gezira merits a page to itself. Situated on Gezira Island, in the middle of the Nile, it is the social centre of the English community in Cairo. It is best summed up in the phrase "all that money can buy". Every branch of sport is catered for, from horse-racing to bridge - though come to think of it I didn't see a shove-ha'penny board there. There is a fine swimming pool, with a sun terrace, lounges and changing rooms. There is a very fine dining room in a separate block of buildings. The whole place swarms with attendants, who come at the clap of a hand. All very luxurious, but a bit nauseating, somehow. I played tennis here four times in all, and enjoyed it very much. I also had one swim in the pool whilst on leave, and got quite badly sunburnt, though I thought I had been very careful. I had a slight attack of tennis elbow, too!

I don't propose to give a detailed description of our time at Cairo; it was much like any other holiday. I saw several good pictures, amongst them "Tunisian Victory" and "Now Voyager' with Bette Davis; air conditioned cinemas made a visit to the pictures a good way of spending a hot afternoon. I also visited a couple of cabarets - expensive but dull - and dined at one or two of the well-known hotels and clubs. The finest of these is the Turf Club - a very exclusive English Club, which the members very kindly opened to serving officers on leave. Here we had an excellent dinner in very quiet surroundings - no band, no nattering crowd of drinkers, and no waiters hanging round for tips, which are expressly forbidden by the Club rules. I also spent a pleasant afternoon and evening at Mena House Hotel, where we swam in the pool and then had dinner on the terrace.

I spent my four days' leave at the Continental Savoy Hotel with Popeye, the survey officer. I was in two minds whether to go at all, as Cairo is very noisy and hot at night, but I decided to go in the end in order to avoid the long and expensive taxi-ride back to camp late at night. Our bedroom was certainly noisy, it looked out on the main street. The tram conductors in Egypt don't use a whistle or bell, but a tooter rather like the children's toy trumpets distributed at gala dances and other festive occasions; the result is that Cairo street noises resemble nothing so much as a permanent jamboree; the flies were a nuisance, too. After so long roughing it in the field I found I had to be more than usually careful with both my language and manners. One afternoon I went for a bath and found the door was locked. I rattled the handle and was just about to shout "Have you nearly finished in there, you old so and so" when I remembered where I was, which was fortunate, for after about a minute the door opened and the most gorgeous female emerged! I expect she wondered why I blushed so deeply! After so long away from them, we found the sight of so many smart women a bit distracting, and I'm afraid we stared at them rather longer than strict good manners would allow; I hope they forgave us, and some of them even seemed to enjoy it.

I visited the Mohamed Ali Mosque, and the Citadel, but wasn't very much impressed by them, and also looked in at one or two museums and went to a concert of recorded music one evening. I spent a lot of time browsing in book shops too; all the latest English novels and books were on sale, all at about double the published price.

Whilst we were in Cairo I had a letter from John Armstrong, the American Ambulance driver who had been with us for so long last winter. He had returned to America, and his letter contained his impressions after a year away from home. It was very bitter indeed - the letter of a man ashamed of his own countrymen. He painted a picture of adolescent over-confidence, hero-worship, and irresponsibility; the general attitude was that the war would be over as soon as we set foot in Europe. I thought his description exaggerated at the time, but in view of what has since taken place it looks as though he was right. He wanted to return to Italy, but was unable to do so for various reasons and had settled down to a desk job, which he hated. I hope to keep in touch with him, but it is difficult; that is one thing I hate about these war-time friendships - they cannot be kept up. I don't suppose Johnny and I will ever meet again; I certainly shan't be able to go to America after the war, and he is unlikely to come to England.

We left Cairo on the evening of June 29th, when we boarded a troop train for Palestine. We crossed the canal at El Kantara in the middle of the night, and stopped there for a meal. We then puffed our way on up the coast, with the blue Mediterranean on our left and desert on our right, to Gaza, where we stopped for breakfast at the NAAFI. Here, there were undreamt of luxuries for sale - tinned fruits, sweets, chewing gum, etc. We also made contact for the first time with that masterpiece of Middle East journalism, the Palestine Post. After breakfast, we continued our journey up the coast in high spirits, till we turned inland and stopped at the Jewish settlement of Rehovoth, a centre of the citrus fruit-growing country. We had an hour to wait at the station till the trucks arrived to take us out to our camp. This was on rising ground beyond Gedera, and near the battleground where David slew Goliath and the Israelites defeated the Philistines; there is an aerodrome now on the site of the battlefield.

The camp area had permanent buildings for workhouses, messes and offices, but sleeping accommodation was in tents - much cooler during the hot weather than wooden huts. I had a very nice little Medical Inspection room, with running water laid on. The camp was one of several in the area, and there was a local cinema, which showed very old films, with a change of show every night. We were thirty miles from Jerusalem and about fifteen miles from Jaffa and the new seaside resort of Tel-Aviv, of which more anon.

The first few days were mainly spent settling in and taking over new equipment and motor transport. In connection with the latter there were several amusing incidents. None of the vehicles were new and of course nobody knew which were good and which were bad, so a coin was tossed and the battery captains took it in turns to choose vehicles; the first one chosen wouldn't go at all! I got a good fifteen hundredweight Ford, in excellent condition, and quite a reasonable motor cycle. I also got a complete new issue of medical equipment, which was of a utility pattern, and lacked an auriscope and other essential instruments. As we were in a non-operational area these extras took ages to arrive.

We now embarked on an era of peace time soldiering, with parades, guard mounting, button polishing, etc. All webbing had to be scrubbed white; as a result, it showed up so clearly in the dark that the guards had to take it off at night, so that they wouldn't be seen by any intruders in the camp area! We had been warned of the danger of thieves, but were very lucky and lost very little kit during the time of our stay, chiefly, I think, because we were fairly well away from the main road.

We soon settled down to a very pleasant routine. Reveille 6.30 am; a nice tepid shower to wake you up. Breakfast 8 am, sick parade 8.30-10.00. 10 am TEA (very important) then a tour of inspection round the camp area, or a visit to one of the other MOs. 12.30 - a long cool drink in the mess. We had some wonderful soft drinks laid on, mostly grapefruit and orange juice. 1 pm lunch. 1.30 to 3.30 siesta. 4 pm tea, followed by either a game of cricket, a ride out on the motorbike, or a quiet read in the tent as the day got cooler. 6 pm hot shower and change. 7.30 pm gin-up. 8 pm dinner, after which we played bridge, read or went to the pictures. It was no good going to bed before 11 as the camp was noisy till then, when "lights out" was the order.

As soon as we were settled in, I went through my kit and discarded all the worn-out stuff. I now have hardly anything left of the kit with which I left England; some of the discarded clothes had happy associations - these shoes - very expensive - bought with almost the first money I earned after I became a doctor; that pair of boots - my first pair after entering the army, etc, etc. I was able to get rid of quite a lot of junk too, which I had been carting round for some time.

This area of Palestine has been pretty extensively cultivated and developed in recent years, principally by Jewish residents and immigrants. Where irrigation has been installed, the sands of the desert have flowered and given generously. But this new Promised Land has been rendered hideous by the hands of the men who created it, for the houses are ugly; built mostly of cheap concrete they conform to no pattern or style of architecture whatsoever, and many are already showing signs of cracking and falling to pieces; they stretch across the land like some hideous eruption, which reaches its climax in the town of Tel-Aviv. This is a very new township, all built within the last twenty years on the shores of the Mediterranean, a couple of miles north of Jaffa. Intended as a luxury seaside resort it combines the worst features of all our British seaside towns with none of their virtues. Here is private enterprise and big business run riot. What a chance there was to plan a beautiful garden city, with some style and uniformity in its buildings and streets. The site was almost perfect. But none of this happened, and apart from a few well laid out streets, there is no pattern at all; again, reinforced concrete has run riot, and the few handsome buildings are completely spoilt by the shoddy ones which flank and surround them. The beach is narrow and dirty, with little or no accommodation for bathers. The bathing is dangerous anyway! Even the sea front fails to display any sign of forethought in its architecture.

One of the redeeming features of Tel-Aviv was the excellent stock of books in the shops; it is the same all over Palestine, and the prices were far more reasonable than in Egypt, being controlled at the published price plus twenty-five per cent. I bought several good medical text books both in Tel-Aviv and Jerusalem, as well as some fiction. Prices of clothing etc, were very high, though quite a lot of the stuffs were home-produced in Palestine. There were few attractions in the way of amusements in Tel-Aviv; there was a fairly reasonable NAAFI Officers' Club and several very expensive ones run privately. I only visited the town a few times on shopping and picture expeditions. I spent a few pleasant hours at a bathing club at Bat Yam, south of Jaffa; the bathing all along this coast is very dangerous, and the under-tow terrific. The water was tepid and the sun too fierce for anything but the mildest sunbathing. In any case, the part-time dwellers in the tropics, such as I, soon come to hate the sun. I spent most of my days in camp, where I did a prodigous amount of reading; I read the whole of Sterne's "Tristam Shandy", a work which I had often meant to read but had never got down to; I also started reading Medicine and Surgery, but found them hard-going in the absence of sick bodies on which to practise.

Of course, we all visited Jerusalem on several occasions, and I spent four days leave there with Ken Pople. The modern Jerusalem is a fine city, built on the hills round the old city. Most of the larger buildings are carried out in the off-white local stone, reminiscent of Cotswold stone. This is a very cheap and durable building material, and, together with low ground rents, renders living in Jerusalem very cheap, in peace time at any rate. There are many fine modern churches, erected by all the Christian nations, and also a very fine museum. The YMCA building, opposite the King David Hotel, dominates the skyline on one side of the city and from its tower there is a marvellous view over the city.

I must say that the old city disappointed me, especially that part connected with Christ's life and crucifixion. Everything was on a much smaller scale than one had imagined, and the whole area of Calvary was completely messed up by the Crusaders in the eleventh century. Using their equivalent of a bull-dozer, they levelled the small hill that was Calvary, and later built the Church of the Crucifixion on the site. So that now all that is left is a lot of tradition - "Here, traditionally, Christ was crucified - there is the crack in the ground which opened at the moment of his death - here (a marble slab) he was laid to rest". The whole is symbolism and fetishism run riot, and in my opinion quite contrary to all Christian teaching.

The same may be said of the Church of the Nativity at Bethlehem, though in this case the building itself has some historic interest. It started life as a pagan temple, when the Romans attempted to stamp out Christianity; traces of the old temple still remain in the pillars of the church nave and in the mosaic of the floor. The manger and birthplace of Christ were just as disappointing to me as calvary had been. The modern Roman Catholic church is very beautiful. Many of the people in Bethlehem have the fair hair and complexion of the Northern races; I was told that many of them were the direct descendants of the Crusaders, but they all showed the shrewd commercial instinct of the Jewish race. The Padre took a party of us to Bethlehem, and made the place live again as it had done in Jesus' time - not as difficult as it sounds, for the natives still dress and till the land much as they did in ancient days, winnowing the grain in the wind and threshing it with flails.

We spent one day of our leave in a journey to the Dead Sea, in which we bathed - a most interesting experience. The water was more buoyant than any brine bath and stung my face and neck. I believe a spot in the eye can be agonising, and the taste is terrible. One feels very braced after a bathe, and we did full justice to an excellent lunch which we took at the restaurant attached to the BOAC Flying Boat Station. The journey from Jerusalem is most interesting and very hot, becoming positively oppressive as one gets below sea level. The road winds through deep passes and over hills, all in a landscape of red and barren rock. We visited the site of ancient Jericho, - just a heap of earth - and passed on the way a big area of derelict camps in which Allied troops had been quartered until a year ago.

We had a devil of a job to get sleeping quarters in Jerusalem, and were finally reduced to what was really no more than a high-class doss house. We had two beds in a room containing eight, and the population changed every night, except for one individual who snored very loudly and kep us all awake; the heat was terrific and there was one wash-basin for all of us, so we didn't spend much time there, and had most of our meals at the Officers' Club, a pleasant place on one of the hills.

Just before we had our leave some terrorists, members of the notorious Stern gang, blew up a block of offices in Jerusalem, and soon after our return from leave the same gang attacked the High Commissioner, Sir Harold MacMillan, wounding him and killing his aide-de-camp. The active Jewish terrorists are said to number only a few, but in each of these outrages they escaped without trace, so that one cannot help wondering just how much the Jews as a whole connived at the conspiracies. The Arab-Jewish problem in Palestine is now so complicated that it is practically unsolvable without injustice to one side or the other. The Jewish population has increased enormously since the outbreak of war, and many industries have been built up in Palestine; these industries have done much to supply Allied needs in the Middle East, as a result of which Jewish interests now have a substantial sterling balance. This is bound to influence British policy. The Arabs are opposed to any further Jewish immigration, and will no doubt do something about the matter, once the war is over. They promised Britain that revolts on their part would cease during the war, and they have kept this promise loyally. The Jews have been buying and stealing arms for some time, and can muster fifty thousand or so trained men. It doesn't take an expert on Palestine to see what is in the wind. If immigration were instituted on a large scale, the land could support many times its present population. But it seems doubtful whether many Jews who went to Palestine as refugees from Europe will want to stay there permanently. Most of them seem to regard themselves primarily as citizens of countries from which they fled, and only secondarily as Jews. If this happens the problem MAY solve itself, but I doubt it. The Jews are persistent in their demands to rule Palestine; the Arabs are determined that they shall not.

Dear me, we seem to have wandered somewhat. However, there is little more to tell about our stay in Palestine. Life just went on, till one day, three weeks before we expected it, we got orders to get ready to move again. All this was very annoying, as we had been given a firm date by which to be ready, and everything was at sixes and sevens. However, somebody found they had half a ship at Haifa empty (or should I have said a ship at Haifa half empty?) (or half full?) (who started this anyway?), and we were detailed, with half the other medium regiment, to fill it. Once more I had to leave Bombardier Jones and all my medical equipment behind, to follow with the truck. We had to get up at 4 am and spent a very disturbed night. The Arabs knew we were moving (they always do, somehow!) and an officer was detailed to stay up all night and scare them off with training grenades (noisy, but harmless), Very lights, and a tommy gun. He performed his duties very efficiently, but we might just as well have been on the same job, for the noise he made deprived us of all but the most fitful sleep. We climbed wearily aboard the three-tonners just as the sun rose, and were in Haifa by 10.30, where we had to wait some hours before embarking. We reached the ship at 2 pm and I shared a very comfortable cabin with five others. So once more we were on our way, back to Italy, and the war.

No more for now. Chin chin.

BULLETIN TWENTY-ONE

"Italia Rivisita" — September 1944

Our ship for the return journey was a very modern Dutchman, the *Willem Ruys*, which in peacetime plied between Holland and the Dutch East Indies; she was fitted with forced draught ventilation in every cabin. Being chiefly a cargo-carrier, what cabins there were were large and airy; I shared one with five other people, but we weren't a bit cramped. The lounge and dining room were superbly appointed, but the food was not really either adequate in quantity or well cooked, and the place was alive with cockroaches.

There was plenty of work to do and the voyage passed pleasantly enough; we had a cinema show twice during the trip. There was a large contingent of French troops on board, and I had several interesting talks with their doctor. He had a great grudge against what he called "those bludee Americans", and very much resented their friendly attitude to the German prisoners, after the Tunisian campaign had ended.

We landed again at Taranto, and it was depressing to be back again in dirty, smelly Italy. Our camp site was dirty and very dusty; a strong wind from the sea stirred up the red, sandy soil, and spread it in a fine film over everything and everybody. The heat was intense, and everybody who could do so got out of the area during the heat of the day and went into Taranto. It was the same old place - effete men, firm figured young women and - smells! The first morning I was in town an Italian committed suicide by flinging himself from one of the piers of the swing bridge. He made an error of judgement, falling on the jetty instead of into the water and making a nasty mess. Crowds were still staring at his body hours later.

Our depressing surroundings were rendered even worse by the mail situation; all our mail was still going to MEF and it was now ruled by "higher authority" that we must continue to use the MEF address till we had been in Italy for three weeks, thus causing further delay. We later found that this order was quite wrong and should never have been given.

I should have explained before now (I may have done in bulletin twenty, but I forget) that we were without our transport, which was on its way in slower ships together with the drivers and quite a large number of people who made up the rear party.

After a few days we moved our tents to another and less dusty area, and no sooner had we done so than we had to prepare for yet another move. Somebody, thank goodness, had found that there was a body of troops at a loose end, and decided to make use of us till the rest of the Regiment arrived. We were to go to Bari and do guards in the railway station and various other military objectives. Once again we went through the familiar (by now) routine of packing our luggage and dumping it at a central spot in the camp for collection by the luggage party - unfortunate fellows! Again we had to march to the station, and again I dodged the column and had a ride in the front of an ambulance which was taking some of the fellows who were unable to march for one reason or another. It was a blazing hot day, and when the main column arrived at the station they were in pretty poor shape. One barrel-shaped officer was undoubtedly the hottest individual I have ever seen; his bush-jacket was dark with perspiration, and the sweat actually dripped from the hem of this garment. (Sorry, I forgot, only horses sweat. Men perspire, and ladies just "feel a little warm!").

The train journey was quite pleasant; the railway wound upwards over rolling hills, which looked quite green and fertile, and there was little sign that war had passed over the land, for there was hardly any fighting in this area. The way gradually got steeper, till at one time it took the united efforts of two engines to get us over the highest ridge; thence we had an exhilarating, though somewhat alarming, swoop down to the plain on the other side, and arrived at Bari in the middle of the afternoon. The station did not look very prepossessing, nor did the cobbled streets through which we marched to the transit camps where we were to be quartered during our stay. However, first impressions turned out to be misleading, as they so often are. On arrival at the transit camp we had to put up our own tents, but after a few days everybody was in buildings, which was a blessing, for the weather was breaking up, and we had several very heavy thunderstorms.

We now settled down to a better-than-peacetime routine. I had a sick parade at 8.30 after which I had nothing else to do all day, so there was plenty of time for reading and for sampling the fleshpots of Bari, such as they were.

Bari (pronounced "Bar-ee"; but by the English "Barry") is a town which has grown rapidly under the fascist regime, so that there are sharp contrasts in the layout, though not so sharp as at Taranto. Mussolini was trying to make Bari the transit port between Europe and the Levant, substituting it for Brindisi. To this end, a large and very fine harbour and docks were built, and also a new promenade lined with fine buildings, as at Taranto. The newer part of the town is laid out in fine wide streets, intersecting at right angles.

Amenities for the forces were a great improvement on Taranto; there are two quite good cinemas, and there is another theatre where weekly symphony concerts and opera are performed. It was pleasant to hear and see good music performed again, and the orchestra was quite competent. I also went to see "Tosca", but the scenery and costumes were very shabby and the cast not up to much. After one well-known aria, I was startled to hear loud and definite boos coming from a large party of Italians in one box; it was only later that I was told that the boo in Italy is a sign of extreme approval, analogous, I suppose, to the loud belch of approval at the end of a meal in China. The party in the box turned out to be relatives of the prima donna, and made rather a nuisance of themselves.

The Officers' hotel and restaurant in Bari was in pleasant contrast to that at Taranto. It was in the chief hotel on the sea front, and was very well run; part of the routine was a morning walk to the Imperiale for coffee and buns, and if one hadn't the energy for the walk back, one could always stay for lunch, and even tea. There were plenty of comfortable chairs in the lounge, and quite a few girls in uniform, new out from England. Quite what they did, except dine and dance with the officers, I never found out, but no doubt they contributed something to Britain's war effort or they wouldn't have been there.

Despite all the amusement, time hung heavy on my hands. I had quite a pleasant room in the transit camp, shared with three others;

the ceiling, as always, was decorated, in this case by cupids, and there was a balcony. There is certainly something to be said for the fashion of balconies, at least in countries where the weather is warm for the greater part of the year. One can pass a pleasant hour in the cool of the evening watching the parade on the pavements below; it was late summer, and the women looked very pretty in their summer frocks, especially on Sundays, when they have on their best bibs and tuckers, and often very little else! I started trying to read medical text books again, but found it difficult to concentrate on them in the absence of clinical material.

One snag about living at the transit camp was the almost complete lack of hot water, except for shaving in the mornings; the cold water remained icy even on the hottest day, as it came direct from an Artesian well beneath the building. We used to go for our baths to an Albergo Diurno (literally "Hotel for the Daytime") beneath the promenade of one of the main streets. Here one could get a hot bath, shave, haircut, etc. These places are to be seen in most Italian towns, and are an eloquent testimony to the lack of ablution facilities in even the middle-class Italian houses. A small comedy was enacted each time we went for a bath. There was nearly always a long queue of "other ranks" waiting for baths, and the two girls in charge always tried to push us in ahead of the queue; they could never understand why we always insisted on waiting our turn; from which I gather that democracy does not yet exist in the Italian armed forces!

It was three weeks after leaving Palestine before we got any mail; then it started to arrive in dribs and drabs, and of course all the letters were in the wrong order; I never really got straight till the rear party caught us up. They came over on the same ship, but this time it was crowded with women, and most of the officers had to sleep in the holds. In addition, they were landed at a different port, and had a most uncomfortable train journey down to Taranto, where they settled into the dust to wait for us. The day before we left Bari to rejoin them a whole heap of surface mail came in and I was snowed under with bundles of magazines; this always happens before a journey, somehow. One of the officers had a letter from his former batman which contained the following gem of

English prose "You will be sorry to hear that my brother has been wounded in the Second Front".

We travelled back to Taranto by road; it was grand to travel in our own trucks again and to see the rest of the Regiment when we arrived; there were three very new officers amongst several surprises, and also some really up-to-date mail.

We had only a couple of days in which to shake down before starting our long journey North - the next step on our way into battle again. I took over my new motor-bike - reconditioned BSA with a slipping clutch - and laid in a stock of comforts for the journey, and we were ready. All we knew of our destination was that it was somewhere just south of Rome and under canvas - not a pleasant prospect in view of the autumn rains.

We started on our way at 7 am, on a nice brisk sunny morning. It was the first time for nearly four months that the Regiment had been on the move with all the transport, and everybody was in high spirits. We got along very well whilst we were on the main road north, but we were soon diverted to a bumpy and very dusty secondary road, which was rough on motorcyclists. We passed through one village where all the streets were named after men who fell in the last war - the first time I had seen such war memorials. I imagine they will have to enlarge the place a bit if they adopt the same scheme for this war's casualties. All the usual scenes were visible en route, - the teeming children, the slouching men, and the groups of women gossiping in doorways or searching each other's heads for lice. It came on to rain heavily during the late afternoon, but I managed to keep dry except for my neck. We had a long journey on the first day, and it was after dark when we pulled into our staging area west of Foggia. The advance party had everything "laid on" and we soon had a hot meal and turned in for an early night.

Our next day's journey lay over familiar roads, which we had traversed just ten months before on our way back from the Sangro battle. The road abounded in steep hills and grand mountain scenery. I had omitted to use my camera last time we came that way, but didn't make the same mistake this time. The results were some of the finest photographs I have taken since leaving home.

Owing to the hilly nature of the road and our previous experience of the journey, it was decided to send all the guns ahead, starting half an hour before the rest of the vehicles. This was done because the tractors and guns had to crawl up the hills in very low bottom gear, thus holding everybody up, and splitting the column badly. The new arrangement worked like a charm, and tempers at the end of the day were much less frayed than on the same trip ten months before. We stayed the next evening near Caserta, and arrived in good time to have a good clean-up before darkness arrived.

When we started again the next day we did not know our destination; we were to receive orders, appropriately enough, at Vairano, the railway junction from which we had said good-bye to the Italian front four months previously. Only when we reached Vairano did we know that we were bound for Valmontone, thirty miles south of Rome on Route Six.

It was really a perfect day for main-road travel; it was so warm that after mid-day all I needed when riding the bike was my ordinary KD without pullover or any top covering. We went bounding up Route Six at a steady thirty miles an hour. We staged a breakdown and had a brew-up near one of our old gun positions, where we renewed acquaintance with some of the locals. Since we left Italy in June, nature has passed a healing hand over the scars of battle. The trees put forth new shoots - even the broken off stumps had flowered anew - and standing crops and grass hid the tracks our guns had made in the mud of the previous winter. Only the houses and ragged hedges showed that war had been that way; and, of course, the Eighth Army roadside slogans, which stretch all the way from Cairo to Ravenna, "No Double Banking", "Dust means Death", "Slacks and Long Sleeves at Sundown beat Mosquitoes" and, relic of last winter's mud "No chains on this road". Cox's Corner and the Mad Mile still showed traces of the constant shelling they had undergone, but most of the bridges were already being rebuilt, largely by female labour; the famous Bailey Bridge over the Rapido at Cassino was still in place, however. A week later it was washed away by floods caused by the autumn rains - just like last winter.

Even Cassino looked better than when I had last seen it, though it can never lose the awful atmosphere of desolation. The awful stench had gone, and grass had started to grow through the chinks in the rubble. The road through the town had been cleared and re-made, but all the ruins had been fenced off because of the danger of mines and booby traps. But that wasn't stopping various Ities from grubbing about in the ruins near the road. The old town is to be preserved as a memorial and the famous crypt in which our men lived and which withstood several direct hits from large bombs, was already on show. I suppose British tourists will be paying Italians good money to see the place after the war! A new town is to be built further down in the valley.

So, marvelling at the lush greenness of the countryside, we rumbled on northwards. The further north we got, the more frequent were the signs that there had been a war in those parts. Even after three months, when everything salvageable would have been removed, there was a gratifying amount of Boche transport lying about, mostly burnt or bombed. All the Allied stuff I saw was an occasional "brewed-up" tank. Hardly a mile of the road was without a bomb crater either very close to the edge or dead on it. Nearly every bridge had either been demolished by Jerry or bombed by us, so that diversions were many and dusty.

Our pitch at Valmontone was in a field - no houses at all, so out came our bivvies. The estate belonged to an Englishwoman but she never put in an appearance; the place was run by an Italian manager. A public footpath ran through our camp area, so you had to be careful when having a bath. The site was in a narrow valley, beside the main road and railway. Oil-burning locomotives puffed up the steep incline at all hours, covering everything outside with black smuts. The valley filled each night with a dank mist, which made all our clothing clammy; the place was degrees colder than Bari OR Rome, owing to its peculiar situation. We never saw the sun until 7.30 am (on fine days) and it disappeared behind the hills again at 4.30. The weather, already deteriorating with the approach of autumn, was particularly bad in our area, as the place was a natural rain-trap; often we found it had been raining at camp when the roads a few miles away were quite dry. The rain was a source of worry to me, for I had no tent or lean-to on my truck; all we had as an R.A.P. was a far-from-waterproof canvas sheet. Tents were quite unobtainable so far from the fighting front.

Naturally, we were all agog to visit Rome. I shall deal with the city more fully when I describe my leave there. The entry to Rome along Route Six is most disappointing, lying as it does along narrow cobbled streets and past jerry-built blocks of tenements. On the first day in I felt completely lost, though the military have the place pretty well signposted. As a result, I didn't see much, but quite enough to whet my appetite for further visits.

We were getting colder and colder and wetter and wetter at Valmontone, but after about a fortnight we moved in to new billets five miles south of Rome. Before we left, I took a closer look at Valmontone, or what was left of it. A key point in the last defence line south of Rome, it had been terribly handled by our heavy bombers. Less than 50% of the houses were habitable, and the church inevitably suffered. The inhabitants were insistent that all the Germans had left before the raid took place; whether this is true or not I cannot, of course, say, but it is quite possibly so, as the town was pretty well outflanked by our troops on both sides.

Our new billets were in a partially completed glassworks, at Ceccignola, south of Rome and near the buildings which were being built for the 1940 World Trade Exhibition. The place was in an awful mess, with nearly all the windows broken. Apparently partisans had held it in September 1943 when it was expected that the allies would land at Rome, and had been cleared out by the Germans, who systematically wrecked the place. This didn't stop the caretakeer, after we had been there a fortnight, from alleging that our men were breaking the electric light fittings!

It was pleasant to be under a roof again and I had a very nice room to myself, with real glass in the windows and a sub-balcony. I was able to get out all my books and arrange them neatly on a table for the first time since leaving home. I had a good R.A.P. too, and was able to get all the equipment off the truck and use it as a runabout. We had changed from KD to battledress just before leaving Volmontone, and we certainly needed it now, for the nights got quite cold, and there were no fireplaces in the mess.

Rome being only twenty minutes away in a jeep, we often went there either to the pictures or the opera in the evenings. Nevertheless, I found time began to hang very heavy on my hands; you can't go into Rome every day, and there was little else to do. Contrasting my comfortable quarters with the prospect of another winter in the line just tipped the scales in favour of applying for a hospital transfer. I had been toying with the idea for at least a year, but kept on putting off the decision. I hated the idea of leaving the Regiment, after getting to know it so well, and I was afraid that, after only a short spell in hospital, I might be posted to some Unit in which I would not be happy. In fact, I had got to the stage of leaving things to fate because I was afraid to make a definite decision. Now, however, I weighed the pros and cons very carefully for the last time, and decided to go ahead. I reckoned that the war would be over by March 1945 at which time I would still be in Hospital. The CO gave me his blessing, and I put in my application. I must say my record looked good on paper - two years with one unit and two-and-a-half years unbroken service with another, and I had high hopes that my application would be approved. Fortunately for me, nearly three months were to elapse before that approval was made known; otherwise, I might now be awaiting posting to a front line unit again, the war being still with us at the time of writing.

There were one or two diversions in addition to visits to Rome (which I shall describe next time). We had an exercise, our first for some time, which was unanimously nicknamed "Rupture"; we went away into the countryside and got all warlike and pretended to fire our guns. During this exercise a most extraordinary accident occurred; one of the men slipped on the wet grass and was run over by a gun, the one wheel of which passed right over his chest. He looked pretty pale when I got to the scene of the accident, and I rushed him off to hospital as quickly as I could. He was completely unharmed and was fit for discharge in less than a week. He said his chest felt a bit sore!

We went to Anzio one day to see the famous battlefield. The whole place was in a terrible mess, and I should think the ground will be dangerous for many years to come. We entered the battle area along the straight road, from Route Seven to Anzio; in some places close undergrowth and trees lined the road, whilst elsewhere there was no cover at all. The fields and road verges were lined with miles of old signal cable, wrecked vehicles, graves and slit-trenches. The little village of Carrocetto had virtually ceased to exist. As we neared Anzio itself, we passed the area where the hospitals had been located. Here was a large graveyard, with, in the next field, the rotting goal-posts of what had been a football ground.

Anzio town, on superficial inspection, appeared surprisingly whole but close inspection revealed that hardly a single house had escaped damage. We climbed the famous lighthouse, from which we could see for miles around. It was practically the only good OP in the whole beachead, and the German artillery made frequent but unavailing attempts to demolish it by gun fire. We went along to Nettuno to have a look at the famous air strip, the only one on the beachead and operated under almost constant shellfire. But it was only when we got out into the country behind Nettuno, on the road to Cisterna, that we realised to the full what the men of the Allied Beachead forces had been up against. The area was just like our own Lincolnshire fenland, cut up by dozens of dikes, and with few roads and hardly a stitch of cover for man or machine. From the hills to the south, east and north the Germans commanded the whole of the beachead with their super-heavy guns, which were out of range of most of our artillery. Nowhere in the area could a man rest in the knowledge that he was out of shelling range. Every house had at least one shell hole in it. On the road we passed a wrecked "Ferdinand" 88 millimetre self-propelled gun. Weighing about sixty tons, it will probably stay there till it rusts away. Cisterna, when we got to it, was in a worse state than Cassino. Lying on Route Seven, it was bombed time and time again by our heavies. The inhabitants were still living in what was left of their houses.

Rather an abrupt ending, I'm afraid, but more next time. Cheerio folks.

BULLETIN TWENTY-TWO

"Roman Holiday" — September to October 1944

Many people had told me that Rome was at its best in the autumn, and I can well believe them. I am told that the city seldom gets uncomfortably hot, owing to the cool breezes which blow in from the sea, but the weather when I was there was as delightful as I could have wished; it never got uncomfortably hot OR cold, and there were only a few showers of rain, mostly at night.

I could describe my visits to the Eternal City by quoting the guide-books in extenso but I see no point in doing this. For one thing I have already sent all my guide books home, and you can all read about the places for yourselves. So I will just tell of the places I saw and of how they impressed me. You all know me as an impatient and critical sightseer, prone to scoff at the stories told by the guides and guide books, so that when I say that Rome fascinated me you will realise what a wonderful city it must be. And the more I saw of Rome the more fascinating I found it; I wished that I had read more of the Latin classics about Roman Life and a little less about Caesar's Gallic wars!

Having decided to see Rome whilst the opportunity offered, Popeye (the Surveying Officer) and I hired a guide from Thomas Cook's for the day. He took us fairly rapidly round all the chief places of interest, and we were able to examine them in detail later on. The places can be divided for purposes of description into ancient Roman monuments and ruins, and the many beautiful Churches and sacred buildings, in which a large number of the greatest works of art are preserved.

The place for which one instinctively makes a bee-line is the Forum; actually there are several fora, all very close together, but THE Forum is known as the Forum Romanum. It lies in a valley about half a mile long and quarter of a mile wide, between the Palatine and Capitoline hills. Little remains of the buildings which once stood there, but it needs only a moderately vivid imagination to build it up again into what it used to be - the centre of Roman life, law-making, trading and culture. Unfortunately, a good many of the finest sculptures and statues were still enclosed in their protective sandbags, but what was visible was well worth seeing. I was chiefly surprised at the smallness of the place. In very ancient times, the site of the forum was a green and rather swampy valley; into it from their living quarters on the Capitoline and Palatine hills the Romans and Etruscans would descend for what I presume was their equivalent of our Teheran conferences. Later, the same valley was the obvious place to build a common meeting ground and market place, and so the forum arose. Close by are the fora of Trajan and Caesar (which one I don't know). At the Palatine end of the Forum is the Palatine hill, now topped by pleasant ornamented gardens, the Arch of Titus (boarded up for the duration) and the Basilica of Maxentius. This last is all that remains of an enormous market hall; the ruins are tremendous, and I can't imagine how enormous the original building must have been. Near by is the Temple of Venus - sounds exotic, but contains nothing except some pleasant looking trees - cypresses, I think.

Just across the road - literally - is the Colosseum, or Flavian Amphitheatre, in which the Christian martyrs are supposed to have been thrown to the lions. Actually, most of the torturing of Christians probably took place in the Circus Maximus, which we didn't see. The Colosseum looks rather like an enlarged and ruined version of the Albert Hall. About half of it was pulled to pieces by the ruling families of Rome, who used the stone to build their houses. On performance days the whole amphitheatre was roofed over by one colossal silk canopy.

From the Colosseum up to the famous Piazza Venezia runs the Via Imperatore - a fine new promenade built by Mussolini, which opens up the heart of ancient Rome. The Piazza Venezia is bounded on one side by the Palazzo Venezia; this building contains the famous balcony from which the Duce harangued the crowds. I had always visualised this balcony, from the newsreels, as being an imposing edifice on the third floor. Actually, it's a silly little shelf about three feet deep and six feet long on the first floor. I visited the room from which the balcony opens when I went to see an exhibition of world-famous paintings held in the Palazzo Venezia. Along one side of Via Imperatore were bas-reliefs showing the empire at various periods of Italian history; that of the fascist empire had been liberally daubed with red paint. One end of Piazza Venezia is occupied by the Vittorio Emmanuele Monument, commonly known as the "sugar-cake". Executed (that's the word) inwhite marble and bronze, it is supposed to be the finest of the modern Roman monuments. Personally, I think it rivals the Albert Memorial in ugliness.

Of the earlier Christian relics, by far the most interesting to me were the catacombs. There are several sets of these just to the south of Rome; those we visited were the catacombs of Saint Callixtus. When they were chased out of Rome the early Christians lived and died in these passages hewn in the rock anything up to 100 feet underground. We were shown the niches in which they had been buried. Each niche was roughly five feet by three feet by one foot, and I was unable to see how any adult body, living OR dead, could possibly be placed in such a cavity without being dismembered first. Near this set of catacombs, which stretches for several miles underground, are the Ardeatine caves. At the time of our visit they had just finished exhuming the bodies of a large number of Italian men and women who had been shot by the Germans and buried there some months previously. After identification, the bodies are to be buried in a memorial graveyard on the spot. The shooting was in reprisal for the killing of several Germans by partisans in a certain street in Rome. I forget the exact number of Italians who were shot, but there were over a hundred of them.

Whilst at the catacombs we went out along the old Appian Way, the original Roman road, still bearing the marks of chariot wheels and lined on each side by the tombs of the Patrician families of ancient Rome. The view looked lovely in the reddish light of a waning autumn day, till the guide spoilt it for us by saying that it used to be one of Mussolini's favourite walks!

Of the sacred buildings in Rome, the piece de resistance is of course St. Peter's. It really is magnificent, and no words can do justice to its perfection. I believe it is the largest Christian Church in the world, yet it is all so perfectly proportioned that the casual observer loses all sense of its immensity. Marble statues of angels look life-size at a distance, and it is only when one gets really close to them that one realises that these figures of children are over ten feet high, and the rest of statuary, mosaic and gilding is in the same proportion. Here are kept some of the greatest art treasures in the world. Finer than any statue I have ever seen is Michelangelo's "Pieta". Done when the artist was only twenty-four, it depicts the dead Christ after His removal from the cross; every tiniest detail is correct, down to the attitude of the limbs and muscles and the markings of the veins and finger-nails. There are many other fine pieces of sculpture, as well as much magnificent mosaic work. There is a fine bronze statue of St. Peter; the right foot is partly worn away by the kisses of the millions of pilgrims who have been to St. Peter's over the centuries.

From St. Peter's we naturally went to the Vatican where we were in time for the daily audience which the Pope gives to the Allied Forces. These public audiences were never given to the Germans, who were also excluded from St. Peter's except when in couples and accompanied by an armed Guard from the Vatican's picturesque Swiss Army.

The audience chamber was a fine room, about two hundred feet long and twenty feet wide, beautifully decorated with a simple mosaic ceiling, cream walls and rich hangings and curtains. In this room is the famous balcony from which His Holiness blesses the crowds in St. Peter's Square below. The room, when we arrived, was crowded with representatives of nearly all the allied forces, including many women in uniform. Many catholics had with them rosaries and other trinkets of a religious nature for the Pope to bless. There was much setting up of cameras, flourishing of exposure-meters and squinting through view finders. On the stroke of mid-day, an expectant hush fell over the crowd, about two hundred and fifty strong, and the head of the entourage entered the chamber. First to appear were the bodyguards, dressed in brightly coloured costumes with slashed breeches and leg-o-mutton sleeves, steel cuirasses, and armed with pikes. The Captain of the Guard was beautifully dressed in a dark blue uniform, pantaloons, and black boots. He had a full, fair beard and wore a glossy black helmet; he looked for all the world like an Elizabethan courtier. His Holiness Pope Pius XII rode in a chair, borne on the shoulders of four bearers. He was dressed in robes of beautiful cream cloth and a white silk cap covered his tonsure. As he passed between the rows of men and women he bent down and touched their heads and the trinkets which they held out to him. At the top of the chamber the chair was lowered, and the occupant stepped gracefully out of it, and ascended the steps of a small throne, on which he took his seat, facing us all against a background of cloth and gold. He made a very good speech of welcome, speaking in fluent English, and then repeating his address in French. He then descended from his throne and talked with many of the audience. His Holiness struck me as a practical and realistic man, with a charming manner and a pretty shrewd observer of the world and its troubles.

The Vatican itself contains thousands of valuable art treasures. One could spend weeks going through all the departments; we managed to see one or two of the better known sculptures - the Discus thrower, the Laocoon and the Apollo Belvedere.

We also visited the Sistine Chapel and saw the Michelangelo frescoes depicting the Last Judgement, the birth of Adam and many other biblical episodes. These frescoes are seen at their best only when the sun shines in and illuminates them. We were lucky and had the light just right; others who went came back very disappointed at what they had seen. There are many other fine paintings and frescoes in the Vatican, notably Raphael's "Transfiguration". Whatever opinion one may have about the Roman Catholic Church, there is no doubt that it preserved for posterity the finest examples of renaissance art; but for its patronage, many of the greatest artists would have died of starvation or discouragement. There are many other fine churches in Rome. The most notable among them are St. John Lateran; Santa Maria Maggiore and the Church of St. Paul outside the Walls. This last is a comparatively modern church built on the site of an older church destroyed by fire. The Church contains the portraits, in mosaic, of all the Popes of Rome, and there is a very fine XVth century cloister, which fortunately escaped destruction in the fire. The Pillars in the nave of the Church are of alabaster, and the sunlight shines through them at certain times of the day.

One of the finest sights of Rome in peace time are the many fountains, which are floodlit at night; they inspired Respighi to music. Unfortunately, there was no electricity power to work the pumps or the floodlights, so we had to use our imagination; even without the water many of the fountains looked lovely. The most elaborate one I saw was the Trevi fountain, tucked away in a little square by itself. Another well-known fountain (by Bernini) is the "Barraccia" in Piazza di Spagna. Keats knew this fountain well, for the house in which he lived is just opposite. It is now preserved as a monument to both Keats and Shelley. We saw the graves of the two poets in the Protestant cemetery, near the Pyramid of Caius Cestius. A bomb landed in the cemetery, fortunately without doing much damage.

A very fine view of Rome is to be had from the Janicular Hill, on the north bank of the Tiber near the Vatican City. I was at once struck with the clearness of the air over the city; there are no grimy factories to pollute the air and soil and eat away all the buildings and statues - the finest argument I have ever seen for a campaign of smoke abatement in London. On the Janicular is a fine equestrian statue of Garibaldi, which I saw finely silhouetted against the afternoon sun.

I could go on for hours writing about the ancient monuments of Rome; the Pantheon, first a public bath, then a pagan temple, now a burial place of the Kings of Italy; the Capitol, with its fine staircase and statues of Castor and Pollux etc, etc. But its time to deal with some of the modern aspects of this most fascinating of all cities.

We spent our four days leave quartered in the Hotel Inghilterra, near Piazza Spagna, fairly quiet and handy for all the amusements. For me, the greatest of these was opera; I started by seeing the Barber of Seville and was delighted with it; the scenery and costumes were superb, and the cast were admirable actors as well as singers. I later saw "Tosca" - very spectacular, and "I Pagliacci"; the latter had the most attractive prima-donna I ever hope to see, very slim and with a beautiful figure. Yes, she had a good voice as well! "I Pagliacci" being only a short work, the extra time was devoted to the ballet "Coppelia". This I found one of the most delightful entertainments I have ever witnessed. The decor was beautiful and most elaborate, and the large stage gave both the principal dancers and the corps de ballet full scope. I later went to a full evening of ballet at a smaller theatre, where I saw Petrouchka, Four Seasons and Prince Igor Dances. On this particular evening we met up with three American Red Cross Girls, one of whom knew an officer in our party. We took them to dinner after the show, and had quite an enjoyable evening. They left for Florence the next day, so there were no repercussions!

Another wonderful experience, to me, was a visit to an exhibition of pictures in the Palazzo Venezia; here were collected together for the first (and probably the last) time many world-famous pictures which would normally be dispersed all over Italy. Amongst many others, I saw the original Holbein of Henry VIII (sorry, I mean Charles Laughton), Titian's "Sacred and Profane Love", the Botticelli Venus (hideous, I though) and Tintoretto's "Christ and the Woman Taken in Adultery". There were many others, whose names escape me for the moment, but I was most impressed by the portrait of a Pope, by Velasquez, and by an enormous canvas, "The Martyrdom of St. Matthew" by Caravaggio. Having been twice round the exhibition, I returned to the car, explained about it to my driver, and told him I would wait if he would like to go and see the pictures. His reply was "No thanks; I'd rather go and have a cup o' tea"! Comment is superfluous.

We used to dine out a lot in a restaurant in the famous Pincio Garden; it was pleasant to have lunch on the terrace, from which there is a fine view towards the Tiber and St. Peters; near by is the Villa Borghese, in which a lot of jiggery-pokery and murder went on in the ancient days. The gardens looked a bit faded and dusty, but must have been beautiful before the war when properly cared for. At least they hadn't been ploughed up, as have a lot of English parklands.

Returning from Rome to the camp late at night had its amusing side; every mile or so along the road one would meet an Italian car or lorry with a prostrate figure beneath it, changing a wheel or mending a puncture. Tyres are getting very threadbare in Italy, and new ones are unobtainable. It can't be much fun travelling by car just now. One day an enormous lorry with huge balloon tyres had a "blow-out" just outside the camp area. The driver dismounted, removed the tyre, mended the puncture and laboriously blew the tyre up with a hand-operated pump. The whole operation took him about one and a half hours. With a grin and a wave he climbed into the cab, and was just about to move off when BANG! Wheeeee....went the tyre; another puncture. Never have I seen a grown man nearer to tears without actually crying. We felt so guilty at our own immoderate laughter that we gave him a hand with the repairs and saw him on his way, but I don't suppose he got very far.

A word or two about the Italians we saw in Rome. There seemed to be the usual large gap between the well-to-do, dressed in the height of fashion, and the beggars and the poor. But even the well-to-do are now in dire straits; for food is scarce - scarcer than when the Germans left Rome, for there was a black market then, and at least the rich could eat. The biggest headache for the Allied Control Commission is transport to get the food from the fields to the shops. The Germans took most of the serviceable lorries with them. There is very little electric power or gas for civilian consumption, and crime and prostitution were becoming rife. The Romans are now beginning to pay dearly for their aggressiveness of past years, and of course, all their misery is put down to the Allied occupation. Personally I remember the way Italians treated our men when they were prisoners, and their barbarity towards the Abyssinians, and I can really find little pity for them.

Soon after my return from leave, the usual "grape-vine" brought news of an impending move, and in a few days it was confirmed. We were off once more to the war, the mud and the rain, to fight with our first and greatest love, the Eighth Army.

Cheerio, folks.

BULLETIN TWENTYTHREE

"Once more into the breech" (sorry!)
October to November 1944

We had not been given a firm date for our departure from the rest area, but only that travesty of army administration, a "warning order". This gets everybody really thoroughly unsettled, and leads to very little constructive work. We all had that nasty unsettled feeling, and realised that the time when one could look ahead with certainty was over, at least for some time to come, and probably for the duration of the European war. There were some half-hearted attempts to suck the last pleasure from the flesh-pots of Rome, and to get in a little last-minute Christmas shopping. This latter was, indeed, a major operation; two or three days had to be spent in reconnaissance of all the shops before any purchases could be made, for fear something good might be overlooked. There was little fear of this, as the shops were filled with trashy goods at iniquitous prices. One day I received a large dollop of surface mail in the form of bulky magazines and books; I unhesitantly forecast a move within forty-eight hours and, sure enough, orders came through that same night. A last day spent getting things ship-shape, and we were ready for the final trek.

On the morning we moved off I sported, for the first time of wearing, a natty pair of "issue" riding breeches. These fitted me perfectly, except at the knee; apparently my calves are "OS"; I had to let out the seams of the legs before I could get the breeches on at all, and the first two days of motor-cycling were agonising. My feet kept going to sleep, and I had to rise in the saddle frequently to ease the pressure and get a little blood down to my toes, much to the amusement of the gunners. However, it was well worth the trouble, as the garment in question was a godsend in the mud and slush which we later encountered.

Things went wrong from the word go. The Regiment had been given a very complicated route in order to avoid going through the centre of Rome, but the column got split up in the general civilian traffic. I was travelling in my usual position at the rear. We came to a full stop near the Colosseum, so I went ahead on the bike and found one of the sergeants scratching his head and wondering what the next move was. It gave me great pleasure to be able to lead the column right through the Piazza Venezia and down Corso Umberto, sweeping aside all other traffic with an authoritative air and getting salutes from a couple of carabinieri. We found the rest of the column still milling around on the south side of the Tiber because a bridge on our route had been closed without warning. Ah, well, its all part of the fun, I suppose.

Once clear of Rome, we set off in cracking style along the narrow but well-surfaced Via Flaminia, running north east to Terni and Fano. Hills and congested village streets soon slowed us down, however; a fine drizzle had been falling, but this cleared away before the lunch time halt. We pulled off the road, and I gave the welcome signal to "brew up" (conveyed by raising the right hand, with thumb and forefinger pressed firmly together, towards the mouth. To be distinguished from "How about a pint?" in which the same motion is used, but all the fingers are curved as though affectionately clasping a bottle!) But we were not even allowed to have our lunch in peace; a despatch rider appeared with a panic message "MO wanted urgently; there's been an accident further up the road". No details, of course! So I hared off on the bike leaving the others to follow in their own time. One of our trucks had skidded, left the road and rolled down a fifteen foot bank. I don't know why it is so, but these accidents invariably happen to a key vehicle, which can ill be spared at the end of the day; this case was no exception, as the vehicle in question was the officers' mess truck. It speaks well for the packing of the china, for only one plate was broken. Our batman broke his collar-bone! I stopped a passing ambulance and packed him off to hospital.

Soon after lunch we started to climb; the weather let us down again, and it started to pour with rain, so that I was very glad I had handed the bike over to Bombardier Jones, who had rather a wet ride. The rain made the road extremely treacherous, especially for our heavily-laden vehicles. We were lucky to arrive at the little town of Foligno without another accident. It was nearly dark by the time we got in, and we sloshed round in the wet, trying to find somewhere to put the truck. As usual, we had been forgotten in the rush for billets, and all the good ones had been pinched; a lot of the men slept on beds with clean sheets, and I expect some of the men found the beds ready-warmed for them! We slept in a barn with a leaky roof, but it was better than under canvas.

The next day we had a leisurely start, as the road ahead was closed until 10 am for repairs. Whilst we were waiting at the roadside a dear old Itie gentleman came up to me and said "You go to Rome?". In my best Italian I replied with a flourish "No, No! Adiamo al Norte" (I go northwards). The old boy clasped my hand between his two and said in a fervent tone of voice "Goooood luck; goooood luck", as one bidding farewell to a friend who was going to certain death. I was no end cheered by this little encounter; I felt as I imagine the Christian martyrs felt as they heard the first yowls of the lions!

The weather remained fine and brilliantly sunny; we left the Via Flaminia after the luncheon halt and climbed up over the Appenines; on this part of the journey we encountered the finest mountain scenery yet. The hills were bare of trees and were covered with short and very green grass, so that the place looked like some giant's golf course. On the other side of the mountain range the road dropped down very steeply to the plain below, where it ran through narrow valleys and gorges. At one point the road appeared to end in a solid wall of rock; at the last moment a narrow cleft appeared in the rock-face. It was less than one hundred feet wide, and through it passed a river, a railway and a road! Every railway bridge we saw had been demolished by bombing, and every rail-junction or station had been bombed well and truly, and the area in the vicinity of all these targets was covered with the craters of "near misses".

We arrived at our staging post in good time that night, and I held my sick parade in the town square, much to the amusement of the local populace. There was a big aerodrome close by, and it was grand to see combat aircraft of many types flying around in the evening sky. Late that evening we received an order to send a representative ahead to contact a Beach Group; this set everybody a-twitter, and vague speculations that we might be about to take part in an amphibious landing operation went the rounds.

Fortunately, such was not the case.

We had a fairly late start the next day, so I went on ahead and spent an enjoyable hour watching operations at the airfield. Soon after we got on the move our road joined highway number sixteen, which runs alongside the eastern seaboard for many miles between Ancona and Pesaro. This latter town was our destination for the day, and we had an uncomfortable and irritating journey to it. There were many delays owing to road and bridge repairs, and there was a tremendous amount of traffic on the road. The old familiar unit and formation signs began to make their appearance again, and became more frequent the nearer we got to the fighting. It was nearly dark when we reached Pesaro. We were quartered in a great barrack of a place, which had been partially wrecked by the Germans before they left. It had few windows or doors, and a good part of the roof leaked, as we soon found out. Altogether an unpleasant contrast to our lebensraum of the last few months. We were to stay in this haven of rest for three days, after which it was "into battle"!

It was pouring with rain when I awoke the next morning, and the downpour continued, almost without ceasing, all day. I still had no tent for my R.A.P. and decided that something drastic would have to be done without further delay, so as soon as sick parade was finished, I climbed into the truck and made off for the DDMS office, forty miles forward. It was a devilish journey, over muddy and flooded roads crowded with traffic, and with long hold ups at every bridge and diversion. We were "stuck" for very nearly an hour in Rimini. This town has "had it" in a big way; I didn't see one whole building on the streets through which I passed, and the roads were full of craters. After much delay I managed to get a release note for a tent; by the time I had got the tent and returned, tired but triumphant, to Pesaro, it was nearly dark. In the end, we never needed the tent, and it was still in its original packing when I left the Regiment; nevertheless, it was a comfort to have it as a standby.

Recce parties had been forward to the new gun area to make contact with the Regiment which we were due to relieve; they had a gloomy tale to tell, when they returned, sodden and weary, after dark. The gun positions were ankle-deep in semi-solid mud, and most of the Regiment was living under canvas. The enemy shelled the positions each day, and his artillery was very active. The advance had come almost to a standstill, and we looked like spending some time in the position. Allowing for the usual amount of exaggeration that always occurs on those occasions, the outlook certainly didn't seem very bright; the whisky and gin were strongly in evidence that night! The next morning I was awakened by a loud explosion; we later found it was caused by engineers destroying mines on the beach, but it really frightened me, and I wondered how I was going to stand up to the noises of battle after so long away from them. Mercifully, the weather had cleared and it was a reasonably fine day. I gave a last clean out to my kit, and had a bath at the local Mobile Bath Unit (shades of Gedera and our own hot showers!). In the evening we went out to (of all things) a symphony concert! This in a town which had been in enemy hands five weeks ago. Pesaro is the birthplace of Rossini, and boasts quite a creditable orchestra, composed of amateur players who are the butcher and the baker, etc, during the day. I thought they played extremely well; later on in the winter ENSA adopted the orchestra and it toured the front line towns giving concerts to the troops which were very well attended.

This musical evening really was our last fling; the next day was spent packing up again for our move into the battle. As usual, it was a night move, and we had to leave at 3 am. There was a nice bright moon, which made driving easy, but it was bitterly cold on the bike, and my hands and knees rapidly became numb. It was about dawn when we bumped and ground our way through Rimini. As usual, there was a last-minute change of plan, and new gun positions had to be recced near the little town of Forlimpopoli, which had been captured a few days before. When we rolled into the town at about 10 o'clock in the morning a fierce battle was going on for the possession of Forli airfield, about two and a half miles away down the road. Guns had been going off all round us, and we could see our own fighter bombers going in just over our heads to bomb strong points along Route Nine. They were using one thousand pound bombs; the noise frightened ME so I don't know how the Germans stood it.

I was at once confronted with an awkward job in the selection of my R.A.P. The two batteries were a couple of miles apart, the roads were vile, and the nearest ambulance car was also two miles away; I had no ambulance of my own. I wasn't at all happy about the prospect of dealing with casualties in a set-up such as this; the country was flat, like the fens, and I felt sure the Germans would have our guns "taped" as soon as we opened fire. So I ground my way over the muddy roads, trying to find a suitable place to lay my head; it was an experience I was to repeat several times in the weeks to come. Just before Christmas I got fed up with it, and from then on the recce party chose and reserved an R.A.P. for me, instead of my having to take what was left after the others had got in somewhere.

The Regiment had a terrible time getting the guns into action; the roads were narrow with a deep ditch on either side, and most of the fields were soft and boggy because of the recent heavy rains. The problem was to get the guns off the road without getting them hopelessly bogged down. The only way was to put them in the farmyards, and even before that could be done the bridges over the ditches had often to be strengthened. The farmers naturally took a dim view of all the proceedings, and with good reason; the bang of a medium gun is enough to shake the tiles from the roof of any Italian farmhouse. So all in all, it was a trying day, and everybody's temper was the worse for wear by the time it was ended. I finally ended up by having my R.A.P. in the front room of a half-wrecked house; before we could move in we had to fill up an enormous hole in the floor, dug by the enemy for use as an air-raid shelter. There was no room for me to sleep there, so I pitched my magnificent new bivvy against the wall at the back. Unfortunately, I failed to look up at the roof before doing this, and a few nights later, when it rained heavily, I was kept awake most of the night by the water from a broken down-spout thundering on the roof of my canvas home. Incidentally, this was the very last time I had to use a bivvy that winter.

As soon as it became dark we were introduced to a new dodge of warfare - the so-called artificial moonlight. This is made by dozens of searchlights, set at a low trajectory, and with their beams focussed on the clouds over the German lines. By this means it was possible to walk about in reasonable comfort and confidence on nights which were cloudy and moonless; anybody who has fallen into a slit-trench full of muddy water on a dark night will agree with me when I say that artificial moonlight was the best single innovation on the Italian front during the whole wretched campaign.

Being the last regiment to move in, we were naturally pushed rather far forward; at least, we THOUGHT that was the reason at the time! Later we found that ideas seemed to have altered since we were last in Italy, and medium artillery was nearly always pushed up to within less than four thousand yards of the enemy line. On this occasion, there seemed to be very little between us and Jerry except one rather muddy river!

As I had feared, long absence from the line had made me extremely "gun shy"; I think everybody finds themselves affected in this way to some degree, but it seemed to me that I was worse than average. There was a heavy regiment of 7.2's and "Long Toms" behind us, and for the first night or two I got hardly any sleep because of the din they made. The flatness of the terrain probably made things worse, as there were no hills to mask the sound. Before coming into action we had all said "Ah, well, it won't be as bad as last winter. No hills, old boy! Jerry won't be able to look down at us all the time like he did last winter!" Well, he couldn't, but the flat country gave no cover to the enormous flash from our guns, and the Germans sound-ranging was perfect, as we found out. In sound-ranging, the noise of the enemy gun is picked up by a sensitive microphone, and by various intricate calculations the position of that gun or guns can be worked out with great accuracy; especially so when there are no hills to distort the sound or give an echo effect. On the whole, I think I prefer fighting in hilly country, from the gunners' point of view, but I expect the Infantry think otherwise!

The very first night we fired, the other battery of the Regiment had a load of iron back from the Germans; one round of really big stuff landed very near a command post, and only the fact that they were in a good solid house saved the boys from casualties. All through the winter we were able to get nearly everybody into houses, and there is no doubt that we were saved a considerable number of casualties; if you have room between you and the enemy and a room above, you are safe from anything except a bomb or a very large shell. Time and again we occupied houses which had been shelled by our own guns, and even a two hundred pound shell never penetrated more than one room that I ever saw.

Two evenings later the enemy got the battery I was with thoroughly taped; he put three big air-bursts in the sky right above the gun positions, and when you see that you know what's coming. He laced into the place for nearly half an hour; a lot of the rounds were duds, but there were still far too many live ones. We could hear three guns firing in salvos - boomp - boomp - boomp - wheeeeeeeee - crump-crump-crump. The old familiar sounds, and how they frightened me! However, as usual, the bark was worse than the bite; they knocked one or two chaps' kits sideways, but the sole casualty was one fellow who thought he knew a better 'ole, and sustained a flesh-wound of his arm whilst running towards a house; its fatal to get up whilst the metal is flying! The wound healed perfectly, and he was back with us again in a couple of weeks. After this incident, the position was shelled regularly without further damage. And it went on like this all through the winter. Whatever the Germans were short of, it certainly wasn't guns OR ammunition! We were shelled in every position in which we opened fire, and had to resort to all sorts of dodges, like moving the guns frequently, in order to avoid too many casualties.

Just to complete the picture, Bombardier Jones, my medical orderly, suddenly produced a temperature of 101° and a sore throat, and I had to pack him off to hospital. It was the first time we had been parted for two years, except for periods of leave, and I missed him badly. I had got to rely on him too much and found I didn't know where half the odds and ends of the medical equipment were packed. He came back to us after about a week.

Well, here my story ends for this time; the next incident takes more than a page to tell.

Next time I shall tell the tale of our dreary Italian winter, in the all-too-familiar mud and slush. I would skip this as being rather too much of a bore, but for the fact that I know nobody at home really has much conception of what the conditions are like, and no wonder! But, for now, Cheerioh.

BULLETIN TWENTY-FOUR

"More mud and misery" — November 1944

We moved again in the middle of November. Our new position was on the north bank of the Ronco river, just a mile out of Forli, capital of the province of Romagna. The town had only fallen thirty-six hours before we moved in; the Germans were known to be only just north of the town, and nobody knew just how far away they were on our right flank, which seemed to be resting on the thin air. The main road bridge had, of course, been blown, so the route up was over a detour miles long, much of it in view of the enemy. The military police kept on altering the one way traffic circuit, just to make things more awkward and complicated. I went forward after lunch, and had a rough ride; mud kept jamming between the tyre and mudguard of the front wheel, necessitating frequent stops to clear it away. I made a firm resolve to make my own modifications to the bike to prevent a recurrence of this trouble; its no fun trying to clear mud away in a hurry when enemy shells are landing in the neighbourhood. I finally remedied the trouble by a very simple dodge; send a sixpenny postal order for the answer.

After a lot of dickering I managed to secure a very safe R.A.P. in a stable with good thick walls. Owing to the mess-up in the traffic arrangements, it seemed doubtful if the guns would get through in daylight; the wireless communication broke down, so I went back on the bike to tell the boys what the position was. As I was the only officer on the spot who knew the route to the gun positions, I was deputed to lead the way forward. This was probably the only occasion during the Italian campaign, and possibly in the whole war, when a gunner regiment was led into battle by a doctor on a motor bike! We got moving straight away, and on crossing the river found the traffic route had been altered yet again. We took the whole column right across Forli airfield, the scene of much heavy fighting in the days just past; nobody felt inclined to loiter and admire the view, however; we all felt horribly naked on that bare expanse of grass and tarmac. The evening hate was on as we went through the back-end of Forli; shelling on the road was very accurate, and a salvo from six-barrelled mortars landed just after our column had passed.

Our recce parties had been practically the first allied troops to appear in the new gun area, and they received a royal welcome from the locals, who dined and wined them in great style. It was here that we saw, for the first time, some really constructive work by Italian partisans. The side roads were fairly well mined, and the local partisans had watched carefully where the mines were placed, and marked them with sticks and white bunting as soon as the Germans pulled out. They missed one or two, however; the RE's came along a few days later with detectors, and found a mine right in the middle of the road along which nearly all our transport had travelled. It was a glass mine - the first I had seen. Rather like a flattened goldfish bowl, it contained practically no metal, and was very difficult to detect, except with a bayonet or other prodding device.

Forli was the centre of a good deal of partisan activity, and before they left the Germans strung up six of the ringleaders, five men and a woman, in the square. Oddly enough, some of the earliest disorders associated with Mussolini's rise to power also took place in Forli; the horrid man's birthplace is in the little village of Predappio, quite near Forli. All the people on our gun area had buried their most treasured possessions under the floors of their outhouses - away from the Germans, so they SAID, but I feel it more likely that the Boche told them WE would steal everything and that they really hid their goods for that reason. It is a tribute to our honest open faces that the people started digging up their treasures again within a few hours of our arrival.

The German counter-battery fire continued to be as fierce as in the previous position. Within a few hours of opening up, lots of old iron was coming back at us and it was unpleasantly accurate, too. A couple more gun tyres were punctured, and a lot of people had narrow squeaks; fortunately, the guns were very well spread out. For once in a way RHQ came in for more than their fair share of shelling. Usually they are back behind the guns, but that would have meant having the river in between, so they were half a mile on the right flank of the guns, and just in front of some Long Toms

- hundred-and-fifty millimetre guns. They had shells all round them on several occasions, and the CO, who sleeps in a caravan, had quite a narrow squeak one night. One of the battery command posts also had a near shave; they were in a house which had once been a German HQ and the enemy went for it one morning about 6.30. Fortunately, his range was just a shade too long, and the shells - big ones - fell in a line about twenty yards away.

To our great joy, Bombardier Jones returned to us a few days after this; he had been at a Field Ambulance in Cesena, and admitted that when he left us he had been looking forward to a few days away from the cold and the shelling. Alas for his hopes - the building he was in was windowless, and the town was shelled several times by the German heavies!

Since our return to the line, a steady build-up of livestock had taken place; Nearly every gun-sub had its own poultry farm. One rascal had the effrontery to beg some corn from the farmer on whom he was billeted. I suppose the poor innocent Italian throught he might as well provide food for OUR poultry, rather than have his own hens stolen. The very same afternoon, I came across a neatly laid hen-trap, baited with this same corn. Unfortunately, we couldn't run a chicken farm in the R.A.P. owing to lack of space on the truck during moves.

Life continued to be quite pleasant, in spite of the rather noisy nights; the rainy days became more frequent, but in between the showers the sun shone brilliantly, and it was pleasant to sit out in the afternoon with a book. People dropped in for a smoke and a chat and there was always something to fiddle with; I fitted the bike with a very good pair of carrying-cases, and also, as previously mentioned, dealt with the question of mud and jamming under the mudguards. I have a note in my diary of three telephone calls, all of which were made to me on the same day. The first was from a sergeant in one of the batteries, who had a knotty point about aircraft recognition, which he wanted me to settle. The second was from the Signals; THEY wanted to know the length of a man's intestines, and much money hung on the answer. The third call came late in the evening from one of the Command Posts. They hummed a few bars of music, over the phone, and wanted to know if they were from Lizt's Hungarian Rhapsody Number Two or from Dvorak's New World Symphony. Such is fame!

My civilian practice began to increase again. There was a great deal of diphtheria among the civilian population, and this had to be dealt with owing to the danger of our own men becoming infected. Some of the people had the most frightful throats, with a yellow slough as big as a two shilling piece on the tonsil. Fortunately, general effect on the body seemed to be mild. Often I would be called to a house to find half a dozen adults and children infected, and they all had to be carted off to hospital. The civilian hospitals were snowed under with cases; the usual treatment was three days in bed, with some shots of serum, and then back home again.

In connection with diphtheria, I had an interesting talk with some American MOs whom I met one afternoon. They came round with me to see some of my patients, and were most interested. There were five of them, and only one had previously SEEN a case of full-blown diphtheria. Immunisation in America is so universal that the disease is rarely seen, and then only in a very mild form. Would that it were so in our own country, where thousands of children die from diphtheria each year.

Meantime, the war on the Italian front was slowing down to its winter pace. The rains had come three weeks earlier than expected, and the allied plan to winter on the line of the river Po was foiled. The Americans just failed to reach Bologna, and on our own immediate front we were stuck at the river just above Forli. Everywhere it was the same tale, just too few men to do the job, and a determined and fiendish enemy, fighting very well and in first-class defensive country, at any rate during the bad weather. There was little sign of deteriorating enemy morale, and all he was short of was motor transport and aircraft - neither of them a deciding factor in the trench-warfare conditions in which we were now fighting. We had plenty of armour, including flame-throwing tanks, but it was hopelessly road-bound, and a sitting target for enemy anti-tank guns. The ground never stayed hard enough for a sufficient length of time to mount an attack before the rain came on again and turned the fields into quagmires.

At this time was announced the LIAP (Leave In Addition Python) leave scheme; it caused more misery and heartburning and dissatisfaction than it was worth. The Regiment was allocated four vacancies in November, and these went to men who had been wounded or who had been exposed to more danger than most of us by reason of their jobs - men at the OP etc. This seemed fair enough, but there were many who thought the vacancies should be decided by ballot, especially in view of the fact that we had all been overseas about the same length of time. People at home got all worked up, and obviously hadn't a clue as to the individual chances of getting home. The scheme was a sop to those who had been agitating for better leave facilities for the CMF, and it tasted pretty vinegary to us. Especially in December, when it was announced that the BLA men in Europe were to get seven days leave every six months. Nobody in CMF wanted the BLA leave cut down, but we all felt that something more could have been done for us. Coming on top of criticisms of the conduct of war in Italy, and shortage of manpower and certain items of equipment, all this was enough to make anybody feel frustrated and bitter, and the tales LIAP men brought back with them - D-Day Dodgers, etc - didn't help at all. And I've no doubt that in years to come the war in Italy will be written off as a side-show, just as Gallipoli was last time. Well, maybe it was, but that doesn't make the mud any more solid or the rain drier. When I say this I am speaking for the infantry and the gunners, who were up to their eyes in slush all the time. For my own part, life could have been a lot harder, and I would be ashamed to complain on my own behalf. All this tirade may seem very much by the way, but when you read in the papers from home that VE Day in Europe meant, for Montgomery's men of the BLA, the end of long weary YEARS of fighting (I quote) - well, it makes yer think! At any rate, they had to have Monty to lead them, and most of the old Eighth Army to take the beaches!

Let's see, where was I? Oh, yes. In spite of the mud and bad weather, there was some very slow progress. Forli airfield was in use by fighters within ten days of its capture, and this attracted the German fighters at dusk - quite like old times. In order to support another attack we moved still further over to the left flank and forward till we were on a line between Forli and the sea. During the move one of the tractor drivers drove his gun into a ditch at a corner past which everybody had managed to manoeuvre without trouble. He was suspected of being drunk, and was sent along to me. Of which more anon.

My R.A.P. was in the back room of the little village store; the wall was one brick thick, and we were right on a cross-roads. We didn't like the set-up a bit, and I was never really happy in the place; it was very cramped too, if we had had many casualties. After a lot of argument, I managed to persuade the ADMS to give me an ambulance car which eased my mind a little, for we were a long way from the nearest dressing-station, and the roads were very bad. Every bridge had been demolished by the retreating enemy, which is a damn nuisance in a terrain criss-crossed with drainage dykes and canals.

Talking to peg-leg - the old man who owned the shop - I had my first concrete instance of how the allies have debased the Italian currency. The old man's price for a new glass for our hurricane lamp was ten lire - two shillings at the pre-war value of the lira, but only sixpence by our military government currency. We were the first troops to attempt to buy anything from him and he didn't know the position until I told him. We railed at the Germans for doing just the same thing in occupied Europe!

Being well away to a flank, we hoped for a little less attention from the enemy, and it certainly was less noisy for a few nights than it had been at the last position. The attack which we were to support had to be put off because of bad weather, so one of our troop of guns was moved even further forward to a sniping position, so that their fire would not give away our battle positions. There was really very little doing, but I had a good many civilian patients, so the time didn't drag too badly, and my fees kept the men in eggs. The people here had a far greater pride than down south, and always insisted on giving me something, though I didn't like taking it, for there was little I could do for them. One poor old soul lay dying of cancer, with one of our guns in the front yard of the farmhouse.

The daughter of the house in which we had the R.A.P. was a

schoolteacher in Forli, and used often to bring one of her friends in for a talk in the evening. This last-named young lady was a saucy piece, and far too free with her eyes and dress for our peace of mind. She spoke French and German very fluently, a fact which I found very suspicious, and she had a lot of dirty stories to tell about the Fascists and the Italian Royal family. The people of the north speak a much purer Italian than those of the south, and I was able to understand pretty well all that was said. To me there is something particularly foul about the way in which the Italians discuss those who have let them down - witness particularly the disgusting desecration of the bodies of Mussolini and his mistress, after they had been quite rightly, killed. Good clean hatred is understandable, but this beastliness was purely Italian, somehow. I very soon got sick of the conversation and stayed away; the others didn't speak Italian, and doubtless found other reasons for staying. There is much less of the early Victorian atmosphere in the north than in the south, where chaperones were the rule. I know of at least one "grand passion" which occurred in the Regiment last winter, when some of the men were in the same billets for weeks on end.

The weather closed right in now; wet days began to outnumber the dry ones, and progress on the ground became slower and slower. Low clouds cut down our effort in the air, and bombs sank into the mud, where they did less damage. The war squelched forward in rain-sodden boots. Objectives of attacks got nearer and nearer the start-lines, and it became obvious that progress would very soon come to a dead stop till frost could make the ground really hard. No attack ever went just as planned; there was always some last-minute hitch due to weather or simply to the inability of the weary infantry to cope with the enormous tasks thrust upon them. How those boys stuck to the job I shall never understand. The wonder is not that there were some desertions but that these were, comparatively speaking, so infrequent.

Our next move took us well forward, across the next river north of Forli; Route Nine, the main road, was a shambles. Every house had been turned into a strong point by the enemy, and most of them had been flattened into rubble heaps by our fighter-bombers. Later, the RE took the rubble to make up the roads, and any returning householders were confronted with their front gate posts, a few laths of timber and a large hole in the ground!

One-way traffic was the rule on all side roads, where vehicles, especially tanks, kept sliding sideways, into the steep ditches. Everybody was moving up, and there were traffic jams galore. The final touch was added by German shelling of all the principal crossroads and junctions; they knew what they were doing, too! I ran out of petrol (bad show!) at rather an awkward point, and had to fill up whilst a really thorough German bombardment was falling unpleasantly close. I shan't run out of petrol again.

I think I had better break off here, before we get involved in another episode.

Chin chin till next time.

BULLETIN TWENTY-FIVE

"Mainly about keeping warm" — December 1944

I ended Bulletin twenty-four just at the point where the Regiment had moved into a very muddy position a mile or two south of Faenza. We had one battery on either side of Route Nine and I stayed in the middle, with the RHQ for once in a way, leaving each battery to the tender mercies of an MO who happened in each case to be quite handy. I had what was unquestionably the dirtiest R.A.P. ever. It was in a sort of cart shed, with only an earth floor, so nothing in the way of dressings or instruments could be left out, as they became covered in dust. However, it was the only place I could find which had a roof, and there was an excellent wine cellar next door, which made a safe dormitory for the chaps, and I also had a small room with a leaky roof.

It was the last day in November when we moved in, and the weather was becoming very bad; it rained two days out of three, and it was quite cold except when the sun was out. Once again the problem of stoves loomed up and had to be tackled. This year we were issued with a Valor stove; unfortunately, fuel for it was rationed to the equivalent of two evenings' consumption, so alternative means of heating had to be improvised. You would think, wouldn't you, that after one wet winter in Italy some basic design of wood-burning stove would have come into use, and that all the snags would have been ironed out. But no! Everybody had their own ideas on just how the stove should be improvised and erected; I think we had more rows and displays of bad temper over this subject amongst the R.A.P. staff than over anything else, except possibly, the beer ration. The first stages are easy. You beg, borrow or steal a five-gallon oil drum, and burn it out with petrol to get rid of the paint and oil-fumes. You also steal some down-spouting from the wall of an Italian house; straight bits are easy, but joints and bits with right-angle bends in them are hard to come by. Having collected all this, you start to make the stove, and here's where all the argument develops.

First of all, the oil-drum. There are several schools of thought about how this should be treated. One says that all the air-holes should be punched in the bottom, a large hole cut in the top, for stoking, and no other apertures or orifices allowed, except that for the chimney (of which, more later). Another school is all for holes all over the lower part of the sides of the drum, a stoke hole in the upper part of the side, and no hole in the top at all, on the grounds that smoke always leaks round the edges of the metal bedroom utensil (filled with earth to weight it) which, by tradition, is always used as a lid for the aforesaid hole. Then, of course, there is the important point as to whether the chimney take-off shall be from the back of the drum or from the top.

When the drum has been suitably dealt with, there remains the thorny question of the chimney. Shall it go through the roof or the window? That having been decided, one has to work out how to use the various lengths of pipe and junctions to the best advantage. This is very important for two reasons. Firstly, it is advisable to have as few joints as possible; they always leak, and have to be covered in wet clay, which always cracks as the evening wears on. Obviously, the fewer the joints, the less smoky the atmosphere is by the end of the evening. Secondly, it is important that the chimney should be easy to take down for cleaning. The wood we burn has a lot of tar in it, which soon clogs the pipe. When this happens after dark, there's hell to pay. The final blockage usually occurs quite suddenly, and almost always when you've got a roaring fire going; the atmosphere rapidly thickens, and the situation is difficult to cope with. You can't open the doors till the fire dies down a bit, because of the blackout; you certainly can't continue to exist in the rapidly thickening atmosphere. The only thing to do is shove off to somebody else's fire for the evening, and deal with the matter by daylight, by which time everything in the room is covered in smuts and even one's bedclothes reek of smoke. After this has happened once or twice, you learn to judge the coking-up time of the chimney, and arrange to anticipate disaster by a timely clear-out during the warmer part (if any) of the day.

The stove having been designed, constructed, and set up, the time comes to light the first fire in it. This ceremony has an atmosphere all its own, in more senses than one. There is a tension in the air worthy of the House of Commons on the eve of some world-shaking pronouncement. First, a shallow tin of petrol is placed in the bottom of the stove, and wood is piled over and around this. The officiating individual then stands well away and casts a match into the petrol.

If all goes well, there is a dull explosion, and the billet rapidly fills with smoke and fumes; this always happens at first before the chimney gets warmed up and provides a good draught. As the smoke clears, the tension in the rival camps reaches its climax; those who designed the stove stand by to make excuses for any snags that crop up, whilst those who disagreed with the designers get ready to jeer. Spectators from other billets keep quiet, if they are wise; they may be grateful for a warm at the stove one evening when their own is misbehaving!

It is always amusing to visit a billet a few hours after the troops have moved in. Stove pipes of every shape and size belch smoke from every window, and search parties are looking out for new pieces of chimney and wood for fuel.

If I have been somewhat garrulous on the subject of stoves, you must forgive me; but the subject is one which occupies a lot of our time and thought during the colder weather, and I don't believe I have given it more space than it deserves.

The weather grew steadily worse, and so did the enemy shelling; we were on a fairly obvious traffic route, and there were lots of gun positions round about, so we were smartened up regularly every night, and sometimes during the day as well. After about a week the AIR OP people came and used a field about a quarter of a mile in front of my R.A.P. as a landing strip, which furnished the Boche with an even better reason for shelling the whole area. One night we had a record stonk; I counted two hundred and ten rounds, fire in seventy salvos from three guns. Quite fifty per cent were duds, but it was noisy just the same; all the rounds sounded quite close, but we weren't worried - just academically interested. The house we were in had already stood a couple of direct hits from two hundred pound shells, so we felt quite secure. The air OP landing ground was still untouched next day, much to our surprise.

Air activity on our side was on a very much reduced scale, owing to bad visibility, but if a clear patch appeared, our fighters would be over to strafe the enemy infantry. We had an excellent view of some of the proceedings, and it was here that I first saw aircraft rockets in use. I was glad we weren't on the receiving end; you can see the rockets all the way down to the target, and unlike cannon shells, they move faster as they get nearer.

The weather being very depressing, we were really lucky to have a "character" to keep us amused. "Wally" came to us an an ambulance orderly. He was a genuine and very typical cockney, with a pawky wit and a telling phrase for any and every situation; it was impossible to be gloomy for long when Wally was about. I remember one cold and dreary night. We were sitting in the R.A.P. The stove was smoking very badly, and we were all fed up to the back teeth. "Now then, chaps" says Wally, "Let's have two minutes' silence for the poor bloody war-workers at 'ome. Just think of them, getting ready for bed. Nice gas fire in the room, carpet on the floor, nice clean sheets." In addition to keeping us cheery, Wally was a first class handyman, and we were very sorry when the time came for him to leave us. He had a small pup called "Jacko" which he bequeathed to us, but unfortunately Jacko only remained with us for ten days. I think he was pinched by some New Zealanders one afternoon; anyway, we never saw him again.

Very little happened for the rest of the three weeks we spent in this position; the weather grew more and more miserable, and it became obvious that there would be little or no advance on this part of the front for some weeks to come. I had a fair number of civilian patients, mostly with trivial complaints. The Regiment was unfortunate enough to have two "prematures". Technically, the term "premature" means that the shell explodes at some instant other than that at which it is meant to explode. Sometimes the explosion takes place in mid-air, outside the barrel, but in medium guns the explosion nearly always occurs whilst the shell is still in the gun, which is much worse, as the force of the explosion bursts the barrel, and the crew stand a good chance of being seriously hurt. As a matter of fact, it is surprising how often the crew escape without injury, and it is all a matter of luck. In one of the aforementioned prematures a man was killed; in the other, all the crew except one escaped, and his injuries were minor ones. Oddly enough, the injured man had been the only casualty in another premature explosion just over a year previously. Its all in the luck of the game.

During this time I attended a court-material in Forli, in the capacity of an expert witness. I am not supposed to say much about the case, but I would like to emphasise that in a court martial the scales are weighted heavily in favour of the accused, and he is given every chance. In this case my evidence was held to be invalid because I had conducted certain tests for drunkenness, which, it seems, are prohibited by King's Regulations. But it was the PROSECUTOR who pointed out that my evidence was invalid, just in case the defending officer might not know, and as a result, the whole case against the man fell to the ground, and he was found "not guilty". It is difficult to see how any man could be unjustly found "guilty" with such a procedure, which is a comforting thought.

I finished up our stay here with a sharp attack of flu; I felt very ill for a couple of days, and had quite a high fever, but it soon went away again and I was up and about in a few days. During my illness, I conducted the morning sick parade from my bed.

As the days drew on towards Christmas, with no signs of a move, we became more and more depressed. With the Regiment so spread out, it would be difficult to get any communal Christmas spirit into the festivities. In the end it was a close shave, and after several false alarms we really did move, on the day before Christmas Eve - and what a move! We went right up to Faenza - captured a few days before - and then off a mile or so to the east of the town. Our guns were all along a main road (goody-goody), and within two thousand yards of the enemy - closer than we had ever been before, if my memory serves me correctly. One of the higher-ups had evidently boobed; I gather that the Boche was expected to retire completely behind the line of the river Senio, but he did not do so, and left a large pocket on our side of the river. However, we were told that we would not be expected to fire unless a German attack materialised, which was as well, for we had several small bombs from enemy mortars on one gun position while the chaps were settling in; no casualties, but much surprise!

We all had good strong houses, fortunately; I lived with one of the batteries again and had my R.A.P. in the back kitchen of a good solid Fascist tile-works. I slept in the R.A.P. and the other fellows slept in a small room which opened off it. The place was very dirty, but quite weatherproof, and was certainly a great improvement on our last billet. Some of the houses around about had been in use as German HQ's and in a cupboard in one of them we found some German propaganda leaflets which were so attractive that the enemy had evidently hoarded some for himself. They were small facsimiles of the American magazine "Life"; on one side was a rather Germanic but none the less attractive nude in a suitable "artistic" pose, on the other side a grinning skull dressed in a British tin hat, with the heading "Death". I saved a few of these leaflets, but lost them somewhere later on. Talking of nudes, etc, I saw a few German pin-ups at odd times, and the German idea of ideal feminine beauty didn't impress me much; mostly the women had plain faces and long straggling hair. But the face isn't important!

We started off badly in this position by having a fatal casualty on the day we moved in. One of the fellows was walking up the road when a one-seventy landed right beside him. He wasn't discovered till five minutes later, when he was just recovering consciousness, and at first they thought he was only concussed. I had not yet arrived, so they wheeled him off to the nearest dressing station. Here he was discovered to have a minute wound in the small of the back; he had such severe internal bleeding that he died early next day, despite all that could be done for him. A very small piece of metal had penetrated one of his kidneys.

The casualty had its effect on a good many people; the chief sympton was a tendency for people to hang around the command post when they were off duty; instead of getting out in the fresh air and taking a walk. I felt a bit this way myself, I must admit, and had to drive myself out for a day or two; once that sort of thing really gets a grip on you it is very difficult to break it again.

Wel, well, that's all this time, folks. Sorry to end on such a gloomy note but I will cheer you up next time, when I describe our Christmas festivities. Cheerio.

BULLETIN TWENTY-SIX

"End of story" — December 1944 to June 1945

You will recall that in the last bulletin we were near the town of Faenza and in a very forward position. We remained here for several weeks, including Christmas, our third away from England.

Christmas celebrations started with a bang! We had all been around the battery position cadging drinks, and turned in very late and rather the worse for wear. I was woken in the early hours of Christmas morning by the unmistakable sound of aircraft and falling bombs; a lone German bomber was stooging around, and he later let go a stick of three bombs, each one nearer to our R.A.P. than the last. The second one fell about ten yards in front of our billet and the third in the back garden, and the explosion of this last one was accompanied by the sound of breaking glass and muffled oaths from the chaps in the back room. I arose hastily, opened the door, and shone my torch into the room. The floor appeared to be covered by a mass of plaster of Paris, from which protruded five white faces. The ceiling had come down en masse on the sleepers on the floor below, and the air was thick with plaster dust and bad language. Everybody was coughing and spluttering, and I was the only one who felt like laughing. It took a couple of hours of hard work before we could think of getting any more sleep, and bad tempers and sore heads were still in evidence when we awoke on Christmas morning. Much the most upset was Johnny Ellard, my batman, who had mislaid his upper dentures; as he suffers from a cleft palate, this was a major disaster and he spent half the morning going round all the places where he had had a drink the night before. Nobody had found his teeth and they eventually turned up amongst his blankets, much to his relief.

After all this, the rest of the Christmas celebrations passed more or less in the usual way, with plenty of food and drink, a bit of a sing-song, and an early night. The next day I moved my kit into the top room of a nearby disused railway signal box, so that the R.A.P. staff could have my old room to sleep in, the back room now being completely uninhabitable. A few days later I developed a severe attack of tonsilitis, complicated by an abscess so I had several days of pain and fever until it burst, and it took me another week before I was really fit again. Whilst I was suffering, a posting order came through telling me that I was to report to the 98th British General Hospital at Bari as soon as my replacement as RMO arrived.

I was fortunate that the Regiment had remained in the same place whilst I was ill, but early in January we moved to an area west of Rimini in support of an Armoured Brigade (British) and a group of Italian troops. The war in Italy had now entered another period of stalemate. The weather was awful, and we began to suffer shortages of ammunition, Jeep spares and other supplies. As the war on the Western Front hotted up the Italian campaign became bottom priority for everything, which didn't help morale. In addition to this we had to suffer a new nuisance from our own mobile guns. Some bright spark had conceived the brilliant idea of mounting guns on tracked vehicles, which made them much more mobile. To add insult to injury, these weapons were named after members of the Church hierarchy, so we had Cardinals, Priests and Bishops depending on the calibre of the gun in question. A troop of these gentry would drive into position near our billets, generally during the night, fire off a hundred rounds or so and then retire rapidly, leaving us to receive the inevitable German return fire. Having survived the war unscathed up to this time, I was not anxious to become a casualty just before being posted to a safe area, and I am afraid that I became very nervous and jumpy at times.

Early in February we had our last move before my departure; we went back to the Faenza area, and were all very wet and cold and miserable, as it had begun to snow and we had frost every night. I was glad when my replacement arrived and I could bid the Regiment a fond farewell. Though glad of the chance to brush up my medicine and become a proper doctor once more, I knew that I would miss the open air life and the friends and companions I had made in the last two-and-a-half years, and I hoped that they would miss me too!

As parting gifts I was given a new battledress, beret and leather jerkin by the Quartermaster and a bottle of whisky by the Commanding Officer, who thanked me for my services. I was also allowed to have a car to take me and my baggage back to Ancona, where I spent the night in a hotel and caught a hospital ship down to Bari the next day.

Here I found myself in quite a different atmosphere, and as security is no longer a problem I can write in the present tense. The 98th British General Hospital is one of three situated in a half-finished polyclinic complex. I am working on the Medical Division under a splendid physician from St. Mary's Hospital, London. We deal with general medical cases, but also with diseases of the chest, mainly tuberculosis, which is very good training for me after so long away from the bedside. I am enjoying the work, but am having to work much harder than I have done for the past five years, as there is a shortage of Medical Officers in Italy.

The Officers Mess is quite pleasant, though the food is, if anything, less varied than it was in the Regiment. All the officers except two are doctors, two of whom I knew in Birmingham before the war. Nobody salutes anybody else very often, and shoes rather than boots are the footwear of choice. My bedroom, shared with four others, is in the living room of a luxurious villa; the ceiling is decorated with lots of cherubs and beautiful ladies in various states of nudity - a sight for sore eyes when I wake in the morning! One of the things I enjoy most, apart from my work, is the ability to have a nice hot bath as often as I like.

There is quite a lot of cultural activity in Bari. There are symphony concerts or operas fairly frequently, and cinemas showing mostly Italian or American films. There is also a minor war crimes trial in progress! In the dock is a local Italian Army General who is accused of atrocities against some of the local partisans.

There are some quite interesting places to visit in the area, notably some newly discovered caves. Nobody knew they were there until part of the roof fell in in early 1944. They are quite as beautiful as our Cheddar caves, but not so extensive. They are near the sea, so we combined the visit with a bathe and a picnic and the weather is now (May) really summery but not too hot. I expect to have a chance of a few days leave in Venice, as we can hitch a flight in the plane which brings our blood supplies.

This will probably be my last Family bulletin, as I am now static and medical rather than mobile and combative! Life is now fairly routine and humdrum, which suits me!

P.S. Famous last words! Just as I was about to finish off and post this, we had the great Bari explosion! They were unloading an American Liberty ship laden with bombs when somebody dropped one. An enormous explosion shook all the buildings in the compound, and within a few minutes large black drops of fuel oil began to rain down on us. A large area in the docks was devastated, and within half an hour the casualties began arriving at the hospital in every form of transport imaginable. As usual, the severity of their injuries varied in inverse proportions to the amount of noise they were making. The air was rent with cries of "Mama Mia" etc. We had over two thousand people altogether in the compound and had to sort out the really seriously injured for priority treatment. The operating team started working at 3 pm and went on non-stop until 8 am the next day. The rest of us spent the night walking the wards and monitoring the progress of the more seriously injured. The hospital did not return to normal for over a week.

On this sensational note I will end, hoping that the rest of my war will be peaceful!

THE END